New Developments in Dementia Prevention Research

New Developments in Dementia Prevention Research addresses a dearth of knowledge about dementia prevention and shows the importance of considering the broader social impact of certain risk factors, including the role we each play in our own cognitive health throughout the lifespan. The book draws on primary and secondary research in order to investigate the relationship between modifiable factors, including vascular and psychosocial risks, that may affect the incidence of dementia.

Bringing together world-leading expertise from applied science, medicine, psychology, health promotion, epidemiology, health economics, social policy and primary care, the book compares and contrasts scientific and service developments across a range of settings. Each chapter presents these themes in a way that will ensure best practice and further research in the field of dementia prevention is disseminated successfully throughout the world. Perhaps most importantly, chapters also question what type of social responsibility we are prepared to embrace in order to address the challenges inherent in dementia prevalence.

New Developments in Dementia Prevention Research includes contributions from leading authorities in brain health and dementia prevention and provides an essential contribution to the discourse on dementia prevention. It will be of great interest to academics, researchers and post-graduate students engaged in the study of the psychological and social aspects of ageing and dementia.

Kate Irving is a jointly appointed Professor of Clinical Nursing and Dublin City University and Dublin North Community Health Organisation.

Eef Hogervorst is Professor of Biological Psychology at Loughborough University and Director of Dementia Research.

Deborah Oliveira is Nurse by background and works as a Research Fellow (Programme Manager) for the Institute of Mental Health, University of Nottingham, United Kingdom.

Miia Kivipelto is Professor of Clinical Geriatric Epidemiology at Karolinska Institutet in Stockholm, Sweden.

Aging and Mental Health Research

Series Editor: Martin Orrell

In the 21st century, the world's aging population is growing more rapidly than ever before. This is driving the international research agenda to help older people live better for longer and to find the causes and cures for chronic diseases such as dementia. This series provides a forum for the rapidly expanding field by investigating the relationship between the aging process and mental health. It compares and contrasts scientific and service developments across a range of settings, including the mental changes associated with normal and abnormal or pathological aging, as well as the psychological and psychiatric problems of the aging population. The series encourages an integrated approach between biopsychosocial models and etiological factors to promote better strategies, therapies and services for older people. Creating a strong alliance between the theoretical, experimental and applied sciences, the series provides an original and dynamic focus, integrating the normal and abnormal aspects of mental health in aging so that theoretical issues can be set in the context of important new practical developments in this field.

In this series

Perspectives on Behavioural Interventions in Palliative and End-of-Life Care
Edited by Rebecca S. Allen, Brian D. Carpenter and Morgan K. Eichorst

Perspectives on Palliative and End-of-Life Care
Disease, Social and Cultural Context
Edited by Rebecca S. Allen, Brian D. Carpenter and Morgan K. Eichorst

New Developments in Dementia Prevention Research
State of the Art and Future Possibilities
Edited by Kate Irving, Eef Hogervorst, Deborah Oliveira and Miia Kivipelto

For more information about the series, please visit: www.routledge.com/Aging-and-Mental-Health-Research/book-series/AMHR

New Developments in Dementia Prevention Research

State of the Art and Future Possibilities

Edited by
Kate Irving, Eef Hogervorst,
Deborah Oliveira and
Miia Kivipelto

Routledge
Taylor & Francis Group
LONDON AND NEW YORK

First published 2019
by Routledge
2 Park Square, Milton Park, Abingdon, Oxon OX14 4RN

and by Routledge
52 Vanderbilt Avenue, New York, NY 10017

First issued in paperback 2020

Routledge is an imprint of the Taylor & Francis Group, an informa business

British Library Cataloguing-in-Publication Data
A catalogue record for this book is available from the British Library

Library of Congress Cataloging-in-Publication Data
Names: Irving, Kate, (Kate Elizabeth), 1974– editor.
Title: New developments in dementia prevention research : state of the art and future possibilities / edited by Kate Irving, Eef Hogervorst, Deborah Oliveira and Miia Kivipelto.
Description: Milton Park, Abingdon, Oxon ; New York, NY : Routledge, 2019. | Includes bilbiographical references.
Identifiers: LCCN 2018034600 (print) | LCCN 2018038682 (ebook) | ISBN 9781351122719 (E-book) | ISBN 9780815358336 (hardback) | ISBN 9781351122719 (ebook)
Subjects: LCSH: Dementia. | Dementia—Prevention. | Alzheimer's disease—Prevention.
Classification: LCC RC521 (ebook) | LCC RC521 .N49 2019 (print) | DDC 616.8/3105—dc23
LC record available at https://lccn.loc.gov/2018034600

ISBN 13: 978-0-367-58320-0 (pbk)
ISBN 13: 978-0-8153-5833-6 (hbk)

Typeset in Bembo
by Apex CoVantage, LLC

Contents

Contributors

Aimee Aubeeluck is Registered Practitioner Psychologist and is currently an Associate Professor of Health Psychology in the School of Health Sciences, University of Nottingham. She is a Senior Fellow of the Institute of Mental Health. Aimee's research interests predominantly focus on the impact of neurological conditions on the quality of life (QoL) of individual's and their families living with disease and disorder.

Lorraine Boran is Assistant Professor in Cognitive Psychology, Law and Neuroscience at the School of Nursing and Human Sciences in Dublin City University, Ireland. Her research work is based on cognitive assessment, executive function and cognitive reserve and capacity across the life course.

Carol Brayne is Medically Qualified Epidemiologist and Public Health Academic. Her main research area is longitudinal studies of older people following changes over time in cognition, dementia natural history and associated features. She is lead principle investigator in the group MRC CFAS studies which have and will continue to inform national policy and scientific understanding of dementia in whole populations. She is Director of the Cambridge Institute of Public Health and Primary Care at the University of Cambridge.

Kay Deckers works as a Postdoctoral Researcher at Maastricht University and was initially trained as a neuropsychologist before becoming an epidemiologist. In his research, he investigates the effects of lifestyle factors on cognitive disorders, with most studies focusing on dementia. Additionally, he is concerned with preventive strategies for a brain-healthy lifestyle.

Hamish Foster has a BSc (Hons) in Neuroscience and an MBBS from Barts and the London School of Medicine and Dentistry. After training in London, he worked as a research assistant in Tanzania, then moved to Glasgow to train as a general practitioner (GP). In 2013–2014, he completed a Diploma in Tropical Medicine in East Africa and worked in rural Uganda. He is now a Clinical Academic Fellow and GP in Glasgow. Research interests include obesity and lifestyle in primary care, prevention in primary care, health inequalities and global health.

Ron Handels is a young talented Researcher on health-economic effects of diagnostics, primary prevention, disease-modifying treatment and care access in AD. He developed various health-economic simulation models in a variety of European collaboration consortia.

Eef Hogervorst is Professor of Biological Psychology at Loughborough University and Director of Dementia Research. She is also a Senior Fellow of the Institute of Mental Health in Nottingham and has three chairs in Indonesia. Her research focuses on diagnostics and risk/protective factors of dementia and she has published over 200 peer-reviewed international publications. Before she came to Loughborough she worked at Oxford and Cambridge University. Eef did her PhD in Maastricht on the modelling of age-related cognitive decline. She is involved in several large multi-million pound projects focusing on lifestyle and dementia prevention.

Kate Irving is a jointly appointed Professor of Clinical Nursing and Dublin City University and Community Health Organisation. Kate has a research interest in the management of dementia in communities and public responses to dementia. She coordinated the FP7 funded In-MINDD study on dementia deterrence and leads a National Dementia Education Programme 'The Dementia Skills Elevator'.

Miia Kivipelto is Professor of Clinical Geriatric Epidemiology at Karolinska Institutet in Stockholm, Sweden. She is also Managing Director for Theme Aging at Karolinska University Hospital. Her research covers the epidemiology, early diagnosis and treatment of dementia-related diseases, including clinical trials.

Martin Knapp is Professor of Social Policy and Director of the Personal Social Services Research Unit at the London School of Economics and Political Science (LSE). He has also been Director of the NIHR School for Social Care Research since 2009. His current research emphases are primarily dementia, child and adult mental health, autism and long-term social care; much of his work has an economic focus, and in all of it, he seeks to tease out the policy implications. He has published almost 600 peer-reviewed journal papers and 15 books. His work has had numerous impacts on policy and practice in these areas.

Sebastian Köhler, PhD, was trained in neuropsychology and in epidemiology and holds a PhD in psychiatric epidemiology from Maastricht University. He currently works as an Associate Professor at Maastricht University, where he studies the aetiology, course and prognosis of dementia, stroke and depression.

Claryn S. J. Kung is an early career researcher at the Personal Social Services Research Unit at the LSE. She is an applied micro econometrician, and is primarily interested in the determinants, measurement, and consequences of cognition and mental health. She completed her PhD in 2017 at the Centre for Health Economics, Monash University (Melbourne, Australia) and has several publications including articles in *Preventive Medicine* and *Personality and Individual Differences*.

Yue Leng is an epidemiologist and Atlantic Fellow at the Global Brain Health Institute, University of California, San Francisco. She received her PhD in epidemiology from the University of Cambridge, where she has been conducting research on sleep and ageing outcomes. Her research program funded by the National Institute on Aging focuses on investigating the relationship between sleep and cognitive ageing.

Lisa McGarrigle is a postdoctoral fellow with Dalhousie University researching patient-centered approaches in the measurement of frailty and dementia. She received her PhD in cognitive psychology from Dublin City University where her research focused on rather than in the construct validity and modifiability of cognitive reserve.

Tiia Ngandu is Associate Professor at the National Institute for Health and Welfare in Helsinki, Finland. Her research focuses on cardiovascular and lifestyle risk factors for dementia and prevention trials.

Catherine A. O'Donnell is Professor of Primary Care R&D. Her research focuses on the organization and delivery of primary care services, particularly for marginalized populations, and the evaluation and routinization of primary care policy into practice. Key areas of work include migrant health, the interaction of individually focused lifestyle interventions with social determinants of health, the implementation of digital health interventions and the organization of out-of-hours primary care. She has a particular interest in the use of theory to understand complex social interactions. Kate was recently awarded an Honorary Fellowship of the Royal College of General Practitioners, the highest honour the college can bestow on someone who is not a GP.

Deborah Oliveira is a Nurse by background and works as a Research Fellow (Programme Manager) for the Institute of Mental Health, University of Nottingham, United Kingdom. Deborah is originally from Brazil, where she worked as a Community Nurse Practitioner and Palliative Care Nurse. She has clinical, research and teaching experience in ageing, dementia and family caregiving. Deborah is the author of the Dementia Quality of Life Scale for Older Family Carers (DQoL-OC) and has multiple publications in the field of dementia and family caregiving.

Maria Pierce is Adjunct Faculty Member, Faculty of Science and Health at Dublin City University, Ireland. She is a social scientist and holds a PhD in social policy and ageing from Trinity College Dublin. Her research interests are in the areas of ageing, dementia and disability. She was a researcher on the European Union FP7 In-MINDD (Innovative Midlife Intervention for Dementia Deterrence) project. Her current research includes an evaluation of intensive home care supports for people with dementia. She co-edited a report titled Developing and Implementing Dementia Policy in Ireland, published in 2017.

Anne Margriet Pot is Professor of Clinical Geropsychology at the Vrije Universiteit, Amsterdam, currently posted in Geneva at the World Health Organization (WHO). She overseas WHO's work on the establishment of long-term-care systems worldwide and the training for caregivers of people with dementia. She is a prolific writer and presenter, with more than 200 publications in peer-reviewed scientific and professional journals, and in excess of 150 presentations and workshops at scientific and professional meetings. Over the past 25 years, she has dedicated her work on improving the care for older people and people with dementia through policy, research, post-graduate education and clinical practice.

Martin Rossor is NIHR National Director for Dementia Research and supports the Department of Health in implementing government dementia research strategy. He is honorary consultant neurologist at the National Hospital for Neurology and Neurosurgery where he established the specialist cognitive disorders clinic, which acts as a tertiary referral service for young onset and rare dementias. His clinical research interests lie in neurodegenerative diseases, particularly familial disease, and he has been involved in various clinical trials and collaborative studies on molecular genetics of the neurodegenerative diseases.

Alina Solomon is Associate Professor at the Institute of Clinical Medicine/ Neurology, University of Eastern Finland in Kuopio, Finland. Her research focuses on epidemiology and prediction models for dementia and brain pathology.

Charlotte R. Stoner is an early career researcher at the Institute of Neurology, UCL. She is a psychologist with interests in psychometric theory, positive psychology and cognition. Charlotte completed her PhD in 2017 at the Research Department of Clinical, Educational and Health Psychology, UCL. Her PhD entailed developing and psychometrically validating outcome measures within a strengths or capabilities framework to be used in dementia research.

Alan Thomas is Professor of Old Age Psychiatry at Newcastle University. Having qualified as a psychiatrist he completed a PhD focusing on the neurobiology of late-life depression and has published extensively on late-life depression and its aetiology and pathogenesis.

Dominic Trépel is a health economist with dedicated interests in dementia, mental health and ageing. Through working with GBHI, *The Irish*

Longitudinal Study on Ageing (TILDA) and related studies, he aims to develop novel approaches to improve dementia care worldwide. Through applying a broad range of health-economic methods, Trépel's work has informed government policies, clinical guidelines and has raised dementia as a health priority. Trépel serves on the International Panel of Scientific Advisors for the *Alzheimer's Society of Ireland*. He is a member of the International Health Economics Association (iHEA) and the Campbell and Cochrane Economics Methods Group (CCEMG).

Martin van Boxtel is medical doctor and Associate Professor at Maastricht University. In the past decades, his research was focused on determinants of cognitive ageing and dementia (e.g. in the context of the Maastricht Ageing Study (MAAS)). More recently, he shifted his focus more towards projects dedicated to health promotion and dementia risk reduction.

Anders Wimo is responsible for health-economic research and epidemiological aspects of dementia care at Karolinska Institutet. He is member of the SveDem dementia registry managing team, researcher in various EU-projects, author of ADI´s World Alzheimer Report 2010 and WHO's dementia report 2012, member of Swedish dementia care guidelines committee, co-organizer for IPECAD conference, co-creator of RUD questionnaire and has over 240 publications.

Marc Wortmann is CEO of Marc Wortmann Consultancy in the Netherlands, supporting Alzheimer and dementia organizations in strategy, advocacy and fundraising. He was Executive Director of Alzheimer's Disease International (ADI) from November 2006 till June 2017. Marc studied Law and Art in the city of Utrecht in the Netherlands and was a member of the Parliament of the Province of Utrecht. He became Executive Director of Alzheimer Nederland in 2000. Marc joined ADI by the end of 2006 and was responsible for external contacts, public policy (especially towards World Health Organization and United Nations) and fundraising.

Kristine Yaffe is the Scola Endowed Chair and Vice Chair and Professor of Psychiatry, Neurology and Epidemiology at the University of California, San Francisco. Her research focuses on the epidemiology of cognitive ageing. As a leading expert in the modifiable risk factors of dementia, she has published over 450 peer-reviewed articles and received several awards for her distinguished, scholarly work.

Foreword

Dementia is one of the most disabling conditions worldwide and its prevalence is increasing, particularly in low- and middle-income countries.[1] Our experience working over the past ten years has shown that evidence on dementia prevention, and risk reduction has only recently become a top priority in public health with the aim to reduce the number of people living with the condition globally. As research has shown, up to half of Alzheimer's Disease and other causes of dementia may be attributable to potentially modifiable risk factors.[2] Reducing exposure to these risk factors can therefore have a significant impact on the number of people with dementia, which will have important benefits not only for the people themselves, but also for health and long-term care systems and society as a whole. More robust, population-based, life-course approaches need to be established if we want to succeed in reducing the number of people living with this condition worldwide. This book is a first of its kind and will help not only to educate people about the importance of risk reduction in dementia, but will also show some strategies to reduce risk factors.

The need for the development and implementation of dementia risk reduction policies has increased in the past few years. In 2011, a study showed that a 10–25% reduction in seven risk factors could potentially reduce the number of cases of dementia by 1.1–3.0 million cases globally. As a result, Alzheimer Associations around the world asked Alzheimer's Disease International (ADI) to pay more attention to risk factors of dementia[2]. ADI started, together with other Non-Governmental Organisations (NGOs), to campaign for dementia risk reduction. It advocated for the inclusion of dementia in the High-Level Meeting of Prevention and Control of Non-Communicable Diseases, organized by the United Nations in 2011.[3] While the original focus of the high-level meeting was on cancer, heart and lung disease, and diabetes only, the final political declaration also included dementia.[4] At about the same time, WHO too raised awareness about dementia. In 2012, the report *Dementia: A Public Health Priority* was published stating that dementia policies and plans should include risk reduction. In 2015, the First WHO Ministerial Conference on Global Action Against Dementia was organized, which also advocated for an accelerating focus on dementia risk reduction. In addition, the Global Action Plan on the Public Health Response to Dementia was approved by all 194 Member States during the World Health Assembly in May 2017.[5] This Action Plan recommends that every country should develop its own plan to make dementia a public health priority, including risk reduction. The WHO has also started the Global Dementia Observatory to collate and disseminate data from Member States on key dementia indicators including risk reduction to strengthen countries' response to dementia.[6] Around 30 countries in different regions of the world have now published a national dementia plan. Some of these have made risk reduction a key area of these plans, for example Finland, Australia and Indonesia. However, the majority of countries worldwide still need to develop a dementia action plan.

In this book, the authors bring cutting-edge research on dementia risk reduction to argue that a lifelong approach of population-based interventions could reduce the number of people living with this condition. Dementia is a multifaceted complex condition, which can no longer be seen as an issue solely for the health departments, but as a public issue that needs to be tackled by multiple sectors. As is the case with current 'dementia friendly' campaigns, dementia risk reduction strategies need to call the attention of groups involved with development and implementation of public strategies in several public sectors, such as educational, financial and environmental sectors. Although many of the known risk factors for some diseases underlying dementia can be reduced by encouraging individual changes in lifestyle they are doomed to fail if the broader environment of individuals is ignored. Investing in social capital from pregnancy to end of life is key to promote longer healthier lives and reduce the number of people living with dementia.

This is the first book to provide a comprehensive approach to dementia risk reduction and involves leading researchers in the field. Research, policy and practice have been brought together to argue for a more holistic approach to accelerate future developments and promote a collective debate in the area. The authors carefully selected key areas for improvement and provide a range of strategies for clinicians, researchers and policy makers to change how we approach dementia risk reduction and increase impact. Every chapter is written in 'accessible language' by which the benefits of psychosocial interventions, health economics and policy can be easily understood by different professionals and translated into practice. We recommend this book for your careful reading. We should all work together and invest our efforts for a world with less dementia.

Marc Wortmann
Former Executive Director of Alzheimer's Disease International
Anne Margriet Pot, PhD
Senior Health Adviser in Long-Term Care and Dementia,
World Health Organization

Notes

1 Prince, M., Wimo, A., Guerchet, M., Ali, G. C., Wu Yutzu, Prina M. & World Alzheimer Report. (2015). *The Global Impact of Dementia: An Analysis of Prevalence, Incidence, Cost and Trends*. London: Alzheimer's Disease International, 2015.
2 Barnes, D. E. & Yaffe, K. (2011). The projected effect of risk factor reduction on Alzheimer's disease prevalence. *The Lancet Neurology*, 10, 819–828.
3 www.alz.co.uk/news/ncd-declaration
4 World Health Organization General Assembly. Political Declaration of the High-level Meeting of the General Assembly on the Prevention and Control of Non-communicable Diseases. Paragraph 18. Available at: www.who.int/nmh/events/un_ncd_summit2011/political_declaration_en.pdf
5 www.who.int/mental_health/neurology/dementia/en
6 www.who.int/mental_health/neurology/dementia/Global_Observatory/en/

List of acronyms

Aβ	Amyloid Beta
AD	Alzheimer's disease
ADI	Alzheimer's Disease International
AF	Atrial Fibrillation
AHI	Apnea-Hypopnea Index
AHMAC	Australian Health Ministers Advisory Council
AHRQ	Agency for Healthcare Research and Quality
aMCI-AD	Amnestic Mild Cognitive Impairment to Alzheimer's Disease
AP	Angina pectoris
APOE	Apolipoprotein E
ARIC	Atherosclerosis Risk in Communities
ATD	All-type dementia
BDNF	Brain derived nerve growth factor
BLT	Bright Light Therapy
BMI	Body mass index
BP	Blood pressure
BRC	Brain Reserve Capacity
CAIDE	Cardiovascular Risk Factors, Aging and Dementia
CDCR	Cognitive Domains and Cognitive Reserve model
CES-D	Center for Epidemiological Studies Depression scale
CHD	Coronary heart disease
CI	Confidence interval
CKD	Chronic kidney disease
CPAP	Continuous Positive Airway Pressure
CR	Cognitive Reserve
CSF	Cerebrospinal fluid
CST	Cognitive Stimulation Therapy
DASH	Dietary Approaches to Stop Hypertension
EF	Executive Function
DHA	Docosahexaenoic acid
DSM5	Diagnostic and Statistical Manual of Mental Disorders, 5th edition
eGFR	Estimated glomerular filtration rate

EDS	Excessive Daytime Sleepiness
ELSA	English Longitudinal Study of Ageing
ESRD	End-stage renal disease
EU	European Union
FINGER	Finnish Geriatric Intervention Study to Prevent Cognitive Impairment and Disability
G8	Group of 8 industrialized countries
HADS	Hospital Anxiety and Depression Scale
HAM-A	Hamilton Anxiety Scale
HATICE	Healthy Ageing Throughout Internet Counselling in the Elderly
Hb	Haemoglobin (Hb)
HBM	Health Belief Model
HDL	High-density lipoprotein
HPA	Hypothalamus-pituitary gland-adrenal
HR	Hazard ratio
In-MINDD	INnovative, Midlife INtervention for Dementia Deterrence
IQ	Intelligence Quotient
LDL	Low-density lipoprotein
LIBRA	Lifestyle for Brain Health
MAPT	Multi-domain Alzheimer Preventive trial
MAX	Mental Activity and eXercise Study
MCI	Mild Cognitive Impairment
MI	Myocardial infarction
MRC CFAS	Medical Research Council Cognitive Function and Ageing Study
MRI	Magnetic resonance imaging
NCDs	No communicable diseases
NGO	Non-governmental organisation
PA	Physical activity
PHQ	Patient Health Questionnaire
PreDIVA	Prevention of Dementia by Intensive Vascular Care
PSG	Polysomnography
PTSD	Post-traumatic stress disorder
QALY	Quality-adjusted life year
RCT	Randomized controlled trial
REM	Rapid Eye Movement
RR	Relative risk
SCN	Suprachiasmatic Nucleus
SDB	Sleep-disordered breathing
SES	Socioeconomic status
SOF	Study of Osteoporotic Fractures
TC	Total cholesterol
TBI	Traumatic brain injury
TILDA	The Irish Longitudinal Study on Ageing

TPB	Theory of Planned Behavior
TNFα	Tumor necrosis factor α
UK	United Kingdom
UN	United Nations
US	United States
VaD	Vascular dementia
VWS	Ministry of Health, Welfare and Sport
WAR	World Alzheimer Report
WHO	World Health Organization
ZonMW	The Netherlands Organisation for Health Research and Development

Book outline

This book considers the broader social impact of a wide range of risk factors for dementia and provides a forum for this expanding research field investigating the relationship between modifiable factors, including vascular and psychosocial risks that may affect the incidence of dementia. The most common forms of dementia have broad multi-factorial pathologies and complex application in policy and practice. Hence, this edition brings together world-leading expertise from applied science, medicine, psychology, health promotion, epidemiology, health economics, social policy and primary care. The intended readership will be experts or post-graduate researchers from any of these fields, needing an overview of the state of the art and the emerging issues in each area.

The introduction (Chapter 1) situates dementia prevention in terms of the major challenges to evidence production, translation into policy, normalization into clinical practice and popularization of the message in general vernacular. This chapter introduces some of the theoretical debates on the framing of dementia. The chapter covers major themes that are referred to later in the book, such as primary, secondary and tertiary prevention; delay of dementia and to what extent this might be the same as prevention; and the population approach to the more common multi-factorial risk factors for dementia. The possible polarization of approaches (population and targeted) and potential for combined approaches, defining risk factors as opposed to protective factors, are discussed. The chapter also explores the methodological challenges in researching dementia prevention; the need for expensive longitudinal studies, ethics of the topic of study, feasibility, efficacy, and effectiveness. In Chapter 2, five risk algorithms are described and the major differences as well as pros and cons of each under different circumstances are examined. These risk algorithms could provide early assessment of overall dementia risk based on multi-factorial profiles. These tools could help identify those who would benefit most from preventative strategies.

In *Section I*, preventative strategies with the most potential benefit are described in more detail. A broad overview of the risk and protective factors is given with the prevalence of the risk factor and suggested impacts and interactions with other risk factors, established and emerging evidence from observational and randomized controlled trials, and possible biological causation. Each chapter also discusses the gaps in the literature and directions for future research.

In Chapter 3, a broad overview is given on demographic factors, such as age and education, followed by a brief introduction to vascular disease risk factors. This is followed by a review on lifestyles that can affect risk factors for dementia and vascular disease, such as smoking, activity and diet. Chapter 4 reviews individual vascular risk factors and vascular disease in more detail, including, among others, high blood pressure, cholesterol, renal disease and diabetes. Chapter 5 discusses the association between mood and psychiatric disorders and dementia. Chapter 6 explores cognitive reserve and activity as potential preventative strategies, and Chapter 7 addresses risk and protective factors with a review of sleep and sleep disorders and dementia. In all the chapters, the complex interplay between these risk and protective factors is discussed as well as other methodological issues. In Chapter 8, the last chapter of this section, theoretical perspectives on health behavioural change are presented. Lessons learned from large European prevention trails are presented, as well as those from related topics, such as smoking reduction to prevent lung cancer, to guide better interventions to prevent dementia.

Section II describes the social, political and economic aspects of prevention of dementia. Chapter 9 addresses inequalities and policy translation issues of existing and future health policies for dementia prevention. This chapter explores the extent to which dementia prevention messages have been translated into policy internationally and identifies the barriers and facilitators to policy translation. Given the fundamental shift in health policy towards community care, the major responsibility to dementia prevention will be with primary care. Practically, this will require that primary care teams are themselves convinced there may be some benefit, that they are knowledgeable about how to help people change behaviour and that dementia prevention is in the fabric of all health promotion attempts. Chapter 10 explores the barriers and enablers to the dementia prevention message in primary care and examines the usefulness of e-health as a medium for dissemination. Chapters 11 and 12 estimate the cost-effectiveness of a potential preventive intervention programme meant to lower the score related to increased dementia risk. The chapters conclude with salient messages for the economic arguments surrounding dementia delay/prevention. Chapter 12 discusses economic modelling. In Chapter 13, the Cognitive Footprint as a framework to guide public policy is outlined. Chapter 14 concludes the book with a summary covering the main points. The jeopardy of the lifestyle message for people who actually have dementia will be discussed. Future directions are given, including the need for collaboration between different stakeholders with different perspectives on the issues at stake.

Chapter 1

Introduction

Kate Irving, Deborah Oliveira and Eef Hogervorst

Why prevent dementia?

Dementia is a substantial public health issue and major societal challenge, and its prevalence is high and increasing. It is one of the conditions most likely to create fear and existential dread in people (McParland et al. 2012). Associations between neuropathology and the clinical condition are not fully understood. Such fear coupled with uncertainty has led to an industry of products and services claiming to 'rewire your brain' or 'delay dementia by 10 years'. Much of this industry has no grounding in research evidence. The creation of myths around dementia prevention has to some extent damaged legitimate sources of evidence. It is tempting to make a plea to ignore such tensions and have a mature and balanced debate on the 'actual evidence'. However, we must acknowledge that fear and dread are as much a part of the experience of being human as brain physiology; the body and mind form a dissociable whole. Much of what we will argue in this book is for population-targeted approaches aimed at behaviour change on modifiable factors, both risk and protective factors. This can only be achieved with a thorough appreciation of the nature of dementia and dementia prevention understandings among the population and how these understandings impact such attempts.

Inevitably, this chapter must start off by talking about what we are trying to prevent. Dementia can be understood as a dialectical interplay between neurological impairment and malignant social psychologies that happen to persons who go through a dementing process (Kitwood 1997, p. 51). The purpose of bringing this particular definition into play here in the context of dementia prevention is because it moves the conversation away from fear and empowers people to look at what is within their control. It shifts us away from awaiting scientific developments and towards action and agency. Kitwood has made an extraordinary impact on care models for people with dementia. However, what is less well understood is the impact of such a definition of dementia on dementia prevention.

A magic pill for the prevention of all but the rarest dementia diseases is not only unlikely – it is challenging to the human condition. This begs the question: Why then have attempts to reduce its incidence through public health interventions been so inadequate? Perhaps the answer lies in the complex jeopardies of ageing and dementia. Age is the largest factor in the development of dementia. Dementia is a disease of ageing, although not in itself part of 'normal ageing'. Like other diseases of ageing, some people will prove very resilient to it; this is partly mediated by lifestyle, a major theme of this book. Perhaps part of the reason for the silence around dementia is ageism. There is a complex relationship between the stigma associated with dementia and ageism, and the two are very difficult to separate. This has been described as the overwhelming fear of an imagined future incapacity and the dread of 'going into care' with the isolation, reduction of autonomy and 'othering' this is perceived to bring (Higgs and Gilleard 2017). From the point of view of younger people working to maintain health and lifestyle, the fourth age 'appears as a horrific apparition that dramatises "lack" in a rather potent way' (West and Glynos 2016, p. 230).

Over many years, the human race has had this particular fixation on staying and being young. The picture from the 16th-century German Court painter Lucas Cranach the Elder (Figure 1.1) demonstrates that this is no new obsession. The picture clearly demonstrates the seductive docility of waiting for the 'Fountain of Youth'. On the left of the picture we see the sick and elderly being wheeled up to the fountain and on the right, they skip out to engage in fun and feasting. So, it would seem fantastical notions of staying and being young are not a new feature of existence.

Figure 1.1 Fountain of Youth, from Lucas Cranach the Elder (16th-century), German Court Painter.

Of course, dementia is not a force for good in anyone's life, but to what extent is dementia existentially worse than other diseases of ageing? What part of our fear of dementia is actually fear of societal response to cognitive impairment? This is not just a theoretical subtlety in the case of dementia. Debate on these issues is vital to furthering our understandings of behaviour in response to dementia prevention and even the allocation of funding to curative research over population-based risk reduction. How we talk about or 'frame' dementia (Van Gorp and Vercruysse 2012) will have a substantial effect upon how we manage to change policy, change clinical and wider community practice and ultimately, change individual behaviour. Building cross-disciplinary collaboration in the context of these understandings is what is required to manage the worldwide public health challenge of the 'dementias'.

To prevent dementia on an appreciable scale, we will need to recruit all available skill and knowledge. This will require an understanding of the biology of dementia, but importantly, if we are to recruit people in anything more than taking a pill (acknowledging, even this can be difficult), we need to understand the sociological aspects of dementia. The editors' endeavour is to create a resource for any medical, health or social researcher interested in the area of dementia prevention. We will present the major concepts of dementia prevention, the state of the art and the promising future trends from science and research to clinical practice and policy.

Health systems across the OECD spend less than 3% on prevention.[1] In the UK, the research impact report from the Alzheimer's Society showed that only 5% of research funding (on average spent between 1990 and 2012) was allocated to studies of risk and preventive strategies.[2] Dementia research still has large emphasis on biomarkers, biochemical mechanisms, treatments and cures. There is a question of balance: What are the marginal benefits of redirecting some research funding away from traditional biomedical research and towards epidemiological and service development research? Redirection alone is not enough in the case of dementia prevention, particularly for those aspects which now have a moderate to strong evidence base. This knowledge needs to be normalized in mainstream prevention discourse. For example, many European healthy ageing policies are vociferous in their approach to cancer, heart disease and stroke prevention, but strangely silent about dementia prevention, despite very similar risk factors being involved. Dementia must be mainstreamed into major chronic disease prevention in order to give it the same legitimacy and standing in the eyes of the public and healthcare professionals alike.

We must ask why is there such invisibility on the subject of dementia prevention. There are, at least, four jeopardies in the dementia prevention message which may have contributed to this silence on the subject. First, it risks disenfranchising those who may or may not have engaged in lifestyles detrimental to their brain health – that is, those who are living with dementia. Clearly, there is a need to avoid any category of 'victim blaming' and use sensitivity regarding the communication of dementia prevention. Second, we know that focusing on individual agency is only a small portion of the issue – lifestyle is largely socially mediated. Lifestyle is not a choice for many living in difficult social circumstances. Third, it is not a simple message of cause and effect, but one of relative risks and population attributable risks and perhaps delay, rather than prevention in the true sense; these complexities are not quite amenable to 'sound bites'. Finally, in popular discourse, dementia has been associated with animalism (McParland 2014), zombies (Behuniak 2011) and social death (Sweeting and Gilhooley 1997). It is unsurprising then that it is the chronic disease most likely to cause existential dread and fear in people.

> *Is also associated with existing perceptions of care, feelings of hopelessness or futility, and a profound fear of developing a condition that appears utterly arbitrary and totally beyond the control of the individual or the world of science and medicine.*
>
> (McParland 2017, p. 86)

In the In-MINDD study, the following quote was typical of the reticence of general practitioners to discuss dementia:

> *I would mention heart disease yes because there are treatments. Ideally you don't want to raise a hair on the head if you don't have something you can do about it.*
>
> GP Interview IE

When we spoke to people with risk factors, it was clear they took the conversation seriously:

> *The GP asked me if I wanted to participate. Then you get such a letter, and it says that you have one or more risk factors. And then I thought oh!*
>
> (Female, Netherlands, Intervention arm, Exit interview)

While there was no evidence that the advice was totally unpalatable, understanding about modifiable risk factors was low, and most believed that modifiable factors were negated by non-modifiable factors, particularly genetics.

In truth, the genetics of dementia are complex, contributing to familial dementia by causing genetic mutations or as a contributing factor towards genetically complex disease. Twenty-five percent of all people over 55 years of age have a family history of dementia (Loy et al. 2014). Very few of these cases are due to a specific genetic mutation, with only just over 500 such families reported (Cruts 2012). Rare single-gene disease is caused by a mutation in one of the 25,000 genes in the genome. Inheritance of this gene is associated with a 95% lifetime risk of dementia (Loy et al. 2014). Multi-factorial diseases are caused by genetic, behavioural and environmental factors, individually and in interaction. These genetic factors are variations that appear in the general population and each factor increases disease risk by a small amount. Families of course share behavioural, environmental and genetic influences, so it is not always the case that familial dementia is genetic. As genetic variations infer a small effect, and environmental conditions are also needed for complex disease, a person with complex disease is unlikely to pass on every one of their many genetic variations to a child. Because genetic variations are common, the offspring might inherit risk conferring genetic variations from the other parent. Genetic testing for complex disease has poor predictive power and is not recommended in clinical practice (Loy et al. 2014).

Studies of rare forms of familial inherited dementia may afford us useful insights into neurocognitive diseases. However, the studies are expensive and complex, and so far have attracted much funding with very little impact on the lives of people with dementia such that the treatment that can be offered now is not significantly different than it was 15 years ago. We do not call for an all-or-nothing approach to dementia risk; we call for a better balance between risk reduction strategies where the cumulative knowledge of multidisciplinary groups is considered outside of the scientific hierarchy of knowledge and firmly within a pragmatic hierarchy of what has the best potential to do the most good for the greatest number of people in the most expedient fashion.

There is some interest in the area of epigenetics in understanding the expression of dementia. Epigenetics mean 'above genetics' and includes mechanisms that involve chemical marking of chromatin (the form in which DNA is packaged with proteins in the cell nucleus). Epigenetic marks can induce chromatin remodelling and related changes in gene expression that are not caused by DNA sequence change. Many factors, including nutrition, age, gender, physiological and psychological stress, chemicals and infections, exert powerful influences on gene expression. It is believed now that epigenetic mechanisms are not one way but also potentially reversible (Ishino et al. 2013). Consequently, there is much interest in the role epigenetic signals play in synaptic plasticity, learning and memory. Many areas are still at the level of fascinating implications, but biological plausibility could lead to some significant development of this field.

Further to these sociological and genetic issues, there have been recent changes in the way dementia is diagnosed. In the DSM5, 'dementia' is replaced by 'major neurocognitive disorder', and less severe cognitive impairment is diagnosed as 'mild neurocognitive disorder'; memory impairment is joined by visuo-spatial, language and other impairments. At present, the epidemiology (incidence, prevalence and risk factors) of these conditions is largely unknown.

This will force a reconceptualization of disease: Does it start with the onset of specific pathological changes in the brain or does it start with the first appearance of specific clinical symptoms? Whilst in other fields of research the pathological changes usually define the disease onset, in the dementia field this is arguable. Many elderly individuals die with intact cognition, but with a sufficient number of pathological signs to be classified as Alzheimer's Dementia. Age has the strongest effect on the risk of late-life cognitive impairment, and it is not clear if the ageing process and the dementia process are two distinct processes (Solomon et al. 2014).

The ability of the brain to tolerate or respond to structural changes is known to differ among people, and this is often known as cognitive reserve (Esiri and Chance 2012; Stern 2012). This forms the major explanation of why pathological changes can accumulate with no significant change in clinical signs or symptoms.

Because most dementia pathology starts decades before clinical symptoms become apparent, much research has attempted to identify biomarkers associated with increased pathology in the brain. However, a combination of markers is required to have reasonable sensitivity and specificity. This is further complicated by findings that not all people with neuropathology will develop dementia (Esiri 2000).

As stated, the most common cognitive impairments in old age probably have mixed aetiologies, and different pathologies share the same risk factors, suggesting that combined, multi-domain preventive interventions targeting several risk factors simultaneously have the highest likelihood of being effective (Solomon et al. 2014).

There is intense debate concerning clinical versus neuropathological disease definitions, but clinical relevance remains a priority (Solomon et al. 2014). A possible exception to this is in rare cases of Alzheimer's disease due to known genetic causes, i.e. mutations in APP, PSEN1 and PSEN2 genes. These are specific and different from sporadic AD, so they may represent another disease altogether.

These discrepancies are echoed in questions about how prevention can be defined, with primary prevention aiming to reduce the incidence of the pathology before disease onset, secondary prevention aiming at very early or pre-clinical phases to prevent more manifest clinical symptoms and tertiary prevention aiming to manage the disease and its complications and promoting quality of life (Figure 1.2).

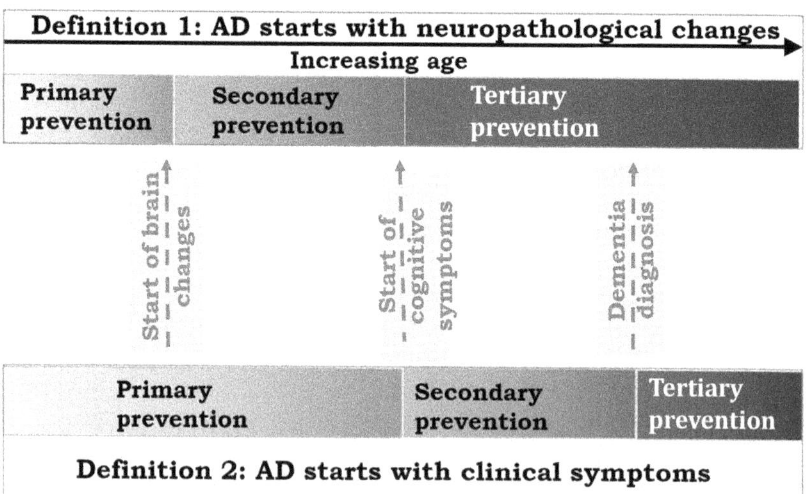

Figure 1.2 Different levels of dementia prevention, based on Dubois et al. (2010)

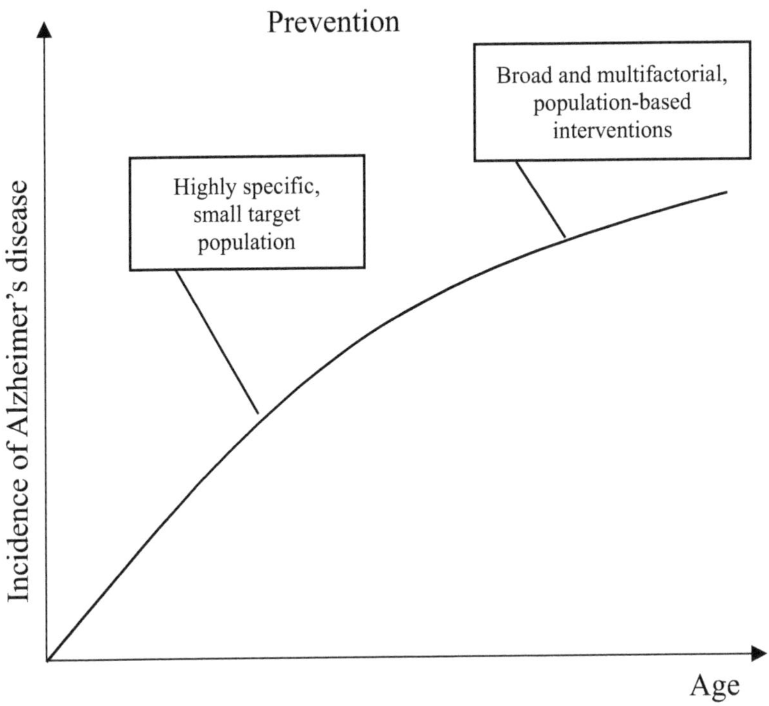

Figure 1.3 Targeting Alzheimer's disease at different points across the lifespan

The prevention paradox describes the seemingly contradictory situation where the majority of cases of a disease come from a population at low or moderate risk of that disease, and only a minority of cases come from the high-risk population (of the same disease). This is because the number of people at high risk is small. This can be seen in the graph in Figure 1.3, demonstrating that the prevention potential to impact on the population level is greatest where there is are multiple causes and pathologies. That said, it is probably the case that there is much transferable knowledge from studies of highly specific much rarer forms of dementia. Rather than polarizing the field, it is important to combine the learning from such studies and ensure that knowledge generation is not stifled by allegiance to one or other end of the curve in the graph in Figure 1.3.

Methodological complexity

Nine considerations proposed in 1965 have had a huge effect on epidemiological thinking around prevention (Hill 1965). These factors were conceived as direct acting causal factors and so are less appropriate but nonetheless interesting to consider in multi-factorial conditions. The methodological complexities in each consideration will be highlighted.

Strength of association

A stronger association is more likely to indicate a cause and effect relationship. In dementia, associations tend to be relatively weak (Lucas and McMichael 2005). Practically, those individuals with very high-risk levels may not survive to older ages where their dementia expression can be studied. This 'selective mortality' make it difficult to assess what 'strong' association should be in dementia prevention.

Environmental conditions in the population can change quite dramatically over a long-term study. For example, in Europe, hypertension and hypercholesterolemia has decreased, while obesity and diabetes have increased among middle-aged populations between the 1960s and 2000s (Finucane et al. 2011). Detailed longitudinal studies combining many risk factors which can be hard to measure need to be measured at regular time intervals if we are to understand the implications of such societal changes.

Consistency

This refers to the stability of results when measures by different people in different circumstances and times. Much dementia research uses different definitions for exposure and outcome, which makes direct comparison of studies difficult.

Specificity

This criterion is based on two assumptions – a single factor should cause a single effect and an effect can only have one cause. Neither of these apply in multi-factorial diseases, such as dementia, where neuropathology does not always translate into clinically diagnosed dementia, and clinically diagnosed dementia is not caused exclusively by neuropathology. In addition, many risk/protective factors are risks for a whole range of chronic disease.

Temporality

That exposure must precede the outcome is an inarguable criterion. Dementia has an insidious onset (either of the associated neuropathology or the cognitive symptoms). The effects of midlife risk are not necessarily observed at older ages, and there is complexity about midlife risk factors mirroring late-life risk (for example, obesity in midlife is a risk factor, but at older ages, it can appear to protect against dementia (Tolppanen et al. 2013).

Biological gradient

The most clear-cut example of this is where there is a linear increase in the outcome with increasing exposure to the risk factor. There is a dose-dependent increase in dementia with increasing number of E4 alleles (Solomon et al. 2014). However, other risk factors have a less clear relationship, and it can be difficult to decipher what is causally related to dementia and what might reflect confounding factors or other biases.

Plausibility

A causal association needs to be biologically plausible, but this is dependent on the knowledge available at a given time point. Absence of knowledge does not make a proposition untrue. There is general acknowledgement that there are different thresholds of knowledge for different types of interventions. For example, treating asymptomatic 'at-risk' individuals with trial drugs will need to point to significantly greater evidence than large-scale population health approaches, such as those which address physical activity or diet.

Coherence

This is the assertion that causal association should not fundamentally contradict existing knowledge about disease pathophysiology. However, Solomon et al. (2014) caution that plausibility and coherence should not be too strictly imposed, as the role of vascular factors in AD would not have been recognized in the 1990s had research avoided contradicting the ridged dichotomy between Alzheimer's and vascular dementias.

Analogy

Analogy can help formulate sound bites for public health campaigns, and indeed there has been some success with the 'healthy heart health brain' message. However, some see dementia prevention as redundant in the discourse of cardiovascular prevention strategies. For complex sociological reasons argued earlier, we should strive for both a piggy backing onto existing public health campaigns but a better understanding of the dementia-specific needs in any campaign.

Experiment

The field of prevention research has been so far the realm of epidemiological research and experimental research where disease treatment has been the primary force. An association is more likely to be causal if it is supported by experimental data. However, many of the experimental trials have had poor methodology, with small sample sizes and short follow-ups. Combined animal models of AD and other common old age pathologies are only starting to be used.

Sufficient evidence

The aforementioned criteria are good touchstones to consider in any dementia prevention research, but as has been pointed out, it should not be taken as doctrine in many cases. Proper consideration of these criteria, however, do mean that legitimate or compelling research into dementia risk reduction will necessitate large, long and complex research studies which will be costly and have some ethical obstacles to negotiate.

A large number of risk and protective factors for dementia have been investigated and these are summarized in the Table 1.1. The remaining question is what should constitute sufficient evidence for prevention recommendations. We need to have a sensible debate about the main danger for dementia prevention, acting on weaker evidence that may turn out not to be a determinant or not acting to reduce the risk of disease. Bradford Hill (1965) proposes that, in the case of prevention, 'the decisive question is where the frequency of the undesirable event B will be influenced by a change in the environmental feature A'. This avoids the question of causation and seems justifiable in the case of dementia prevention. One must also consider if environmental feature A is likely to be detrimental to the population. In most cases, improvements in risk factors and addition of protective factors will have short- and long-term benefit for quality of life with little or no evidence of any potential for harm.

Table 1.1 Proposed risk and protective factors for dementia

Risk factors	*Protective factors*
Genetic (e.g. APOE ε4, familial aggregation) Vascular and metabolic (e.g. cerebrovascular lesions, diabetes, obesity) Poor lifestyle (e.g. smoking, alcohol intake) Poor diet (e.g. saturated fats, low B vitamin) Depression Traumatic brain injuries Occupational exposure (e.g. heavy metals) Pollution Poor sleep quality Hearing loss Social isolation Cognitive and physical inactivity Low education levels	Genetic (e.g. APP, APOE ε2) Psychosocial factors (e.g. high levels of complexity work, social engagement, mentally stimulating activities Lifestyle (e.g. physical activity, low/no alcohol intake) Diet (e.g. Mediterranean diet; Vitamins B_6, B_{12} and folate; vitamin D, antioxidant vitamins) Drugs (e.g. antihypertensive drugs, statins)

Adapted from Solomon 2012 and Livingston 2017

Summary

It is clear that there is stigma around dementia, and it has been argued that this has impacted negatively on knowledge development in dementia prevention. Dementia prevention researchers need to take heed of these complex jeopardies. Funders of research need to wake up to these arguments and look at the massive potential benefits for population approaches to dementia prevention. Dementia prevention approaches can be primary, secondary or tertiary, but it is important to choose sensitive endpoint measures. Notwithstanding changing definitions of dementia and trends in diagnostics, clinical relevance remains a priority and approaches to prevent clinical symptoms are the most desirable endpoints to research as they are most likely to promote quality of life. The fatalism that has plagued dementia prevention is changing and this is a real achievement. Fundamentally, only sustained international commitment and associated funding allocation will accelerate the pace of translating newly emerging or promising results into practical applications. This book is the first of its kind, aimed at medical and related disciplines, science and social science, public health students and researchers to provide a broad basis in the state of the art so that new research may stand on the accumulated research on dementia prevention.

Notes

1 *Organisation for Economic Co-operation and Development*. Available at: www.oecd.org/general/oecdcountriesspendonly3ofhealthcarebudgetsonpreventionpublicawareness.htm [Accessed].
2 *Alzheimer's Society*. Available at: www.alzheimers.org.uk/download/downloads/id/1624/cause_cure_care_and_prevention_impact_of_alzheimers_societys_dementia_research_programme_1990-2012.pdf [Accessed].

References

Behuniak, S. (2011). The living dead? The construction of people with Alzheimer's disease as Zombies. *Ageing and Society*, [online] 31(1), 70–92. http://dx.doi.org/10.1017/S0144686X10000693.

Cruts, M. (2012). *Alzheimer Disease and Frontotemporal Dementia Mutation Database*. Available at: www.molgen.ua.ac.be/admutations/.

Dubois, B., Feldman, Howard, H., Jacova, C., Cummings, Jeffery, L., Dekosky, S. T., Barberger-Gateau, P., Delacourte, A., Frisoni, G., Fox, N. C., Galasko, D., Gauthier, S., Hampel, H., Jicha, G. A., Meguro, K., O'Brien, J., Pasquier, F., Robert, P., Rossor, M., Salloway, S., Sarazin, M., de Souza, L. C., Stern, Y., Visser, P. J. & Scheltens, P. (2010). Revising the definition of Alzheimer's disease: A new Lexicon. *The Lancet Neurology*, [online] 9(11), 1118–1127. http://dx.doi.org/10.1016/S1474-4422(10)70223-4.

Esiri, M. M. (2000). Vascular factors in Alzheimer's disease. *Annals of the New York Academy of Sciences*, 903(1), 239–243.

Esiri, M. M. & Chance, S. A. (2012). Cognitive reserve, cortical plasticity and resistance to Alzheimer's disease. *Alzheimer's Research and Therapy*, [online] 4, 7. https://doi.org/10.1186/alzrt105.

Finucane, M. M., Stevens, G. A., Cowan, M. J., *et al.* (2011). National, regional, and global trends in body-mass index since 1980: Systematic analysis of health examination surveys and epidemiological studies with 960 country-years and 9.1 million participants. *The Lancet*, [online] 377, 557–567. doi:10.1016/S0140-6736(10)62037-5.

Higgs, P. & Gilleard, C. (2017). *Ageing, Dementia and the Social Mind: Sociology of Health and Illness Monographs.* Oxford: John Wiley & Sons.

Hill, A. B. (1965). The environment and disease: Association or causation? *Proceedings of the Royal Society of Medicine*, 58(5), 295–300.

Ishino, F., Shinkai, Y. & Whitelaw, E. (2013). Mammalian epigenetics in biology and medicine. *Philosophy Transactions of the Royal Society B*, 368.

Kitwood, T. M. (1997). *Dementia Reconsidered: The Person Comes First.* Buckingham, England: Open University Press.

Livingston, G., Sommerlad, A., Orgeta, V., Costafreda, S. G., Huntley, J., Ames, D., Ballard, C., Banerjee, S., Burns, A., Cohen-Mansfield, J., Cooper, C., Fox, N., Gitlin, L. N., Howard, R., Kales, H. C., Larson, E. B., Ritchie, K., Rockwood, K., Sampson, E. L., Samus, Q., Schneider, L. S., Selbæk, G., Teri, L. & Mukadam, N. (2017). Dementia prevention intervention and care. *The Lancet*, [online] 390, 2673–2734. doi:10.1016/S0140-6736(17)31363-6.

Loy, C. T., Schofield, P. R., Turner, A. M. & Kwok, J. B. J. (2014). Genetics of dementia. *The Lancet*, [online] 383 (9919) (March 1), 828–840. https://doi.org/10.1016/S0140-6736(13)60630-3.

Lucas, R. M. & McMichael, A. J. (2005). Association or causation: Evaluating links between "environment and disease". *Bulletin of the World Health Organization*, 83(10), 792–795.

McParland, P. (2014). *Dementia: What Comes to Mind?* PhD thesis. Available at: http://dspace.stir.ac.uk/handle/1893/20411#.VaKbuPlViko.

McParland, P., Devine, P., Innes, A. & Gayle, V. (2012). Dementia knowledge and attitudes of the general public in Northern Ireland: An analysis of national survey data. *International Psychogeriatrics*, 24(10), 1600–1613. doi:10.1017/S1041610212000658.

McParland, P., Kelly, F. & Innes, A. (2017). Dichotomising dementia: Is there another way? *Sociology of Health and Illness*, 39(2), 258–269. doi:10.1111/1467-9566.12438.

Solomon, A., Mangaialasche, F., Richard, E., Andrieu, S., Bennett, A., Breteler, M., Fratiglioni, L., Hooshmand, B., Khachaturian, S., Schneider, L. S., Skoog, I. & Kivipelto, M. (2014). Advances in the prevention of Alzheimer's disease and dementia. *Journal of Internal Medicine*, [online] 275(3), 229–250. doi:10.1111/joim.12178.

Stern, Y. (2012). Cognitive reserve in ageing and Alzheimer's disease. *The Lancet Neurology*, [online] 1(11), 1006–1012. doi:10.1016/S1474-4422(12)70191-6.

Sweeting, H. & Gilhooley, M. (1997). Dementia and the phenomenon of social death. *Sociology of Health and Illness*, [online] 19, 1. https://doi.org/10.1111/j.1467-9566.1997.tb00017.x.

Tolppanen, A. M., Soloman, A., Soininen, H. & Kivipelto, M. (2013). Midlife vascular risk factors and Alzheimer's disease: Evidence from epidemiological studies. *Journal of Alzheimers Disease*, [online] 32, 531–540. doi:10.3233/JAD-2012-120802.

Van Gorp, B. & Vercruysse, T. (2012). Frames and counter-frames giving meaning to dementia: A framing analysis of media content. *Social Science & Medicine*, 74(8), 1274–1281. doi:10.1016/j.socscimed.2011.12.045.

West, K. & Glynos, J. (2016). 'Death talk', 'loss talk' and identification in the process of ageing. *Ageing and Society*, 36(2), 225–239. doi:10.1017/S0144686X14001184.

Chapter 2

From prediction to dementia prevention

Alina Solomon, Tiia Ngandu and Miia Kivipelto

What are prediction tools?

Prediction tools are widely used in medicine, where patients and health care providers need to make decisions based on the probability or risk that a certain disease or condition is already present (diagnostic tools) or will occur in the future (prognostic tools) (Collins et al. 2015). Health care providers are trained to identify multiple characteristics and symptoms of a patient and integrate them into an overall clinical profile that forms the basis of highly personalized diagnostic, prognostic and therapeutic decisions. Beyond the 'clinical sense' that develops with experience, prediction tools provide standardized, evidence-based quantitative estimates of probabilities and risks for various short-term or longer-term disease-related scenarios, e.g. presence of a specific pathology requiring more invasive and/or costly tests; development of a specific disease, complications or acute events; faster disease progression; or death. Most prediction tools are based on overall patient profiles and are thus multifactorial, i.e. they take into account several predictors simultaneously (Collins et al. 2015). Such predictors can be sociodemographic (age, sex, education) or other characteristics, symptoms, medical history or results of various laboratory tests or procedures. Examples of well-known prediction tools are Fracture Risk Assessment Tool (FRAX®, University of Sheffield 2008), Systematic Coronary Risk Evaluation (SCORE, Perk et al. 2012), European System for Cardiac Operative Risk Evaluation (EuroSCORE, Nashef et al. 1999), Framingham Risk Score for cardiovascular outcomes (Anderson et al. 1991) and Nottingham Prognostic Index for breast cancer surgery prognosis (Haybittle et al. 1982).

Current research literature includes numerous prediction tools for a wide variety of health conditions. However, only some of these tools become part of standard practice over time. This can be a relatively lengthy process with several steps. First, each predictor needs to have an established, evidence-based relation to the disease or condition of interest. Second, there is a development step where combinations of different predictors are tested to determine performance in the intended context (diagnostic or prognostic) and target population. Assessing the performance of a prediction tool involves two main characteristics: discrimination, or ability to differentiate between people who do or do not experience the outcome of interest, and calibration, or agreement between the predicted and the observed outcomes (Moons et al. 2015). Predictors may be added or removed depending on how much they contribute to the tool performance and on the desired tool complexity (simple, requiring only a brief clinical interview; or more complex, including results from laboratory tests or procedures). In addition, prediction tools need to be validated. Internal validation involves testing the performance in resampled groups from the initial population used to develop the prediction tool. External validation involves testing the performance in independent populations, e.g. different countries, age groups or settings (primary versus secondary care) than the initial population.

With so many available prediction tools, detailed and clear reporting of all information concerning the development and validation process is essential for comparing tools and adequately choosing between different options. However, the overall quality of reporting of prediction tool studies has been surprisingly poor (Collins et al. 2015; Moons et al. 2015). The Transparent Reporting of a multivariable prediction model for Individual Prognosis Or Diagnosis (TRIPOD) guidelines were formulated only relatively recently in 2015 (Collins et al. 2015; Moons et al. 2015). TRIPOD guidelines aim to improve the quality of reporting of published prediction tool studies, so that the strengths and weaknesses of prediction tools can be more easily and objectively judged.

Validated well-performing prediction tools can also be assessed in implementation studies focusing on various scenarios where using versus not using the tool are compared. Examples include impact on the behaviour or health outcomes of patients, on accuracy or speed of decision-making and management by health care providers or on cost-effectiveness aspects of medical care.

Recent technology advancements have brought further important changes in the format and use of prediction tools. Traditional pen-and-paper tools are very accessible and useful in many settings. However, novel computer-based prediction tools based on highly advanced artificial intelligence algorithms are also becoming available on a broader scale. Such tools are capable of handling large amounts of complex data and identifying patterns that may be difficult for a human to see directly. Prediction tools can be integrated into electronic health records for use by health care professionals, but they may also be available online or as mobile apps for patients or the general public for educational, monitoring or self-monitoring purposes.

Prognostic tools for dementia prevention

Cognitive impairment and dementia are the result of many different risk and protective factors acting at various stages across the entire life span (Winblad et al. 2016). Several of these risk factors (e.g. lifestyle-related, cardiovascular or metabolic) are modifiable, thus creating a window of opportunity for dementia prevention. For example, it has been estimated that around a third of Alzheimer dementia cases worldwide would be attributable to seven modifiable risk factors with consistent evidence from observational studies: diabetes, midlife hypertension, midlife obesity, physical inactivity, depression, smoking and low education (Norton et al. 2014). In the context of dementia prevention, prognostic tools have several areas of potential applicability as summarized in Table 2.1.

Two systematic reviews from 2010 to 2014 have identified over 50 different dementia risk prediction algorithms for prognostic or diagnostic purposes (Stephan et al. 2010; Tang et al. 2015). There are many similarities but also differences between these algorithms (Table 2.2).

Table 2.1 Potential applicability of dementia risk scores (prognostic tools)

Clinical	Early identification of at-risk individuals Quantifying an individual's prevention potential Directing at-risk individuals towards the preventive strategies that they are most likely to benefit from (lifestyle-oriented, pharmacological or combined interventions) Monitoring and/or self-monitoring of risk modifications over time, especially in the context of preventive interventions Identifying at-risk individuals who may need more detailed/costly investigations for diagnostic purposes
Public health	Educational and motivational tools for promoting brain health in the general population
Research	Selecting at-risk individuals who are eligible for clinical trials testing specific interventions Tailoring interventions to specific risk profiles Trial outcomes (especially in early prevention where trial duration may preclude dementia incidence from being a feasible outcome)

Table 2.2 General characteristics of current dementia prediction algorithms

Development method	*Data analytical approach* (most algorithms), e.g. using cohort studies to identify predictors and their weights in the algorithm; most common data analysis methods are logistic or Cox proportional hazards regression; more complex and novel methods (e.g. machine learning) are used only rarely. *Evidence-based medicine approach* (a few algorithms), considering extant literature, e.g. systematic review and Delphi consensus process to determine predictors and their weights in the algorithm.

(Continued)

Table 2.2 (Continued)

Predictors	*Easily accessible*: age, sex, education, various cardiovascular factors (e.g. blood pressure, body mass index, cholesterol), medical history (e.g. diabetes, heart disease, stroke, other chronic late-life conditions), lifestyle-related factors (e.g. smoking, physical activity, dietary habits), self-rated health and physical fitness, self-rated cognitive problems. *Requiring more specialized assessments*: cognitive tests, neuroimaging parameters, genetic factors, blood or cerebrospinal fluid biomarkers, electrocardiogram, ultrasound assessment of blood vessel parameters.
Timing	*Shorter-term prediction* (usually up to 10 years) based on late-life predictors (most algorithms) *Long-term prediction* (up to 40 years) based on midlife predictors (a few algorithms)
Target populations	General population Individuals with mild cognitive impairment Individuals with type 2 diabetes
Validation status	Very few are externally validated
Performance range	Discriminative accuracy varies between 0.49 and 0.89 (where 1 is perfect accuracy, and 0.5 is the equivalent of flipping a coin). For comparison, the widely used Framingham Risk Score for predicting risk of coronary heart disease events is considered to perform well with reported discriminative accuracy of 0.75–0.80.

Although there are many dementia prediction algorithms reported in the scientific literature, this area of research is still in its infancy compared to, for example, prediction of cardiovascular disease or diabetes. Beyond data analysis and algorithm development methods, several key methodological issues specific to dementia research need to be considered.

Prognostic or diagnostic algorithms?

Cognitive impairment and dementia are not acute events with a clearly defined onset, and the diagnostic criteria for the underlying diseases are still debated (Morris et al. 2014). For example, Alzheimer's disease (AD) develops over a long period of time, up to several decades. The first asymptomatic brain changes progress gradually, leading to mild cognitive impairment, which is later followed by dementia (Morris et al. 2014). At older ages, traditionally defined at-risk states (i.e. increased risk but the disease is not yet present) are hard to differentiate from pre-symptomatic or pre-dementia stages of an already ongoing disease. These factors can easily blur the distinction between diagnostic and prognostic algorithms (Figure 2.1).

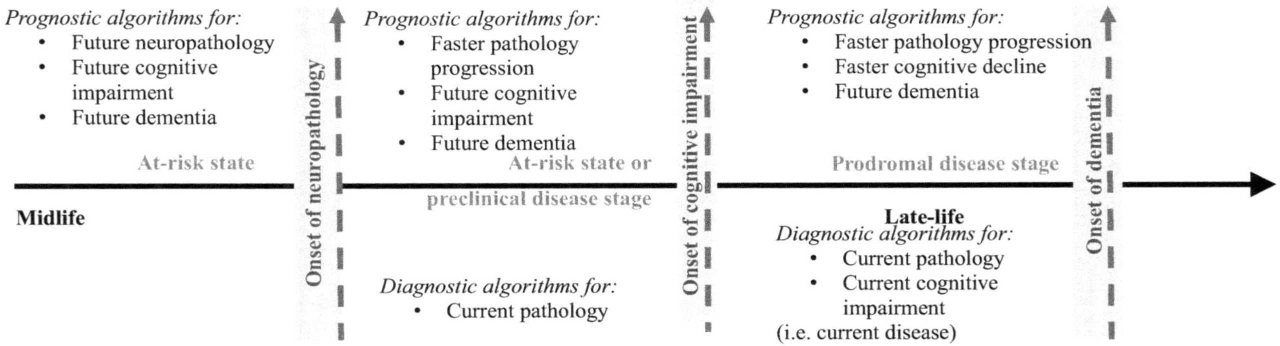

Figure 2.1 Potential purposes of prognostic and diagnostic algorithms in different pre-dementia disease stages

The primary purpose of a dementia risk score must be explicitly stated to avoid confusion and set realistic expectations regarding predictive performance. Requirements for diagnostic algorithms are much stricter than for prognostic algorithms used for general public health education, e.g. to provide guidance about dementia prevention and to motivate individuals to make healthy lifestyle changes and adhere to vascular risk management, or for selection of participants for lifestyle intervention trials. Stricter requirements may be preferable for risk scores aiming to identify individuals who are close to dementia onset and need referral to specialized clinics for detailed cognitive and biomarker testing, or for selection of participants for trials that test disease-modifying drugs with potentially severe adverse effects.

Short-term or late-life versus long-term or midlife prediction?

There is general agreement that interventions to prevent dementia should start as early as possible to be most effective. Long-term prognostic algorithms based on midlife risk factors and covering several decades are usually associated with primary prevention strategies. Midlife dementia risk scores tend to identify 'true' at-risk states before disease onset, because dementia-related diseases are less likely to be present at younger ages. Only a few midlife risk scores for estimating dementia risk 20–40 years later are available (Tang et al. 2015), and they include risk factors such as physical inactivity, unhealthy dietary habits, smoking, hypertension, hyperlipidaemia, obesity or pre-existing medical conditions (e.g. cardiovascular and metabolic disease, depression). By including modifiable risk factors, these prediction algorithms also indicate the dementia prevention potential of an individual, and thus possible intervention strategies, such as modification of lifestyle habits and/or adequate management of pre-existing medical conditions.

Shorter-term prognostic algorithms based on late-life risk factors and covering up to 5–10 years represent most of available dementia risk scores (Solomon and Soininen 2015). They are often associated with secondary or tertiary prevention strategies, given that older individuals are more likely to have brain changes and/or milder degrees of cognitive impairment that may or may not reach the threshold for seeking medical care and receiving a formal diagnosis. Interestingly, the predictive role of lifestyle, cardiovascular or metabolic factors at older ages can be very different compared with midlife/younger ages. Some late-life dementia risk scores include, for example, low blood pressure, low body mass index or low cholesterol as predictors (Tang et al. 2015; Solomon and Soininen 2015). This is perhaps not surprising, as blood pressure, body mass index and cholesterol levels have been shown to decline over time from midlife to late-life in individuals who subsequently develop dementia (Solomon et al. 2014). The exact mechanisms are not fully clear, but difficulties in separating risk relations from reverse causality at older ages are a key source of apparently conflicting findings in dementia epidemiology research. It is thus possible that such late-life dementia risk algorithms are primarily driven not by potentially modifiable risk factors, but by indicators of an already ongoing disease process. These risk scores would be less indicative of an individual's prevention potential and more indicative of a need for further diagnostic assessments.

Work is currently ongoing to develop late-life prediction algorithms that can help quantify prevention potential. Optimal solutions would have to consider not only modifiable lifestyle, vascular or metabolic risk factors, but also indicators of relevant disease processes, so that individuals with elevated dementia risk can be directed to the most appropriate interventions (non-pharmacological, pharmacological or combinations).

What predictors?

Many predictors included in dementia risk scores are also risk factors for cardiovascular disease, diabetes or other chronic late-life conditions. With several established and widely used cardiovascular and other risk scores, it would be relatively easy to use them for estimating dementia risk and motivating people to adhere to healthy lifestyle habits and adequate medical treatments, especially in the context of primary prevention. However, their predictive performance for dementia has not been fully investigated, and many cardiovascular risk scores are not designed for people older than 70 years. It is nevertheless important to keep in mind that pragmatic and effective dementia prevention strategies will have to consider the current background of cardiovascular, diabetes and stroke prevention programs. Integrating such prevention programs, e.g. at the community or primary health care level, would be an essential step towards promoting healthy ageing.

What exactly are we predicting?

Risk algorithms could potentially be used for predicting not only dementia but also cognitive impairment or specific types of brain pathology (e.g. amyloid or tau accumulation, cerebrovascular lesions) (Figure 2.1). Few risk scores have been developed for mild cognitive impairment, and none so far for neuropathology. For example, predicting amyloid accumulation with reasonably good accuracy by using accessible and less costly predictors is much needed for reducing expensive and burdensome screening failures in clinical trials testing amyloid immunotherapy in people with preclinical or prodromal AD. These individuals are currently identified by assessing amyloid in the cerebrospinal fluid by lumbar puncture or on positron emission tomography (PET) scans. A brain amyloid risk score would identify people who are most likely to be amyloid-positive, thus reducing the number of invasive and/or expensive procedures during the trial screening phase.

Dementia risk scores and current prevention-related decision-making

Only two dementia risk scores (Table 2.3) have so far been used in pragmatic contexts, i.e. population-based lifestyle intervention trials. The Cardiovascular Risk factors, Aging and Dementia (CAIDE) Risk Score was developed based on data from a Finnish longitudinal cohort study (Kivipelto et al. 2006; Exalto et al. 2014). The Lifestyle for Brain Health (LIBRA) score was developed based on a systematic review and expert consensus study (Deckers et al. 2014; Schiepers et al. 2018; Pons et al. 2018). Both CAIDE and LIBRA are midlife risk scores meant to estimate dementia risk several decades later based on risk factor profiles in midlife. Both have also been validated in several populations. The CAIDE score has been used in the Finnish Geriatric Intervention Study to prevent cognitive impairment and disability (FINGER) (Ngandu et al. 2015), and the LIBRA score in the Innovative Midlife Intervention for Dementia Deterrence (In-MINDD) study (O'Donnell et al. 2015).

The CAIDE dementia risk score and the FINGER trial

FINGER was the first large multi-domain randomized controlled trial to report significant beneficial effects on cognition for a multi-domain lifestyle

Table 2.3 Dementia risk scores currently used in lifestyle preventive interventions

CAIDE score			*LIBRA score*	
Factors		*Points*	*Factors*	*Points*
Age (years)	< 47	0	*Low-to-moderate alcohol intake*	−1.0
	47–53	3	*Coronary heart disease*	+1.0
	>53	4	*Renal disease*	+1.1
Education (years)	≥10	0	*Diabetes*	+1.3
	7–9	2	*Smoking*	+1.5
	0–6	3	*Depression*	+2.1
Sex	Women	0	*Healthy diet*	−1.7
	Men	1	*High cognitive activity*	−3.2
Systolic blood pressure (mmHg)	≤ 140	0	*(Midlife) hypertension*	+1.6
	> 140	2		
Body mass index (BMI) (kg/m²)	≤ 30	0	*(Midlife) obesity*	+1.6
	> 30	2		
Total cholesterol (mmol/l)	≤ 6.5	0	*Hypercholesterolemia*	+1.4
	> 6.5	2		
Physical activity	Active	0	*Physical inactivity*	+1.1
	Inactive	1		

Total score is calculated as the sum of the listed risk/protective factors. A higher score indicates higher risk for subsequent dementia development. The CAIDE score is available as a mobile phone app (Sindi et al. 2015), and work is ongoing to increase the availability of the LIBRA score.

intervention versus regular health advice (Ngandu et al. 2015). The intervention targeted several risk factors simultaneously: nutritional guidance, exercise, cognitive training, social activity and intensive monitoring/management of metabolic and vascular risk factors. It was thus important to select participants based on a risk profile instead of individual risk factors. Inclusion criteria were age 60–77 years, CAIDE Dementia Risk Score of at least 6 points and cognition at mean level or slightly lower than expected for age. The 1,260 participants were selected from previous national non-intervention surveys conducted since the 1970s. This provided valuable pre-trial data on midlife risk factors that were used to calculate the CAIDE score for each participant. The intervention had significant beneficial effects on overall cognitive performance (the primary outcome), on different cognitive domains (processing speed, executive function and complex memory tasks) and it reduced the risk of cognitive decline. There were also benefits on other outcomes including body mass index, nutrition-related factors, physical activity and quality of life (Ngandu et al. 2015; Strandberg et al. 2017).

The importance of adequately selecting target populations for lifestyle interventions to prevent dementia and cognitive decline, and the key role of validated risk scores were further emphasized by two other large trials testing multi-domain lifestyle interventions. The Multi-domain Alzheimer Preventive Trial (MAPT) study tested whether a combination of nutritional counselling, physical exercise and cognitive stimulation, together with omega-3 polyunsaturated fatty acids supplementation, had benefits on cognition in 1680 frail older adults at risk of cognitive decline (Andrieu et al. 2017). While no significant effect was found when considering all participants, there were benefits in participants with a CAIDE dementia risk score of at least 6 points and in participants with evidence of brain amyloid accumulation on PET scans (Andrieu et al. 2017). The Prevention of Dementia by Intensive Vascular care (preDIVA) trial tested a six-year multi-domain vascular intervention including dietary advice versus usual care in 3,526 older individuals (age 70–78 years) from general practices in the Netherlands (Moll van Charante et al. 2016). The intervention did not result in a reduced incidence of all-cause dementia in this unselected sample of older people in a general practice setting with high standards of usual care. However, some benefits on dementia incidence were noted in at-risk subgroups (e.g. participants with untreated hypertension at baseline who adhered to the intervention).

Findings from the FINGER, preDIVA and MAPT trials thus suggest that preventive interventions may need to be adequately targeted to at-risk populations to be most effective. Validated dementia risk algorithms that can also indicate prevention potential could be particularly useful in this context.

The LIBRA score and the In-MINDD trial

The LIBRA score excludes non-modifiable factors that are commonly part of most dementia risk scores (age, sex and education). It was designed to focus primarily on an individual's dementia prevention potential and consists only of modifiable factors that are promising targets for preventive strategies (Table 2.3). In-MINDD, a multi-centre, primary care-based, single-blinded randomized controlled trial, has been testing the feasibility and acceptability of the LIBRA score and an on-line support environment in France, Ireland, the Netherlands and the UK (Scotland) (O'Donnell et al. 2015). The target population of about 600 participants have been recruited from general practices. Inclusion criteria are age 40–60 years; at least one modifiable risk factor for dementia (e.g. diabetes, hypertension, obesity, renal dysfunction, smoking, high cholesterol, coronary heart disease, history of depression, sedentary lifestyle and low cognitive activity) and internet access. The control group received generic health information material, while the intervention group had access to an on-line profiler and support environment which, based on individualized demographic, clinical and self-reported information on health-related behaviours, can calculate an individual's dementia risk modification score. This information was given to individuals as a personalized LIBRA global score and profile, highlighting areas of health-related behaviour in which they are doing well (e.g. if they are a non-smoker); areas which they cannot change but need to manage (e.g. if they have diabetes); and areas where they could make improvements (e.g. by increasing physical activity). The personalized on-line support environment supported goal setting and gave access to health information. In addition to LIBRA, the study is also investigating participants' views of dementia prevention and exploring the acceptability and integration of the In-MINDD intervention into daily life and routine practice.

Use of risk scores in drug trials for dementia prevention

A possible use of prediction algorithms could be as enrichment tools in drug trials for dementia prevention. A genetics-based biomarker risk algorithm has been developed based on a combination of age, the apolipoprotein E (APOE) genotype and the translocase of outer mitochondrial membrane 40 homolog (TOMM40) genotype (Lutz et al. 2016). The APOE ε4 allele is the strongest known genetic risk factor for AD and dementia (Alzgene.org 2018). The TOMM40 gene is located next to APOE on chromosome 19 and has also been associated with increased AD risk (Lutz et al. 2016). The genetic risk algorithm has been used in the design of the TOMORROW trial testing pioglitazone (a drug used for certain patients with type 2 diabetes) for prevention of mild cognitive impairment (MCI) in cognitively normal individuals aged 65–83 years (Clinicaltrials.gov 2018). In this trial, high-risk participants were randomized to the active or placebo group, while low-risk participants were randomized to placebo only. Stratification for risk of developing MCI due to AD during the study was done using the genetic algorithm at the beginning of the trial, before randomization. The aims of the trial were to (i) qualify the genetic biomarker risk algorithm for assigning five-year risk for developing MCI due to AD and (ii) evaluate the efficacy of low-dose pioglitazone as a treatment to delay onset of MCI due to AD in cognitively normal, high-risk individuals.

Unfortunately, the trial was terminated in January 2018 based on a planned interim futility analysis, which showed an inadequate treatment effect on preventing MCI (Takeda 2018). Further work on the genetic risk algorithm is ongoing.

Conclusion

While much work is still needed until accurate and reliable prediction tools can be used in practice for decision-making related to dementia prevention, the first steps have already been taken, with positive results at least for lifestyle-based preventive interventions. There is great need for a 'dementia prevention toolbox', i.e. a set of tools for different purposes and contexts: midlife or late-life risk profiles and long-term or short-term prediction, public health, primary care or specialized memory clinics. The potential utility of both pen-and-paper and computer-based risk profiling should be tested. With an increasing number of risk factors and biomarkers emerging from observational epidemiological studies, it can become very difficult to easily and quickly identify the most relevant prognostic information hidden within large volumes of data. Computer-based profiling methods and clinical decision support systems have been developed to facilitate early diagnosis of dementia-related diseases (Mattila 2013), and they may also be useful for prevention-related decision-making. In addition, several ongoing large prevention trials, both pharmacological and non-pharmacological, provide opportunities to investigate prediction models for dementia risk and also likelihood of intervention response. This is essential for tailoring preventive strategies to at-risk individuals who are most likely to benefit from specific interventions.

References

Alzgene.org. (2018). AlzGene. [online] Available at: www.alzgene.org/ [Accessed 15 March 2018].

Anderson, K. M., Odell, P. M., Wilson, P. W. & Kannel, W. B. (1991). Cardiovascular disease risk profiles. *American Heart Journal*, 121, 293–298.

Andrieu, S., Guyonnet, S., Coley, N., Cantet, C., Bonnefoy, M., Bordes, S., Bories, L., Cufi, M. N., Dantoine, T., Dartigues, J. F., Desclaux, F., Gabelle, A., Gasnier, Y., Pesce, A., Sudres, K., Touchon, J., Robert, P., Rouaud, O., Legrand, P., Payoux, P., Caubere, J. P., Weiner, M., Carrié, I., Ousset, P. J., Vellas, B. & MAPT Study Group. (2017). Effect of long-term omega 3 polyunsaturated fatty acid supplementation with or without multidomain intervention on cognitive function in elderly adults with memory complaints (MAPT): A randomised, placebo-controlled trial. *The Lancet Neurology*, 16(5), 377–389.

Clinicaltrials.gov. (2018). Biomarker qualification for risk of Mild Cognitive Impairment (MCI) due to Alzheimer's Disease (AD) and safety and efficacy evaluation of pioglitazone in delaying its onset – full text view. *ClinicalTrials.gov*. [online] Available at: https://clinicaltrials.gov/ct2/show/NCT01931566 [Accessed 15 March 2018].

Collins, G. S., Reitsma, J. B., Altman, D. G. & Moons, K. G. (2015). Transparent reporting of a multivariable prediction model for individual prognosis or diagnosis (TRIPOD): The TRIPOD statement. *BMJ*, 350, g7594. doi:10.1136/bmj.g7594.

Deckers, K., van Boxtel, M. P., Schiepers, O. J., de Vugt, M., Muñoz Sánchez, J. L., Anstey, K. J., Brayne, C., Dartigues, J. F., Engedal, K., Kivipelto, M., Ritchie, K., Starr, J. M., Yaffe, K., Irving, K., Verhey, F. R. & Köhler, S. (2014). Target risk factors for dementia prevention: A systematic review and Delphi consensus study on the evidence from observational studies. *International Journal of Geriatric Psychiatry*, 30, 234–246.

Exalto, L. G., Quesenberry, C. P., Barnes, D., Kivipelto, M., Biessels, G. J. & Whitmer, R. A. (2014). Midlife risk score for the prediction of dementia four decades later. *Alzheimers Dement*, 10(5), 562–570.

Haybittle, J. L., Blamey, R. W., Elston, C. W., Johnson, J., Doyle, P. J., Campbell, F. C., Nicholson, R. I. & Griffiths, K. (1982). A prognostic index in primary breast cancer. *British Journal of Cancer*, 45, 361–366.

Kivipelto, M., Ngandu, T., Laatikainen, T., Winblad, B., Soininen, H. & Tuomilehto, J. (2006). Risk score for the prediction of dementia risk in 20 years among middle aged people: A longitudinal, population-based study. *The Lancet Neurology*, 5(9), 735–741.

Lutz, M. W., Sundseth, S. S., Burns, D. K., Saunders, A. M., Hayden, K. M., Burke, J. R., Welsh-Bohmer, K. A. & Roses, A. D. (2016). A genetics-based biomarker risk algorithm for predicting risk of Alzheimer's disease. *Alzheimers Dement (NY)*, 2(1), 30–44.

Mattila, J. (2013). Disease state index and disease state fingerprint: Supervised learning applied to clinical decision support in Alzheimer's disease. *Espoo, VTT Science*, 51. Available at: www.vtt.fi/inf/pdf/science/2013/S51.pdf [Accessed 15 March 2018].

Moll van Charante, E. P., Richard, E., Eurelings, L. S., van Dalen, J. W., Ligthart, S. A., van Bussel, E. F., Hoevenaar-Blom, M. P., Vermeulen, M. & van Gool, W. A. (2016). Effectiveness of a 6-year multidomain vascular care intervention to prevent dementia (preDIVA): A cluster-randomised controlled trial. *The Lancet*, 388(10046), 797–780.

Moons, K. G., Altman, D. G., Reitsma, J. B., Ioannidis, J. P., Macaskill, P., Steyerberg, E. W., Vickers, A. J., Ransohoff, D. F. & Collins, G. S. (2015). Transparent reporting of a multivariable prediction model for Individual Prognosis or Diagnosis (TRIPOD): Explanation and elaboration. *Annals of Internal Medicine*, 162(1), W1–W73.

Morris, J. C., Blennow, K., Froelich, L., Nordberg, A., Soininen, H., Waldemar, G., Wahlund, L. O. & Dubois, B. (2014). Harmonized diagnostic criteria for Alzheimer's disease: Recommendations. *Journal of Internal Medicine*, 275(3), 204–213.

Nashef, S. A., Roques, F., Michel, P., Gauducheau, E., Lemeshow, S. & Salamon, R. (1999). European system for cardiac operative risk evaluation (EuroSCORE). *European Journal of Cardio-Thoracic Surgery*, 16(1), 9–13.

Ngandu, T., Lehtisalo, J., Solomon, A., Levälahti, E., Ahtiluoto, S., Antikainen, R., Bäckman, L., Hänninen, T., Jula, A., Laatikainen, T., Lindström, J., Mangialasche, F., Paajanen, T., Pajala, S., Peltonen, M., Rauramaa, R., Stigsdotter-Neely, A., Strandberg, T., Tuomilehto, J., Soininen, H. & Kivipelto, M. (2015). A 2 year multidomain intervention of diet, exercise, cognitive training, and vascular risk monitoring versus control to prevent cognitive decline in at-risk elderly people (FINGER): A randomised controlled trial. *The Lancet*, 385, 2255–2263.

Norton, S., Matthews, F. E., Barnes, D. E., Yaffe, K. & Brayne, C. (2014). Potential for primary prevention of Alzheimer's disease: An analysis of population-based data. *The Lancet Neurology*, 13, 788–794.

O'Donnell, C. A., Browne, S., Pierce, M., McConnachie, A., Deckers, K., van Boxtel, M. P., Manera, V., Köhler, S., Redmond, M., Verhey, F. R., van den Akker, M., Power, K., Irving, K. & In-MINDD Team. (2015). Reducing dementia risk by targeting modifiable risk factors in mid-life: Study protocol for the Innovative Midlife Intervention for Dementia Deterrence (In-MINDD) randomised controlled feasibility trial. *Pilot Feasibility Studies*, 1, 40.

Perk, J., De Backer, G., Gohlke, H., Graham, I., Reiner, Z., Verschuren, M., Albus, C., Benlian, P., Boysen, G., Cifkova, R., Deaton, C., Ebrahim, S., Fisher, M., Germano, G., Hobbs, R., Hoes, A., Karadeniz, S., Mezzani, A., Prescott, E., Ryden, L., Scherer, M., Syvänne, M., Scholte op Reimer, W. J., Vrints, C., Wood, D., Zamorano, J. L., Zannad, F. & European Association for Cardiovascular Prevention & Rehabilitation (EACPR), ESC Committee for Practice Guidelines. (CPG). European Guidelines on cardiovascular disease prevention in clinical practice (version 2012). The fifth joint task force of the European society of cardiology and other societies on cardiovascular disease prevention in clinical practice (constituted by representatives of nine societies and by invited experts). *European Heart Journal*, 33(13), 1635–1701.

Pons, A., LaMonica, H. M., Mowszowski, L., Köhler, S., Deckers, K. & Naismith, S. L. (2018). Utility of the LIBRA index in relation to cognitive functioning in a clinical health seeking sample. *Journal of Alzheimers Diseases*, 62(1), 373–384.

Schiepers, O. J. G., Köhler, S., Deckers, K., Irving, K., O'Donnell, C. A., van den Akker, M., Verhey, F. R. J., Vos, S. J. B., de Vugt, M. E. & van Boxtel, M. P. J. (2018). Lifestyle for Brain Health (LIBRA): A new model for dementia prevention. *International Journal of Geriatric Psychiatry*, 33(1), 167–175.

Sindi, S., Calov, E., Fokkens, J., Ngandu, T., Soininen, H., Tuomilehto, J. & Kivipelto, M. (2015). The CAIDE dementia risk score app: The development of an evidence-based mobile application to predict the risk of dementia. *Alzheimers Dement (Amst)*, 1(3), 328–333.

Solomon, A., Mangialasche, F., Richard, E., Andrieu, S., Bennett, D. A., Breteler, M., Fratiglioni, L., Hooshmand, B., Khachaturian, A. S., Schneider, L. S., Skoog, I. & Kivipelto, M. (2014). Advances in the prevention of Alzheimer's disease and dementia. *Journal of Internal Medicine*, 275(3), 229–250.

Solomon, A. & Soininen, H. (2015). Dementia: Risk prediction models in dementia prevention. *Nature Reviews Neurology*, 11(7), 375–377.

Stephan, B. C. M., Kurth, T., Matthews, F. E., Brayne, C. & Dufouil, C. (2010). Dementia risk prediction in the population: Are screening models accurate? *Nature Reviews Neurology*, 6(6), 318–326.

Strandberg, T. E., Levälahti, E., Ngandu, T., Solomon, A. & Kivipelto, M. (2017). Health-related quality of life in a multidomain intervention trial to prevent cognitive decline (FINGER). *European Geriatric Medicine*, 8, 164–167.

Takeda. (2018). Takeda and zinfandel pharmaceuticals discontinue TOMMORROW trial following planned futility analysis. [online] *Takeda.com*. Available at: www.takeda.com/newsroom/newsreleases/2018/takeda-tommorrow-trial/ [Accessed 15 March 2018].

Tang, E. Y., Harrison, S. L., Errington, L., Gordon, M. F., Visser, P. J., Novak, G., Dufouil, C., Brayne, C., Robinson, L., Launer, L. J. & Stephan, B. C. (2015). Current developments in Dementia risk prediction modelling: An updated systematic review. *PLoS One*, 10(9), e0136181.

University of Sheffield. (2008). *Fracture risk assessment tool* [online]. Available at: www.sheffield.ac.uk/FRAX/ [Accessed 15 March 2018].

Winblad, B., Amouyel, P., Andrieu, S., Ballard, C., Brayne, C., Brodaty, H., Cedazo-Minguez, A., Dubois, B., Edvardsson, D., Feldman, H., Fratiglioni, L., Frisoni, G. B., Gauthier, S., Georges, J., Graff, C., Iqbal, K., Jessen, F., Johansson, G., Jönsson, L., Kivipelto, M., Knapp, M., Mangialasche, F., Melis, R., Nordberg, A., Rikkert, M. O., Qiu, C., Sakmar, T. P., Scheltens, P., Schneider, L. S., Sperling, R., Tjernberg, L. O., Waldemar, G., Wimo, A. & Zetterberg, H. (2016). Defeating Alzheimer's disease and other dementias: A priority for European science and society. *The Lancet Neurology*, 15(5), 455–532.

Section 1

Established and emerging risk factors

In this section, an overview is given of established and emerging risk and protective factors associated with dementia. In Chapter 3, lifestyle-related risk factors are discussed, followed by the closely related vascular disease risk factors in Chapter 4. This is followed by a review of the association between mood and psychiatric disorders in dementia in Chapter 5 and a discussion of cognitive reserve and activity in Chapter 6. Chapter 7 outlines sleep and sleep disorders and dementia. Each chapter discusses epidemiology and evidence from observational and experimental studies. A brief overview is given for biological plausibility of risk and protective factors and future directions for research. In Chapter 8, theoretical models related to health behavioral change are discussed and evidence from large trials which have focused on prevention of dementia and cognitive decline to better guide development of policy, which is discussed in Section 2.

Chapter 3

Lifestyle factors and dementia

Smoking, exercise and diet

Eef Hogervorst, Deborah Oliveira and Carol Brayne

Introduction

Costs and demographic risk factors for dementia: age and education

Longevity and low levels of education are the largest demographic risk factors for dementia (Launer et al. 1999; Barnes and Yaffe 2011). With an ageing population worldwide, dementia is a growing problem (World Health Organization 2015). Much of this growth (around 60%–70%) is seen in low- and medium-income countries, which are burdened by a lack of financial and specialist resources to cope with this societal need (Prince et al. 2015). In addition, with increasing urbanisation of younger generations, many older adults are left behind without access to both formal and informal care (World Health Organization 2015) (see more in Chapter 9).

Care needs in dementia are significant and increase with its progression, often leading to carer burnout and institutionalisation. Dementia has high human and economic costs, estimated at $1 trillion in 2018. These costs include formal and informal care provided by families and others. Currently, 47 million people worldwide are estimated to be living with dementia, a number which is expected to almost double by 2030 to 75 million and to 132 million by 2050 (Prince et al. 2015).

While an older age might make the brain more susceptible to inflammation, altered glucose metabolism, oxidative stress, hypoxia and plaque toxicity, all proposed as pathogenic influences associated with dementia, the role of low education in dementia is not entirely clear. Having had high education might create more cognitive reserve and having had little education could reduce alternative coping strategies, which are important in having a barrier against functional decline (Brayne et al. 2010). The corollary to this would be earlier clinically apparent manifestation of dementia in people with lower education levels (Brayne et al. 2010). Other mechanisms proposed are related to a build-up of increased connectivity between neurons with higher education levels, so that the physical damage and the loss of neuronal connections are less detrimental in those with higher education (see Chapter 6). This phenomenon has been called the 'brain reserve capacity' theory (Esiri and Chance 2012) (explained further in Chapter 6). Another theory is that higher education levels are associated with a propensity to lifelong learning, which can be protective against dementia. This includes keeping mentally active, which in many observational studies has been associated with lower dementia risk (Hogervorst and Clifford 2013). For this reason, many of the current preventative trials to reduce dementia risk include cognitive or mental stimulation strategies. However, many of these mental stimulating treatment strategies and 'brain games' do not seem to generalise to better every day cognitive functioning (Niederstrasser et al. 2016).

Alternative mechanisms (Hogervorst and Clifford 2013), which could explain the association of education with dementia, include the association of low obtained education with own – but also parental lower socio-economic status (SES). This often means a lifelong lowered access to optimal nutritional, health care, academic and other resources (music lessons, learning another language and other costly extra-curricular activities), more exposure to stressors due to a lack of financial means, more exposure to violence, substance abuse and environmental pollution in poorer areas. In addition, for those with low SES living in the northern hemisphere, this also means less exposure to sun in winter months (and thus less vitamin D). Less education also possibly results in having less knowledge of healthy lifestyles and/or putting this knowledge into practice (Hogervorst and Clifford 2013). Individually based strategies are known to increase inequality for this reason. These factors taken together could result in a lack of protective factors and surplus of potential negative risk factors over the lifespan. For a more detailed discussion on seven models associating low education/childhood IQ with dementia (see Hogervorst and Clifford 2013).

Types of dementia and prevention through lifestyles related to vascular risk

The most common underlying pathology associated with dementia, and clinical diagnosis made, is Alzheimer's disease (AD). This is characterised by distinct pathology of the brain, such as plaques mainly consisting of beta-amyloid and neurofibrillary tangles, which interfere with normal brain function. Clinically, AD shows a gradual and progressive decline in cognitive functions affecting daily and social activities (Mckhann et al. 2011). However, previous post-mortem analysis of people with the more usual dementia of late onset have shown the presence of other pathologies (e.g. vascular disease, Lewy Bodies), meaning that it is unusual to find a single pathology affecting a brain with dementia (e.g. pure AD or pure Vascular dementia) (see Hogervorst et al. 2003). As there is no current effective long-term pharmacological treatment for dementia, prevention is at present the best and probably most cost-effective strategy to reduce dementia incidence.

It has been suggested that preventative measures may be effective if societies, communities and individuals focus on modifiable lifestyle-related risk factors for dementia, such as smoking, lack of exercise and poor diet, which are also risk factors for vascular disease (Hogervorst and Clifford 2013). As the risk factors for vascular diseases overlap with those for most dementias (Kivipelto et al. 2005), reducing the risk factors for vascular morbidities and their related risk factors is likely to be the most beneficial approach in reducing dementia incidence.

It has been estimated that approximately a third of dementia cases could potentially be prevented through lifestyle changes, such as increasing physical activity, stopping smoking, by preventing midlife obesity and by treating midlife hypertension, diabetes and depression, which would result in great cost savings (Norton et al. 2014; Barnes and Yaffe 2011). Although observational studies have generally demonstrated that these factors are associated with dementia risk, there is an overall dearth of high-quality research on the effects of interventions using randomised controlled trails (RTCs) addressing modifiable lifestyle risk factors, such as smoking cessation on the risk of developing dementia (Olanrewaju et al. 2015; Norton et al. 2014).

For this reason, while thus acknowledging the important possibly mediating role of education and SES on dementia risk, this chapter focuses on the relationship between modifiable lifestyles and dementia. In this chapter, we will discuss whether treatments focused on lifestyle factors have been effective in reducing risk for dementia (primary prevention) and have been effective in improving memory functions and other cognitive symptoms in people with prodromal dementia or those at risk for dementia (secondary preventions) and those who have established dementia (tertiary prevention).

Reviews of lifestyle factors and dementia risk

Smoking

It has been estimated that the global prevalence of smoking in the population aged 15 years and over is 31.1% and 6.2% for men and women, respectively (Ng et al. 2014). It is highly biological plausible that smoking plays a significant role in dementia risk, mediated through its association with increased vascular disease risk, as well as the neurotoxins in cigarette smoke (Swan and Lessov-Schlaggar 2007). However, it is a far more effective killer and dementia is clearly more common in women, who live longer. Smoking is thought to be mainly a 'vascular' risk factor for dementia, together with midlife hypertension, diabetes mellitus, midlife obesity, stroke and cardiovascular disease (Mangialasche et al. 2013), and is also associated with increased blood pressure, atherosclerosis, increased total and low-density lipoprotein (LDL) cholesterol and hypoxia. All these factors are implicated in dementia pathology of different types, including amyloid plaques and vascular neuropathologies, such as white matter disease (Hogervorst et al. 2002).

Observational studies

Most observational studies report smoking to be a significant risk factor for dementia (Baumgart et al. 2015). A few studies have shown no association between smoking and dementia onset (Knopman et al. 2001; Strand et al. 2013). One study from Taiwan (Wang et al. 2010) suggested that smoking protected against dementia, but this is likely to have been biased as findings are otherwise consistent (Lafortune et al. 2016; Baumgart et al. 2015; Zhong et al. 2015). A systematic review of cohort studies from midlife with a minimum five-year follow-up found consistent evidence that midlife smoking had a detrimental effect on health across all populations studied (Lafortune et al. 2016).The review identified strong evidence of the association between smoking in midlife and dementia (or cognitive decline) in later life, with less clear associations between smoking and specific types of dementia.The long-term ex-smokers (compared to current smokers and recent ex-smokers) were less likely to have a cognitive deficit, with declines in all cognitive domains being larger as the number of pack-years smoked increased. A meta-analysis of 37 studies confirmed these findings (Zhong et al. 2015), revealing that, compared with never smokers, current smokers have an increased risk for AD and vascular dementia. For all-cause dementia, the risk increased by 34% for every 20 cigarettes smoked a day, whilst ex-smokers did not show increased risk. The study found no difference in risk when comparing different sex, race, study location and diagnostic criteria groups. Another meta-analysis of 2- to 30-year follow-up prospective studies revealed similar findings, with current smokers at baseline having a 1.79 higher risk for AD, 1.78 for vascular dementia and 1.27 for any dementia as compared to never smokers (Anstey et al. 2007).

RCTs

Several prospective studies have shown that smoking cessation can have an overall health benefit, such as causing reduction of anxiety, depression and stress levels, improved positive mood and quality of life (Taylor et al. 2014) and lower cardiovascular mortality (Mons et al. 2015). Nevertheless, there is a lack of high-quality research addressing the effects of interventions focused on smoking cessation specifically for dementia risk reduction (Norton et al. 2014; Olanrewaju et al. 2015). It remains uncertain whether smoking cessation in later periods in life could lead to dementia risk reduction in later life.

Summary

Because of competing risks for mortality, there is conflicting evidence on whether smoking is a risk factor for dementia (see, for example, Olanrewaju et al. 2015; Durazzo et al. 2014); however, the compelling body of evidence suggests it is. Given the toxicity of smoking for health in general it is widely accepted that there is now sufficient evidence to justify immediate action for prevention/ management of vascular and lifestyle-related risk factors (such as smoking cessation) for dementia risk reduction (Smith and Yaffe 2014; Anstey et al. 2007). Indeed, smoking has been recently considered to have the third-highest estimated population attributable fraction of dementia risk, which is partly due to its high prevalence, and interventions aimed at helping individuals to stop smoking are therefore of paramount importance (Livingston et al. 2017).

Exercise and physical activity

Biological plausibility of exercise and physical activity in reducing dementia risk could be related to its association with improved vascular health and angiogenesis, reducing LDL cholesterol and atherosclerosis, reducing central obesity, long-term inflammatory responses and improving glucose metabolism (Trigiani and Hamel 2017). Exercise also has direct effects on brain function, and these have been suggested as helping reduce assumed pathogenic processes associated with dementia, such as amyloid-beta clearance, reduction of oxidative stress, improved cerebral blood flow and cholinergic activity, positively affecting neurogenesis and white matter integrity (Trigiani and Hamel 2017; Voss et al. 2013). Increased physical activity has been reported to be associated with increased neurogenesis (particularly in the hippocampus, which is important for memory) and synaptic connectivity between neurons (possibly through increased levels of brain derived nerve growth factor – BDNF), even in older mammals (Voss et al. 2013).

Observational studies

Many observational studies have shown preventative effects from engaging in exercise, suggesting that those who are physically active have a reduced dementia risk and improved cognition (Soni et al. 2017). Recent meta-analyses for all-type dementia, AD, vascular dementia and cognitive decline including 117,410 longitudinal observations with 32, 21, 8 and 22 cohorts, respectively (Guure et al. 2017), showed that the risk of developing all-type dementia was reduced by about 21% and 24%, from engaging in high levels and moderate levels of physical activity (PA), respectively. A similar meta-analysis conducted by Hamer and Chida (2008) and Blondell et al. (2014) revealed a 28% higher and 16% lower benefit, respectively, in relation to high PA for reduction of dementia risk, as compared to the findings in the most recent meta-analysis, which reported a 21%–24% reduction in risk (Guure et al. 2017). The most recent meta-analysis included over twice the number of studies of those of the earlier report (32 vs 14). This latest review also included several studies that did not report a PA-dementia relationship (regardless of intensity) (see Guure et al. 2017). This meta-analysis also investigated different dementias. For AD, high PA was associated with nearly 40% reduction in dementia risk and for moderate PA this was 29%. In the vascular dementia category, there were only eight studies and no effects were reported. When cognitive decline was the outcome, a dose-dependent effect was found (between moderate and high PA) for cognitive decline.

One study (English Longitudinal Study of Ageing – ELSA) reported that minimal PA just once a week reduced dementia risk by just over a third (Soni et al. 2017) and moderate/vigorous exercise once a week by the same. However, engaging in moderate/vigorous PA more than once a week reduced dementia risk by 50%. Dose-dependent effects were thus reported, in which engaging in more vigorous PA beyond this decreased dementia risk further (Soni et al. 2017). After people in the ELSA study received the dementia diagnoses, memory functions remained better if they continued to exercise, otherwise these showed a decline (Soni et al. 2017). However, causality here cannot be drawn (e.g. people who were more frail and/or more affected by dementia may have felt less able to exercise). The Million Women Study also suggested that the reduction of physical activity may be an early indicator of dementia itself, occurring many years before onset. There are a multitude of other potential reasons for variations in findings, including the nature of the populations studied, differential drop out, whether missing data are accounted for and differences in assessments.

Exercise may also offset some other risk factors and lack of exercise is related to many other known risk factors (e.g. obesity, alcohol abuse). The interplay between these risk factors over time must be understood much better to help tease out the key societal approaches with the greatest promise. Most studies do not address the timing of the physical activity, the duration of follow-up and, most importantly, when people stop exercising and why. As such cause and effect here are difficult to discern. Lastly, while risk models have been used to investigate cumulative effects of dementia risk factors, there is also an urgent need for models, including protective factors, such as exercise, psychosocial activity and diet.

RCTs

Many RCTs have shown that once people have developed dementia, resistance exercise and walking can still improve global cognitive function and activities of daily life. However, a review of reviews showed that evidence for exercise interventions on cognitive function in people with dementia was mixed (Mcdermott et al. 2018). Overall, reviews reported substantial heterogeneity, and there was inclusion of poor quality studies. One review (Öhman et al. 2014) did not perform meta-analysis, but reported positive effects of exercise on global cognition in 5/8 studies of people with dementia (tertiary prevention). In 3/5 of the studies in people with Mild Cognitive Impairment (MCI) improved global cognition was also found (secondary prevention). Other mixed effects of exercise on other cognitive functions in people with dementia or MCI were shown, such as on executive function (in 6/10 studies), delayed recall (3/7 studies, but only in MCI) and attention (5/5 studies, 4/5 in MCI). Combined cognitive and exercise interventions resulted in significant improvement in general cognitive function, although this only included three RCTs at the time (Ohman et al. 2014).

In other reviews (Forbes et al. 2015; Farina et al. 2013; Rao et al. 2014), global cognition after exercise overall was shown to have moderate-to-large effect sizes (tertiary prevention). However, the most recent Cochrane meta-analysis of 17 trials found no overall beneficial effect of exercise on cognition in people with dementia, although activities of daily life were generally improved in six trials (Forbes et al. 2015). Warnings were again given about substantial heterogeneity and poor study quality. Their previous meta-analysis included in the review of 16 studies (Forbes et al. 2013) did show a significant effect on cognition, albeit also with large heterogeneity. In addition, it is a concern to note that when an outlier was removed, the result was no longer significant.

A recent large Swedish trial also found no benefit on global cognition after a high intensity exercise programme (vs a seated control) after four months in people with dementia (Toots et al. 2017). The information taken together suggests that effects of exercise by itself may be most optimal for primary (and potentially to be tested in secondary) prevention, but less effective once people have developed dementia. It may be that some forms of exercise are more beneficial than others for people with and without dementia. There are some indications that a combination of aerobic and anaerobic exercises may have the most optimal results and current guidelines for older people stipulate 75 min vigorous or 150 min/week moderate aerobic exercise with 2–3/week strength improving exercises. However, UK data from 2012 suggest that only half op people over 55 and only 38% of men and 18% of women over 75 reach that target, with fewer people in deprived socio-economic areas (Townsend et al., 2015). However, resistance exercise by itself for 20–30 min, 2–3 times a week was already seen after 12 weeks to improve memory functions in two studies with sedentary older people with and without memory impairment or complaints (Hogervorst et al. 2012).

A recent meta-analysis of 10 RCTs (Karssemeijer et al. 2017) suggested that combined cognitive and physical activity improved global cognition and mood with a small to medium effect size, while effects on ADL were moderate to large. Effects were the same in people with dementia or MCI. Most recent trials (e.g. the Finnish Geriatric Intervention Study to Prevent Cognitive Impairment and Disability – FINGER; the Mental Activity and eXercise – MAX study) also showed beneficial effects of combined interventions (including dietary advice and reducing vascular risk factors) on cognition where more time spend on any physical and/or mental activities was associated with better cognition in people who had not developed dementia yet, but who were at risk (secondary prevention). However, effect sizes in general were small to medium only.

Summary

Exercise is currently considered to be one of the best preventative strategies to reduce dementia risk (primary prevention) and to be incorporated into research into combined interventions in trials of early detection or screening (i.e. secondary prevention). Whether group-based exercises are more beneficial than individual approaches remains to be investigated. Duration, frequency and type (aerobic/strength) may require a more personalised approach. More research is needed to establish this and to include potential offsetting effects of exercise (against known risks, such as alcohol abuse, in those who are obese, smoking and/or have a poor diet).

Diet: micro and macronutrients and whole diets

For dietary factors, associations with dementia risk reduction are also mixed. Antioxidant vitamins, such as vitamin A, C, D and E, could affect brain function by reducing oxidative stress, an important factor in ageing and dementia. There is good biological plausibility for folate combined with vitamin B12 and B6 to affect neuronal function, most likely through reduction of homocysteine, a toxic amino acid, which is a risk factor for both cardiovascular disease and dementia (Smith et al. 2010; Smith and Refsum 2016). Treatment with B vitamins can reduce homocysteine levels by an average 30% (Malouf and Grimley Evans 2008).

Many other foods or food compounds, such as fatty fish, nuts, fruits, olive oil, soy products, turmeric and multiple other condiments, have had beneficial effects ascribed to them through numerous biological pathways implicated in cognitive ageing and dementia. However, biological plausibility does not always lead to beneficial effects being observed, given the difference between laboratory based effective dosages and the smaller amounts found in diet.

Observational studies

A meta-analysis of 116 observational studies showed that people with AD have lower cerebrospinal fluid (CSF)/brain availability of vitamin B12, folate, C and E, and other nutritional compounds, which can affect brain function, such as choline and docosahexaenoic acid (DHA) (De Wilde et al. 2017). Conversely, higher levels of antioxidant levels of vitamin A, C and E have also in observational studies often shown to be associated with reduced dementia risk (Gillette-Guyonnet et al. 2013). However, treatment trials with such anti-oxidants have also shown increased mortality risk. There is insufficient evidence for vitamin D3 currently, but overall mortality risk may be reduced with vitamin D3 treatment. Low folate and/or vitamin B12 status have been associated with increased dementia risk in many observational studies (Hogervorst et al. 2017).

There is always the possibility, and indeed probability, of residual confounding in studies observing lifestyles including diet. Despite biological plausibility and observational data suggesting a direct association, it may be that low blood folate and/or other vitamins have been associated with an increased risk for dementia in observational studies for other reasons (Smith et al. 2010). For instance, people who have memory problems and may be at risk for dementia could forget to eat, which then affects nutrient intake and vitamin blood levels. Memory problems can also result in forgetting to brush your teeth, which can affect dental health. Research found that having fewer than 10 teeth doubled dementia risk (Hogervorst et al. 2008). Importantly, however, good dental care is often accompanied by high costs in most countries, and hence SES could be an important confound. Even if this is controlled for statistically, systematic differences between the affluent and non-affluent could account for these findings. Dental disease is also associated with inflammatory markers, which have been recognised for their importance in promoting diabetes and dementia (Daly et al. 2017; Harding et al. 2017). In two studies these inflammatory factors (interleukins) were found to have independent associations with worse cognition and did not mediate the association of having few teeth with increased dementia risk (Hogervorst et al. 2008). It may be that lifetime exposure to these inflammatory factors is more important, which could have occurred during years of periodontitis or gingivitis, rather than the levels measured once the teeth have fallen out. The end-stage of this lifelong infectious process results in less infection as the tooth no longer encapsulates the underlying infectious process. This highlights the importance of understanding life-course risks and life-course patterns, such as the manifest importance of good free dental hygiene and care in early life.

Many folate rich foods are fibrous, chewy and not easy to chew with few teeth. Green vegetables, liver, fibrous oranges and legumes, such as lentils, can contain high levels of folate. Vitamin B12 treatment has also been associated with improved cognitive function in middle-aged people who did not have dementia yet (Lehert et al. 2015) and is difficult to obtain for people who do not eat meat or animal protein as only small levels are present in whole grains and potatoes.

In China, both green vegetables and meat consumption have been reported to have independent positive associations with memory function and a lower risk for dementia (Xu et al. 2015). It may be that low folate and/or low vitamin B12 as a risk factor for dementia are associated with not having enough masticatory ability to break down foods to obtain these and other micronutrients. Anaemia is associated with dementia and a lack of these B vitamins. Low (but also high) haemoglobin (Hb) (low or malfunctioning Hb is an indicator of anaemia) and iron (a major component of Hb) have been found to be a risk factor for AD (Shah et al. 2011)

Alternatively, interactions of micro- and macronutrients may be more salient than looking at single vitamin levels. Observational work from Indonesia,

China and Hawaii (Xu et al. 2015; Soni et al. 2014; Soni et al. 2016) suggested that high consumption of tofu was independently associated with increased risk of dementia, where tempe, a fermented soy product, may offer beneficial effects and reduce risk. In these studies, possible confounding by low SES and intake of other foods (e.g. eating no meat) were controlled for in analyses. Tempe and tofu both contain high levels of phytoestrogens. In studies in Oxford, high levels of oestrogens in older women were associated with a higher risk for dementia. However, if women had sufficient folate, negative associations of high oestrogen levels were not seen (Hogervorst and Smith 2003). Because of fermentation, tempe contains both folate and cobalamin. After successful animal trials showing reduction of dementia markers (Kridawati et al. 2016), human treatment trials with tempe are now underway.

Whole diets may be more important than individual foods. Evidence from observational studies suggests that a Mediterranean diet with fruit, vegetables, fish, whole grains, legumes, nuts and olive oil, but limited meat, sugar and dairy may prevent cognitive decline and dementia (Hogervorst et al. 2017). Observational studies from India also suggest lower dementia prevalence, which could be, at least partly, attributed to the consumption of turmeric (Mazzanti and Di Giacomo 2016). These studies are problematic as without understanding who in which SES strata eats what and why, systematic confounds can be introduced, and these cannot be controlled for statistically. However, little curcumin (the active ingredient) is found in the amount of turmeric normally consumed, and its biological availability is limited. Other spices, which have anecdotal human and some animal/basic sciences support (such as garlic, ginger, and other herbs and spices), are often used alongside turmeric in dishes prepared. Again, interactions (e.g. black pepper could improve biological availability of curcumin) may be more important than looking at single aspects of a food individually.

Alternatively, other foods used in conjunction with turmeric may be responsible or amplify its beneficial effects, such as lentils to make the popular dahl in India. Lentils contain high levels of folate, iron and also fibre (which could reduce cholesterol) (Mitchell et al. 2009). Until relatively recently, levels of obesity were also not high in rural India and risk of diabetes was low. Observational studies of the oldest old in the Japanese island Okinawa, along with rodent research, have reported that that caloric restriction may be beneficial for cardiovascular disease, dementia and overall mortality rates (Wahl et al. 2017). This is a challenging finding, as in those populations with caloric restriction due to socio-economic deprivation, life expectancy is traditionally below that of dementia risk (Gillette-Guyonnet et al. 2013). Alternatively, the more traditional lifestyles, including physical exercise, low caloric intake especially of processed sugars, less meat, smoking, alcohol use and sedentary behaviour, as well as the survival into age groups at greatest risk of the fittest in those societies could be responsible for initially finding lower prevalence of dementia in rural India and Okinawa. With regards to alcohol consumption, a large French study has shown that alcohol consumption significantly increases dementia risk

(Schwarzinger et al. 2018), and a meta-analysis has shown that this risk increases on a dose-response basis (Xu et al. 2017). Alcohol abuse is also associated with dehydration which, when treated, can positively affect cognitive function in dementia (Hogervorst et al. 2017). Coffee and tea probably have a net hydration effect and have been found to be protective against cognitive decline in some cross-sectional and longitudinal studies, and possibly dementia, but longer studies need to be carried out (Panza et al. 2015). In this review, no dose-dependent effect was found and effects were stronger in women. Some studies with a midlife baseline assessment also found no association with AD.

Lastly, cohort effects are important as the people investigated in previous studies had a childhood without antibiotics, experienced world wars and periods of famine, and thus were well equipped genetically/physically to survive to an older age with its concordant risks for age-related morbidity.

RCTs

While consumption of fruits and vegetables is generally associated with reduced cardiovascular and dementia risk (Xu et al. 2015), not all studies have reported such associations. It is not clear whether individual compounds other than vitamins, such as fibre and/or minerals or interactions between food components or whole foods, may be responsible for the positive associations identified. However, vitamin supplement treatment trials have generally shown disappointing results in improving cognition. According to a Cochrane meta-analyses there was no overall benefit of vitamin E for secondary or tertiary prevention of dementia (Farina et al. 2017), nor were clear effects seen of vitamin C, although mixed effects were seen of the combination of vitamin E and C (Boothby and Doering 2005). However, as vitamin E can also lead to increased mortality, its use as a supplement is not recommended (Boothby and Doering 2005).

Cochrane (Farina et al. 2017) and other reviews have also shown that folic acid treatment does not always improve cognition in people with or without dementia (Kane et al. 2017). Several reviews have suggested that folic acid supplementation may only have positive effects on cognitive function when people are folate deficient and/or have not developed dementia yet (Hogervorst et al. 2017; Lehert et al. 2015). A meta-analysis showed that homocysteine levels (a risk factor for cardiovascular and AD) could be reduced through treatment with folic acid and vitamin B12 (Malouf et al. 2003). However, as high dosages of folic acid also have possible negative effects, such as increased risk of colon cancer (Smith et al. 2010), trials should screen folate levels to establish whether addressing deficiency detected through screening is beneficial or not. Once folic acid was added to flour in the United States as a naturalistic experiment, the association between homocysteine and cognition was no longer significant in an observational longitudinal study and nobody in the cohort had homocysteine levels suggestive of increased dementia risk in later life (e.g. over 14 umol/L) (Hogervorst et al. 2017). Dementia prevalence has declined in the

United States, but there are many other changes across generations which could also be responsible (Langa et al. 2017). Folic acid treatment trials to improve cognitive function in people with dementia (tertiary prevention) did not prove beneficial (Malouf and Grimley Evans 2008; Hogervorst et al. 2017).

With regards to macronutrients, as with cardiovascular disease, much focus has been on fats, such as omega 3 and cholesterol. Pure supplementation with omega 3 does not improve symptoms or progression of dementia (Burckhardt et al. 2016; Farina et al. 2017). However, it has been suggested that omega-3 levels may need to be taken into account in studies investigating folic acid treatment, as this may modify outcomes (Oulhaj et al. 2016). Cochrane reviews also showed that medical attempts to reduce cholesterol by using statins did not improve cognition in people with dementia (Mcguinness et al. 2014) or in people at risk for dementia (Mcguinness et al. 2016).

For foods containing saturated fats which can increase cholesterol, such as eggs, red meat and dairy products, including cheese, the picture is unclear with conflicting scientific and public health advice (Solfrizzi et al. 2017; Grant 2017). However, cheese is often high in sodium (salt), which could increase dementia risk, possibly through its effect on hypertension (Faraco et al. 2018). Dietary Approaches to Stop Hypertension (DASH) may be of benefit, especially when combined with the Mediterranean diet called MIND (Solfrizzi et al. 2017). Limited RCT evidence suggested that additional olive oil combined with nuts with a Mediterranean diet may reduce dementia risk in older people with cardiovascular risk (Hogervorst et al. 2017; Abbatecola et al. 2018). Olive oil contains oleocanthal, which has shown many neuroprotective effects, including reduction of plaques and inflammation (Angeloni et al. 2017; Batarseh and Kaddoumi 2017).

More recently, much of the focus has shifted from fats to reduction of sugar intake. AD has been called 'diabetes type III' because of its altered brain glucose metabolism and insulin regulation. Having diabetes type II can also increase dementia risk by 39% (Barnes and Yaffe 2011). Treatment studies with intranasal insulin to normalise glucose levels have shown some promise in improving memory (but not other cognitive functions) in people with dementia or mild cognitive impairment (Avgerinos et al. 2018), and this approach requires more research.

Summary

Interventions using dietary supplements have generally not shown beneficial results in studies for secondary and tertiary prevention of dementia. Unless there is a deficiency (e.g. as for folate), using vitamin supplements is probably not advisable, e.g. some also contain copper, which was found to have negative associations with brain function, (Manivannan et al. 2015). Instead, whole diets, such as the traditional Mediterranean diet with additional olive oil and nuts, which is high in omega 3, may be more beneficial and more trials are underway. Whether other diets (e.g. Japanese, traditional Indian, low sugar, caloric restriction) could play a role in dementia prevention remains to be clarified.

Discussion

In sum, healthy lifestyles, including exercise and staying mentally active at all stages of life and addressing cardiovascular risk factors and nutritional deficiencies in midlife at the latest, may be the most cost-effective ways of delaying dementia onset in later life. As stated in the introduction, the previous and next chapters, several longitudinal observational studies suggested that risk factors for vascular disease and dementia (such as high blood pressure, central obesity, and high total cholesterol levels) overlap. Importantly, some longitudinal studies following people over time suggest that these vascular risk factors can change over the lifespan, with a drop in blood pressure, loss of body weight/muscle mass and decrease in total cholesterol levels being more predictive of impeding onset of dementia in later life than when these vascular risk factors are raised in midlife (Skoog and Gustafson 2003; Mielke et al. 2010). It is unclear why this is the case. It may be that pathology in the brain affects these parameters or other organs indirectly. It has been hypothesised that these changes may also be caused by people with early signs of dementia forgetting to eat, which would lower body weight, blood pressure and total cholesterol, and result in vitamin and mineral deficiencies (Hogervorst et al. 2017).

The change in direction of these physiological parameters over the lifespan highlights that there are likely to be optimal windows of opportunities for interventions. We need far better understanding of interactions with genetic polymorphisms and their relationship with the behavioural environment. Behaviours are influenced by an individual's whole environment including the physical, cultural and psychological. Thus, approaches to changing these requires a range of different types of research (e.g. of exercise, particular supplements). We need to understand better the interplay between genes, early, mid and later life influences on brain health with ageing. Here we have shown the rich tapestry of findings in the domains of the so-called lifestyle factors. These are also intimately related to socio-economic status and cultural influences. Research which only focuses on one area, assuming that one approach will somehow work for something as complicated as dementia seems unlikely to be the way forward, and even less likely to influence whole populations positively in the future. Thus, biomedical research will need to be integrated with individual-, community- and society-level approaches which can see the value in activities, such as screening alongside those of whole community preventive measures using neonatal and early childhood interventions in order for us to gain maximum value for populations of the future.

References

Abbatecola, A. M., Russo, M. & Barbieri, M. (2018). Dietary patterns and cognition in older persons. *Current Opinion in Clinical Nutrition and Metabolic Care*, 21(1), 10–13.

Angeloni, C., *et al.* (2017). Bioactivity of olive oil phenols in neuroprotection. *International Journal of Molecular Sciences*, 18(11), 2230.

Anstey, K. J., *et al.* (2007). Smoking as a risk factor for dementia and cognitive decline: A meta-analysis of prospective studies. *American Journal of Epidemiology*, 166(4), 367–378.

Avgerinos, K. I., *et al.* (2018). Intranasal insulin in Alzheimer's dementia or mild cognitive impairment: A systematic review. *Journal of Neurology*, 265(7), 1497–1510.

Barnes, D. E. & Yaffe, K. (2011). The projected effect of risk factor reduction on Alzheimer's disease prevalence. *The Lancet Neurology*, 10(9), 819–828.

Batarseh, Y. S. & Kaddoumi, A. (2017). Oleocanthal-rich extra-virgin olive oil enhances donepezil effect by reducing amyloid-β load and related toxicity in a mouse model of Alzheimer's disease. *The Journal of Nutritional Biochemistry*, 55, 113–123.

Baumgart, M., *et al.* (2015). Summary of the evidence on modifiable risk factors for cognitive decline and dementia: A population-based perspective. *Alzheimer's & Dementia*, 11(6), 718–726.

Blondell, S. J., Hammersley-Mather, R. & Veerman, J. L. (2014). Does physical activity prevent cognitive decline and dementia? A systematic review and meta-analysis of longitudinal studies. *BMC Public Health*, 14(1), 510.

Boothby, L. A. & Doering, P. L. (2005). Vitamin c and vitamin e for Alzheimer's disease. *Annals of Pharmacotherapy*, 39(12), 2073–2080.

Brayne, C., *et al.* (2010). Education, the brain and dementia: Neuroprotection or compensation? Eclipse collaborative members. *Brain*, 133(8), 2210–2216.

Burckhardt, M., *et al.* (2016). Omega-3 fatty acids for the treatment of dementia. *Cochrane Database of Systematic Reviews*, (4).

Daly, B., *et al.* (2017). Evidence summary: The relationship between oral health and dementia. *BDJ*, 223, 846–853.

De Wilde, M. C., *et al.* (2017). Lower brain and blood nutrient status in Alzheimer's disease: Results from meta-analyses. *Alzheimer's & Dementia: Translational Research & Clinical Interventions*, 3(3), 416–431.

Durazzo, T. C., Mattsson, N. & Weiner, M. W. (2014). Smoking and increased Alzheimer's disease risk: A review of potential mechanisms. *Alzheimer's & Dementia*, 10(3) (Supplement), S122–S145.

Esiri, M. M. & Chance, S. A. (2012). Cognitive reserve, cortical plasticity and resistance to Alzheimer's disease. *Alzheimer's Research & Therapy*, 4(2), 7.

Faraco, G., *et al.* (2018). Dietary salt promotes neurovascular and cognitive dysfunction through a gut-initiated th17 response. *Nature Neuroscience*, 21(2), 240–249.

Farina, N., *et al.* (2017). Vitamin e for Alzheimer's dementia and mild cognitive impairment. *Cochrane Database of Systematic Reviews*, (4).

Farina, N., Rusted, J. & Tabet, N. (2013). The effect of exercise interventions on cognitive outcome in Alzheimer's disease: A systematic review. *International Psychogeriatrics*, 26(1), 9–18.

Forbes, D., *et al.* (2013). Exercise programs for people with dementia. *Cochrane Database of Systematic Reviews*, (12).

Forbes, D., *et al.* (2015). Exercise programs for people with dementia. *Cochrane Database of Systematic Reviews*, 4(CD006489).

Gillette-Guyonnet, S., Secher, M. & Vellas, B. (2013). Nutrition and neurodegeneration: Epidemiological evidence and challenges for future research. *British Journal of Clinical Pharmacology*, 75(3), 738–755.

Grant, W. B. (2017). Modifiable pathways in Alzheimer's disease: Mendelian randomisation analysis. *BMJ: British Medical Journal*, 359.

Guure, C. B., *et al.* (2017). Impact of physical activity on cognitive decline, dementia, and its subtypes: Meta-analysis of prospective studies. *BioMed Research International*, 13.

Hamer, M. & Chida, Y. (2008). Physical activity and risk of neurodegenerative disease: A systematic review of prospective evidence. *Psychological Medicine*, 39(1), 3–11.

Harding, A., *et al.* (2017). Exploring the association between Alzheimer's disease, oral health, microbial endocrinology and nutrition. *Frontiers in Aging Neuroscience*, 9, 398.

Hogervorst, E. & Clifford, A. (2013). What is the relationship between higher levels of education delaying age at onset of dementia? *Journal of Alzheimers Diseases & Parkinsonism*, 3(e128).

Hogervorst, E., *et al.* (2002). Plasma homocysteine levels, cerebrovascular risk factors, and cerebral white matter changes (leukoaraiosis) in patients with Alzheimer disease. *Archives of Neurology*, 59(5), 787–793.

Hogervorst, E., *et al.* (2003). The validity and reliability of 6 sets of clinical criteria to classify Alzheimer's disease and vascular dementia in cases confirmed post-mortem: Added value of a decision tree approach. *Dementia and Geriatric Cognitive Disorders*, 16(3), 170–180.

Hogervorst, E., *et al.* (2012). Exercise to prevent cognitive decline and Alzheimer's disease: For whom, when, what, and (most importantly) how much? *Journal of Alzheimers Diseases Parkinsonism*, 2(e117).

Hogervorst, E., *et al.* (2017). Nutrition research in cognitive impairment/dementia, with a focus on soya and folate. *Proceedings of the Nutrition Society*, 76(4), 437–442.

Hogervorst, E. & Smith, A. D. (2003). The interaction of serum folate and estradiol levels in Alzheimer's disease. *Neuroendocrinology Letters*, 23(2), 67–72.

Hogervorst, E. A., Ageing & Dementia. ed. (2008). *Depok Seminar Day on Ageing, Gender and Health*. Depok Indonesia: University of Indonesia.

Kane, R. L., *et al.* (2017). *Interventions to Prevent Age-Related Cognitive Decline, Mild Cognitive Impairment, and Clinical Alzheimer's-Type Dementia*. Rockville, MD: Agency for Healthcare Research and Quality.

Karssemeijer, E. G. A., *et al.* (2017). Positive effects of combined cognitive and physical exercise training on cognitive function in older adults with mild cognitive impairment or dementia: A meta-analysis. *Ageing Research Reviews*, 40, 75–83.

Kivipelto, M., *et al.* (2005). Obesity and vascular risk factors at midlife and the risk of dementia and Alzheimer disease. *Archives of Neurology*, 62(10), 1556–1560.

Knopman, D., *et al.* (2001). Cardiovascular risk factors and cognitive decline in middle-aged adults. *Neurology*, 56(1), 42.

Kridawati, A., *et al.* (2016). Tempereversed effects of ovariectomy on brain function in rats: Effects of age and type of soy product. *The Journal of Steroid Biochemistry and Molecular Biology*, 160, 37–42.

Lafortune, L., *et al.* (2016). Behavioural risk factors in mid-life associated with successful ageing, disability, dementia and frailty in later life: A rapid systematic review. *PLOS One*, 11(2), e0144405.

Langa, K. M., *et al.* (2017). A comparison of the prevalence of dementia in the United States in 2000 and 2012. *JAMA Internal Medicine*, 177(1), 51–58.

Launer, L. J., *et al.* (1999). Rates and risk factors for Dementia and Alzheimer's disease. *Neurology*, 52(1), 78.

Lehert, P., *et al.* 2015. Individually modifiable risk factors to ameliorate cognitive aging: A systematic review and meta-analysis. *Climacteric*, 18(5), 678–689.

Livingston, G., *et al.* (2017). Dementia prevention, intervention, and care. *The Lancet*, 390(10113), 2673–2734.

Malouf, R. & Grimley Evans, J. (2008). Folic acid with or without vitamin b12 for the prevention and treatment of healthy elderly and demented people. *Cochrane Database of Systematic Reviews*, (4).

Malouf, R., Grimley Evans, J. & Areosa Sastre, A. (2003). Folic acid with or without vitamin b12 for cognition and dementia. *Cochrane Database of Systematic Reviews*, (4).

Mangialasche, F., Weili, X. & Kivipelto, M. (2013). Prevention of Alzheimer's disease: Intervention studies. *In:* Zerr, I. ed. *Understanding Alzheimer's Disease.* Open, London: InTech.

Manivannan, Y., *et al.* (2015). Role of environmental contaminants in the etiology of Alzheimer's disease: A review. *Current Alzheimer Research*, 12(2), 116–146.

Mazzanti, G. & Di Giacomo, S. (2016). Curcumin and resveratrol in the management of cognitive disorders: What is the clinical evidence? *Molecules*, 21(9).

Mcdermott, O., *et al.* (2018). Psychosocial interventions for people with dementia: A synthesis of systematic reviews. *Aging & Mental Health*, 1–11.

Mcguinness, B., *et al.* (2014). Statins for the treatment of dementia. *Cochrane Database of Systematic Reviews*, (7).

Mcguinness, B., *et al.* (2016). Statins for the prevention of dementia. *Cochrane Database of Systematic Reviews*, (1).

Mckhann, G. M., *et al.* (2011). The diagnosis of dementia due to Alzheimer's disease: Recommendations from the national institute on aging-Alzheimer's association workgroups on diagnostic guidelines for Alzheimer's disease. *Alzheimer's & Dementia*, 7(3), 263–269.

Mielke, M. M., *et al.* (2010). The 32-year relationship between cholesterol and dementia from midlife to late life. *Neurology*, 75(21), 1888.

Mitchell, D. C., *et al.* (2009). Consumption of dry beans, peas, and lentils could improve diet quality in the us population. *Journal of the American Dietetic Association*, 109(5), 909–913.

Mons, U., *et al.* (2015). Impact of smoking and smoking cessation on cardiovascular events and mortality among older adults: Meta-analysis of individual participant data from prospective cohort studies of the chances consortium. *BMJ: British Medical Journal*, 350.

Ng, M., *et al.* (2014). Smoking prevalence and cigarette consumption in 187 countries, 1980–2012. *JAMA*, 311(2), 183–192.

Niederstrasser, N., *et al.* (2016). Approaches to cognitive stimulation in the prevention of dementia. *Journal of Gerontology Geriatric Research*, S5(005).

Norton, S., *et al.* (2014). Potential for primary prevention of Alzheimer's disease: An analysis of population-based data. *The Lancet Neurology*, 13(8), 788–794.

Öhman, H., *et al.* (2014). Effect of physical exercise on cognitive performance in older adults with mild cognitive impairment or dementia: A systematic review. *Dementia and Geriatric Cognitive Disorders*, 38(5–6), 347–365.

Olanrewaju, O., *et al.* (2015). A multimodal approach to dementia prevention: A report from the cambridge institute of public health. *Alzheimer's & Dementia: Translational Research & Clinical Interventions*, 1(3), 151–156.

Oulhaj, A., *et al.* (2016). Omega-3 fatty acid status enhances the prevention of cognitive decline by B vitamins in mild cognitive impairment. *Journal of Alzheimer's Disease*, 50(2), 547–557.

Panza, F., et al. (2015). Coffee, tea, and caffeine consumption and prevention of late-life cognitive decline and dementia: A systematic review. *Journal of Nutrition Health and Aging*, 19(3), 313–328.
Prince, M., *et al.* (2015). *World Alzheimer Report 2015: The Global Impact of Dementia: An Analysis of Prevalence, Incidence, Cost and Trends*. London: Alzheimer's Disease International (ADI).
Rao, A. K., *et al.* (2014). Systematic review of the effects of exercise on activities of daily living in people with Alzheimer's disease. *The American Journal of Occupational Therapy*, 68(1), 50–56.
Schwarzinger, M., *et al.* (2018). Contribution of alcohol use disorders to the burden of dementia in france 2008–2013: A nationwide retrospective cohort study. *The Lancet Public Health*, 3(3), e124-e132.
Shah, R. C., *et al.* (2011). Hemoglobin level in older persons and incident Alzheimer disease: Prospective cohort analysis. *Neurology*, 77(3), 219–226.
Skoog, I. & Gustafson, D. (2003). Hypertension, hypertension-clustering factors and Alzheimer's disease. *Neurological Research*, 25(6), 675–680.
Smith, A. D. & Refsum, H. (2016). Homocysteine, b vitamins, and cognitive impairment. *Annual Review of Nutrition*, 36(1), 211–239.
Smith, A. D. & Yaffe, K. (2014). Dementia (including Alzheimer's disease) can be prevented: Statement supported by international experts. *Journal of Alzheimers Diseases*, 38(4), 699–703.
Smith, A. D., *et al.* (2010). Homocysteine-lowering by b vitamins slows the rate of accelerated brain atrophy in mild cognitive impairment: A randomized controlled trial. *PLOS One*, 5(9), e12244.
Solfrizzi, V., *et al.* (2017). Relationships of dietary patterns, foods, and micro- and macronutrients with Alzheimer's disease and late-life cognitive disorders: A systematic review. *Journal of Alzheimer's Disease*, 59(3), 815–849.
Soni, M., *et al.* (2014). Phytoestrogens and cognitive function: A review. *Maturitas*, 77(3), 209–220.
Soni, M., *et al.* (2016). Phytoestrogen consumption and risk for cognitive decline and dementia: With consideration of thyroid status and other possible mediators. *The Journal of Steroid Biochemistry and Molecular Biology*, 160, 67–77.
Soni, M., *et al.* (2017). Physical activity pre- and post-dementia: English longitudinal study of ageing. *Aging & Mental Health*, 1–7.
Strand, B. H., *et al.* (2013). Midlife vascular risk factors and their association with dementia deaths: Results from a norwegian prospective study followed up for 35years. *Journal of the Neurological Sciences*, 324(1), 124–130.
Swan, G. E. & Lessov-Schlaggar, C. N. (2007). The effects of tobacco smoke and nicotine on cognition and the brain. *Neuropsychology Review*, 17, 259–273.
Taylor, G., *et al.* (2014). Change in mental health after smoking cessation: Systematic review and meta-analysis. *BMJ: British Medical Journal*, 348.
Toots, A., *et al.* (2017). Effects of exercise on cognitive function in older people with dementia: A randomized controlled trial. *Journal of Alzheimer's Disease*, 60(1), 323–332.
Townsend, N., Wickramasinghe, K., Williams, J., Bhatnagar, P., & Rayner, M. (2015). *Physical Activity Statistics* 2015. London: British Heart Foundation.
Trigiani, L. J. & Hamel, E. (2017). An endothelial link between the benefits of physical exercise in dementia. *Journal of Cerebral Blood Flow & Metabolism*, 37(8), 2649–2664.
Voss, M. W., *et al.* (2013). Bridging animal and human models of exercise-induced brain plasticity. *Trends in Cognitive Sciences*, 17(10), 525–544.

Wahl, D., *et al.* (2017). Cognitive and behavioral evaluation of nutritional interventions in rodent models of brain aging and dementia. *Clinical Interventions in Aging*, 12, 1419–1428.

Wang, C-C., *et al.* (2010). Cigarette smoking and cognitive impairment: A 10-year cohort study in taiwan. *Archives of Gerontology and Geriatrics*, 51(2), 143–148.

World Health Organization (2015) Accessed online via: http://www.who.int/mental_health/neurology/dementia/dementia_thematicbrief_executivesummary.pdf on July 2018.

Xu, X., *et al.* (2015). Tofu intake is associated with poor cognitive performance among community-dwelling elderly in china. *Journal of Alzheimer's Disease*, 43(2), 669–675.

Xu, W., *et al.* (2017). Alcohol consumption and dementia risk: A dose – response meta-analysis of prospective studies. *European Journal of Epidemiology*, 32(1), 31–42.

Zhong, G., *et al.* (2015). Smoking is associated with an increased risk of dementia: A meta-analysis of prospective cohort studies with investigation of potential effect modifiers. *PLOS One*, 10(3), e0118333.

Chapter 4

Vascular disease-based risk factors for dementia

Kay Deckers and Martin van Boxtel

Introduction

Various (chronic) health conditions have been linked to the development of dementia (Deckers et al. 2015; Livingston et al. 2017). In this chapter, the epidemiology and current state of the evidence on several disease-based risk factors and their relationship with dementia will be discussed, including diabetes mellitus, renal dysfunction, coronary heart disease (CHD), obesity, high cholesterol and hypertension. Besides ethical considerations, for some conditions, there are major methodological and practical challenges in conducting a well-designed randomized controlled trial (RCT) including a long latency period and comorbidity with other late-life conditions. Therefore, high-quality evidence from RCTs will only be discussed if applicable.

Diabetes mellitus

Epidemiology

Diabetes mellitus has become a major disease challenge worldwide. In 2010, about 180 million people in the world had diabetes, and it has been estimated that the prevalence of diabetes in all age groups will rise from 2.8% in 2000 to 4.4% in 2030 (Wild et al. 2004). The most important change in recent years is the proportional increase in (late-onset) diabetes type 2 in people aged 65 years and older.

Evidence from observational studies

In two recent meta-analyses of prospective observational studies the association between diabetes and all-type dementia (ATD), Alzheimer's disease (AD) and vascular dementia (VaD) was investigated (Cheng et al. 2012; Gudala et al. 2013). The first comprised 19 studies with 38,530 diabetic patients and reported a relative risk (RR) of 1.51 for ATD, 1.46 for AD and 2.48 for VaD (Cheng et al. 2012). The second, more extensive meta-analysis based on 28 studies including

89,708 diabetic patients, reported pooled RRs for ATD of 1.73, for AD of 1.56 and for VaD of 2.27 (Gudala et al. 2013). These studies suggest that for VaD, the risk is higher.

Evidence from RCTs

Given the apparent association between diabetes and both cognitive decline and dementia, several RCTs have compared the effect of different treatments for type 2 diabetes on cognitive outcome. In a recent Cochrane Collaboration review, seven eligible studies using international clinical practice guidelines were identified, of which four could be used for efficacy analyses (Areosa Sastre et al. 2017). The evidence of these trials, which compared intensive with normal glycemic control, showed that there were no evident short to medium term effects of treatment (after 40–60 months) on cognitive decline or dementia incidence. In the ACCORDION MIND study, 2,977 patients with diabetes type 2 (mean age 62 years) were randomized to intensive versus standard management of hyperglycemia or blood pressure (BP) or lipid levels in a 2 x 2 parallel group design (Murray et al. 2017). Initial findings after 40 months showed a small effect of intensive BP treatment on total brain volume and more abnormal white matter on magnetic resonance imaging (MRI) in the intensive hyperglycemia treatment group. No differential effect of treatment was found on cognitive function (measured with the Digit-Symbol Substitution Test). Re-assessment after 80 months (40 months after cessation of formal study treatment) revealed no residual group differences on structural brain MRI or cognitive function. Thus, to date the evidence from RCTs does not show lasting beneficial (or negative) effects of intensive glycemic treatment on cognitive function or the incidence of dementia. However, studies may have been too short to show effects.

Biological pathways and possible interactions

Several biological mechanisms have been suggested to explain the association between diabetes and dementia, including increased vascular risk, toxic effects of hyperglycemia, effects of insulin resistance to the brain, the formation of advanced glycation end products and a competition for insulin degrading enzyme, which could result in a lowered degradation of ß-amyloid, but conclusive evidence for such mechanisms remains elusive (Cole et al. 2007).

Cerebrovascular disease in diabetic patients may increase the risk of stroke. However, among ten studies into the role of diabetes in the development of dementia after stroke, only six studies found evidence of such association (Li et al. 2014). Also, interaction of ApoE4 genotype and diabetes on dementia prevalence has been equivocal (Akomolafe et al. 2006). Based on data from 29,961 patients aged 60 years and older, a dementia risk prediction score was developed, which provides estimates of dementia risk per age stratum, level of education and level of vascular comorbidity (Exalto et al. 2013). Diabetes was associated with a relatively higher risk of dementia in those who were older, lower educated, who showed evidence of depression and had more evidence of vascular comorbidity.

Future directions

Due to the rising prevalence of diabetes, the risk of accelerated cognitive decline and dementia that can be attributed to diabetes is also likely to increase (Biessels et al. 2008). Diabetes tends to cluster with other cardiovascular risk factors, such as obesity and physical inactivity. This makes it difficult for researchers to disentangle the effects of diabetes with those of other risk factors in their attempt to prevent residual confounding (Gudala et al. 2013). Also, to date, it remains unclear whether type 2 diabetes accelerates AD pathology or promotes dementia via increased vascular comorbidity (Biessels et al. 2007). Research into dementia prevention typically requires long follow-up intervals and large sample sizes. Available diabetes intervention studies have used follow-up durations of up to 80 months (Murray et al. 2017), which still may be too short to detect reliable effects on dementia incidence. Theoretically, intensive glycemic treatment may result in more hypoglycemic episodes and thereby more brain-related damage, which therefore should always be closely monitored and carefully gauged against potential health benefits (Lipska and Montori 2013). Also, undetected diabetes can already be present several years before a clinical diagnosis is made. This calls for an adequate and timely screening for glucose-intolerance or diabetes in older individuals in order to prevent early and irreversible diabetes-related neurological damage.

Renal dysfunction

Epidemiology

Renal dysfunction and dementia have in common that their incidence increases with an older age. Individuals at all stages of chronic kidney disease (CKD) have a higher chance of developing dementia in comparison with persons without CKD. The estimated global prevalence of CKD is 11% to 13% (Hill et al. 2016). The incidence of CKD is highest in low-income countries where management strategies (e.g. renal replacement therapies) are less available (Jha et al. 2013). Mortality due to CKD raised between 1980 and 2015 to 1.1 million deaths worldwide (Wang et al. 2016).

Evidence from observational studies

Renal dysfunction (i.e., reduced estimated glomerular filtration rate (eGFR; based on blood test) and albuminuria) has emerged as one of the new candidate risk factors for dementia (Deckers et al. 2015). A systematic literature review and meta-analysis of cross-sectional and longitudinal studies from 2015 indicated that most studies observed an association between CKD and cognitive impairment (Etgen et al. 2012). Meta-analyses of longitudinal studies showed that individuals with CKD (based on eGFR cut-offs) have on average a 39% increased risk of cognitive impairment compared with those without CKD. A more broad systematic literature review and meta-analysis of prospective studies from 2017 showed overall modest evidence for the association between (different markers of) renal dysfunction and dementia (Deckers et al. 2017a). The literature search returned sufficient evidence for albuminuria. Meta-analysis of five studies representing 27,805 individuals showed that albuminuria is associated with a 35% increased risk of dementia. The literature on eGFR was mixed in general and meta-analyses for different levels of eGFR showed non-significant results. There were also mixed effects for other markers of renal dysfunction, including cystatin C (insufficient evidence), serum creatinine and creatinine clearance (both tentative evidence). Another systematic literature review and meta-analysis of all observational studies from 2017 showed that albuminuria is associated with dementia, AD and even stronger with VaD (Georgakis et al. 2017).

Evidence from RCTs

The Veterans Affairs Homocysteine study in 659 patients with end-stage renal disease (ESRD) or advanced CKD investigated whether high-dose vitamin B to reduce high levels of total plasma homocysteine improved cognition (Brady et al. 2009). Treatment reduced homocysteine levels by 26.7%, but there were no differences between the treatment and placebo group on cognitive performance at initial testing or one year later. The Frequent Hemodialysis Network Trials consisted of two RCTs among ESRD patients who received hemodialysis (Chertow et al. 2010). Participants in the 'Daily Trial' received either in-center, 3x-per-week hemodialysis or in-center 6x-per-week hemodialysis, whereas participants in the 'Nocturnal Trial' received either home or in-center, 3x-per-week hemodialysis or home 6x-per-week nocturnal hemodialysis. This study demonstrated that hemodialysis frequency did not improve global cognition or executive functioning.

Biological pathways and possible interactions

There are several possible biological mechanisms underlying the relationship between renal dysfunction and dementia (Bugnicourt et al. 2013). Both conditions have a shared risk profile, including age, cardiovascular disease (e.g. atrial fibrillation (AF), myocardial infarction (MI), smoking, type-2 diabetes, hypertension and high cholesterol (Madero et al. 2008). For instance, diabetes and hypertension are the most common causes of CKD (Jha et al. 2013), while they are also attributable to 2.9% and 5.1%, respectively, of all AD cases worldwide (Norton et al. 2014). Next, both conditions have a high prevalence of cerebrovascular damage, including stroke, cerebral small vessel disease, microbleeds and white matter hyperintensities (Bugnicourt et al. 2013; Madero et al. 2008). By this way, it can be proposed that similar microvascular damage reflect the functional loss of both end organs. Conditions such as cardiovascular disease might even be mediating factors in the kidney-brain relationship. But vascular damage is not the only hypothesis, as uremic neurotoxicity seems to also be involved. People with CKD have higher concentrations of uremic toxins in cognition-related brain areas (De Deyn et al. 2009). It is important to note that it is not possible to relate renal dysfunction to dementia by one single mechanism, but the suggested biological pathways have probably additive or synergistic effects.

Future directions

Understanding the complex underlying pathophysiology between renal dysfunction and dementia-related brain damage is essential in order to minimize the risk for future dementia. One way is to look at interaction and timing effects of vascular disorders and renal dysfunction on dementia risk in large epidemiological cohort studies, preferably including (imaging) measurements of microvascular and neurotoxic pathology of kidney and brain. Another way is to investigate at what stage of the CKD-dementia pathway do certain interventions (low sodium diet, BP lowering medication, hemodialysis, renal replacement therapy) need to be administered to optimize beneficial (kidney and brain) outcomes.

Coronary heart disease

Epidemiology

The total prevalence of CHD in Americans adults older than 20 years of age is 6.2%, with a higher prevalence in men (7.6%) than in women (5.0%). In one year, approximately 660,000 American citizens will have a new CHD event (and approximately 305,000 individuals will have a recurrent event). Nearly every 42 seconds, an American will have a MI (Mozaffarian et al. 2016). It is important to note that the total incidence of CHD has decreased over time in Western countries. Although there is a marked decline in the CHD mortality over the last decades in developed countries, it is still the most common cause of death, with approximately 10 million deaths in 2016 (Livingston et al. 2017).

Evidence from observational studies

Several forms of CHD have been related to cognitive decline and increased dementia risk (Justin et al. 2013). A systematic literature review and meta-analysis of all observational studies from 2017 provided moderate evidence for the association between CHD and dementia. Meta-analysis of 10 prospective studies representing 24,801 individuals showed that CHD (combination of angina pectoris (AP) and MI) is associated with a 45% increased risk of cognitive impairment or dementia (Deckers et al. 2017b). Similar results were found for AP and MI individually. Results from four other systematic literature reviews and meta-analyses showed that there is consistent evidence for an association between AF and cognitive impairment and incident dementia (Kwok et al. 2011; Santangeli et al. 2012; Kalantarian et al. 2013; Stefanidis et al. 2017). For instance, one meta-analysis of seven longitudinal studies found a 36% increased risk for dementia in persons with AF (Kalantarian et al. 2013).

Biological pathways and possible interactions

There are several possible pathways that link CHD and dementia. Besides an older age, CHD and dementia share a number of health factors, including smoking, high cholesterol, hypertension, obesity, unhealthy diet, diabetes and physical inactivity (Helzner et al. 2009). This fits well under the credo '*what's good for your heart, is good for your brain*'. Long-term exposure to these vascular-related risk factors could have deleterious brain effects (e.g. cognitive impairment with a vascular component) (Santos et al. 2017). CHD may lead to reduced cerebral blood flow (with as a consequence hypoperfusion), ischemic brain lesions and other cerebrovascular damage through vascular insufficiency caused by atherosclerosis (Santos et al. 2017). The neurovascular unit ensures that every brain area receives the required blood supply (Van Buchem et al. 2014). Several pathophysiological mechanisms such as lower cerebral perfusion, oxidative stress, inflammation and low cardiac output affect the functioning of the neurovascular unit (Van Buchem et al. 2014), which can lead to cerebral small vessel disease and disadvantageous changes in the permeability of the blood-brain barrier (Gorelick et al. 2011). These processes are in turn associated with increased dementia risk (Santos et al. 2017). In addition, deposition of ß-amyloid in the arterial vessel can lead to cerebral amyloid angiopathy and accompanied vascular brain pathology (Santos et al. 2017).

Future directions

Nowadays, the only interventions available for heart patients to delay the progression of cerebrovascular diseases are secondary prevention strategies (e.g. treating risk factors such as hypertension and high cholesterol) and antithrombotic drugs. Given the large overlap between the target risk factors for dementia and CHD, researchers and policy makers should join forces in developing primary prevention strategies. More knowledge on the causal mechanisms (e.g.

shared genetic associations) or common biological pathways underlying the heart-brain connection are needed to delay or slow the onset of dementia. Epidemiological studies investigating vascular (brain) changes in persons at high risk for both CHD and dementia and cardiovascular interventions studies impacting dementia risk could provide new insights.

Obesity

Epidemiology

The global prevalence of obesity has nearly tripled between 1975 and 2014. In 2014, 10.8% of men and 14.9% of women were obese, compared with 3.2% for men and 6.4% for women in 1975 (Ncd Risk Factor Collaboration 2016). This amounts to more than half a billion obese adults worldwide. The highest absolute numbers are found in high-income countries, while the relative increase is more pronounced in low- and middle-income countries. High body weight (overweight and obesity) was responsible for approximately four million deaths worldwide in 2015 (Afshin et al. 2017).

Evidence from observational studies

Several systematic literature reviews and meta-analyses have shown that midlife obesity is associated with increased dementia risk (Loef and Walach 2013; Anstey et al. 2011; Beydoun et al. 2008; Pedditizi et al. 2016). However, results from individual longitudinal studies are inconsistent (Deckers et al. 2015). Two prospective studies (Albanese et al. 2015; De Bruijn et al. 2015) and two mendelian randomization studies (Ostergaard et al. 2015; Mukherjee et al. 2015) from 2015 found no evidence for this association, while a large retrospective cohort study of almost two million individuals showed that midlife obesity might be a protective factor for dementia (Qizilbash et al. 2015). In contrast, a systematic literature review and meta-analysis of 19 prospective studies from 2017 again showed that midlife obesity was associated with a 33% increased dementia risk (Albanese et al. 2017). Two meta-analyses on the effects of late-life obesity on dementia risk showed inconsistent results, with one reporting no association (Anstey et al. 2011) and another demonstrating a protective effect (Pedditizi et al. 2016).

Evidence from RCTs

A systematic literature review and meta-analysis of longitudinal studies (N = 13) and RCTs (N = 7) from 2017 on weight-loss interventions (e.g. diet/caloric restriction, physical activity or bariatric surgery) and cognitive function in overweight and obese individuals showed that weigh loss has beneficial effects on cognitive performance (Veronese et al. 2017). This builds further on the findings of a systematic literature review and meta-analysis from 2011 with a similar approach that found that weight loss is associated with small improvements in executive function/attention and memory in obese individuals, but not in overweight subjects (Siervo et al. 2011).

Biological pathways and possible interactions

The relationship between obesity and dementia is far from clear. Obesity is an important risk factor for diabetes, CKD, high cholesterol, hypertension, CHD and stroke. Next, it is related to lifestyle factors such as unhealthy dietary habits and physical inactivity. All of these metabolic conditions are also risk factors for dementia (Deckers et al. 2015). High body weight is associated with neurodegenerative and cerebrovascular damage through several interrelated biological mechanisms, including increased presence of adipokines (which induces inflammation and insulin resistance), neuroendocrine abnormalities, oxidative stress and hormonal disturbances (e.g. dysregulation of leptin has an effect on the deposition of ß-amyloid in the brain) (Kiliaan et al. 2014; Gustafson 2006). All of these processes affect brain health and are related to poor cognitive functioning and increased dementia risk.

Future directions

There are still many uncertainties and the influence of obesity on dementia will probably remain a topic of controversy. Possible explanations for the inconsistent findings can be related to methodological issues, such as follow-up duration (e.g. more consistent results in studies with more than 10-year follow-up) and the measurement of obesity in epidemiological studies, in most cases defined by a body mass index (BMI) above 30. The effects of BMI vary during the lifespan. Involuntary weight loss (i.e. a decrease in BMI in late life) starting 10 years or more before dementia onset is associated with increased dementia risk (Knopman et al. 2007), while increased body weight (e.g. higher BMI) in late life is thereby associated with decreased dementia risk (Emmerzaal et al. 2015). More consistent evidence comes from studies where BMI is measured before 60 years of age. Findings from the Whitehall II study with repeated measurements of BMI in more than 10,000 people over more than 28 years showed that the association between obesity and dementia is influenced by age at obesity measurement (Singh-Manoux et al. 2017). Obesity at age 50 was a risk factor for dementia, but no longer at age 60 and 70. Therefore, more studies with several measurements of obesity (e.g. waist-to-hip ratio, waist circumference, BMI, abdominal adiposity) across the lifespan, studies investigating the BMI trajectory in individuals with dementia, and studies including dementia etiology and obesity duration and severity are needed. Additionally, more insight has to be obtained in the neurobiological mechanisms that relate weight loss to improvements in cognitive functioning.

High cholesterol

Epidemiology

In 2008, high total cholesterol (TC over 5 mmol/L) had a global prevalence of 39% and was highest in the WHO region of Europe (54%), but lower in low-income countries (WHO Int/GHO/NCD/risk factors/cholesterol_text/en). Cohort studies have shown good quality evidence that elevated TC levels in midlife are associated with dementia risk later in life. Intervention trials to reduce total cholesterol levels aimed at preventing cognitive decline or dementia have to date been unsuccessful.

Evidence from observational studies

A recent meta-analysis of Anstey and colleagues on the link between serum cholesterol and dementia (Anstey et al. 2017) provided an update and expansion of their comparable study that was done eight years earlier (Anstey et al. 2008). Thirty-four papers on prospective studies were identified, of which 17 could be pooled in a meta-analysis, comprising 23,338 participants. Compared to individuals with normal cholesterol, the RR of AD in those with high TC in midlife was 2.14. High TC in late life was not associated with mild cognitive impairment (MCI), AD, VaD, any dementia or cognitive decline. Levels of high-density lipoprotein (HDL) cholesterol and triglycerides measured in late life were also not associated with an increased risk of VaD, and HDL cholesterol was not linked with the risk of MCI, AD or any dementia (Anstey et al. 2017). Thus, based on currently available evidence, the risk of high TC level may be limited to midlife for the development of AD in later life.

Evidence from RCTs

In 2016, a Cochrane Collaboration study group systematically compiled the available RCTs, in which statins were used for at least 12 months in people at risk of dementia (McGuinness et al. 2016). Two studies were included with 26,340 participants aged between 40 and 82 years. Two different statins were used: simvastatin and pravastatin, with a mean follow-up of 3.2 years in one study and five years in the other study. One study (N = 20,536) reported on dementia incidence, which was not different in treated vs. untreated groups (Odds ratio = 1.00). There were no pooled differences between statin and placebo groups on five cognitive outcome measures. It was concluded that there is good evidence that statins administered in late life do not prevent cognitive decline or dementia at follow-up.

Biological pathways and possible interactions

Cholesterol is the main lipid component of neuronal cell membranes and myelin and can be produced in the brain itself. The link between cholesterol and AD is supported by the identification of clusters of genes (ApoE4, single-nucleotide polymorphisms for clusterin (CLU), ABCA7 and PICALM) that influence lipid binding and metabolism in the brain (Grimm et al. 2013). Cholesterol is important for synapse formation and maturation, and therefore for signal transduction and synaptic plasticity (Van Vliet 2012). Several studies have suggested altered lipid metabolism in brains with AD pathology. Cholesterol has been shown to increase intracerebral amyloid-ß production and aggregation, particularly in midlife (Grimm et al. 2013). On the other hand, high blood cholesterol level is implicated in the development of atherosclerosis and cerebrovascular disease. It has been suggested that cholesterol lowers with age and that low cholesterol levels may precede dementia, which could explain why the association between TC and AD has only been found for midlife TC levels and not for late-life TC levels (Panza et al. 2009).

Future directions

It appears that only elevated TC in midlife is a risk factor for AD (Panza et al. 2006). It remains unclear if this link between midlife TC and AD may vary as a function of factors that can moderate TC level, such as diet, ethnicity or urbanization. Such information can be important for guidelines in clinical practice. Also, in the most recent meta-analysis, it was not possible to address potential interaction of TC with ApoE lipoprotein (Anstey et al. 2017). Furthermore, in trials with statins that have been performed to date, participants were relatively old and were selected based on their vascular risk status, which could limit the generalizability of study findings due to indication bias (McGuinness et al. 2016). Ideally, such RCTs should start at midlife and have a follow-up duration until late life, which would span decades. Without additional pathophysiological insight to support which target group could benefit from statin intervention, it seems unlikely that new RCTs to prevent dementia using statins only will be undertaken in the near future.

Hypertension

Epidemiology

Hypertension is estimated to produce 4.3% of the disease burden in the world and is responsible for one-third of all global deaths (Whitworth 2003). The importance of adequate BP control has become even greater, due to increased longevity and the prevalence of contributing factors, such as unhealthy diet, low physical activity level and obesity in the Western world. Therefore, apart from antihypertensive treatment, lifestyle interventions, such as weight reduction, diet, reduced alcohol intake and sufficient physical exercise, can be supportive (Wexler and Aukerman 2006).

Evidence from observational studies

Two meta-analyses from 2011 found no association between hypertension and risk of AD (Chang-Quan et al. 2011; Power et al. 2011), but they combined studies into midlife with late-life hypertension (Qiu 2012). Evidence from cross-sectional and longitudinal studies suggests that particularly hypertension at middle age is a risk factor for dementia in later life and that lowered diastolic BP (with high systolic BP >180 mmHg) in later life may predict imminent dementia (Qiu et al. 2005). A review from 2011 showed that midlife hypertension was associated with a 61% increased risk for late-life AD (Barnes and Yaffe 2011).

Evidence from RCTs

Some reviews on the impact of antihypertensive treatment on cognitive function found positive evidence of antihypertensive treatment with diuretics (Tully et al. 2016), and renin-angiotensin system blockers (Rouch et al. 2015; Levi Marpillat et al. 2013) and mixed evidence with calcium channel blockers (Rouch et al. 2015; Peters et al. 2014) on dementia outcome. A recent systematic review from the Agency for Healthcare Research and Quality (AHRQ) (Kane et al. 2017) was summarized by the Committee on Preventing Dementia and Cognitive Impairment (Downey et al. 2017). It comprised 16 RCTs on antihypertensive treatment in hypertensive populations, of which 13 were pooled in a meta-analysis. Results were inconsistent in that low-strength evidence found that 3–4.7 years of treatment vs. placebo did not have beneficial effects on cognition in adults with normal cognitive function. There were no clear indications that intensive vs. standard antihypertensive treatment was more beneficial on cognitive outcome. Two trials that reported subgroup data did not find differential effects of treatment on cognition by age or other baseline characteristics. In four placebo-controlled trials in which dementia was measured as a secondary outcome, only one study showed a beneficial effect on reduced dementia incidence after two years (21 vs. 11 patients, $p = 0.05$; Syst-Eur trial). In this trial, treatment was successful on the primary outcome in reducing the risk of stroke (all types) by 42%.

Biological pathways and possible interactions

Hypertension is implicated in the pathogenesis of cardiovascular and cerebrovascular disease (e.g. stroke) via atherosclerotic damage to the arterial vessel wall. Vascular risk rises proportionally along the BP range (Whitworth 2003). Most patients with dementia show evidence of cerebrovascular disease on imaging, including large and small vessel disease, microbleeds and white matter intensities. Such abnormalities are often observed in combination with AD-type pathology (Downey et al. 2017). Also, reduced cerebral blood flow due to atherosclerosis may lead to an increased production or reduced clearance of AD-type proteins, such as ß-amyloid (Zlokovic 2011).

Future directions

As stated, BP may be inversely related to dementia in later life, which complicates the interpretation of observational studies and makes continuation of systematic literature reviews necessary, in which age and other risk factors are stratified (Power et al. 2011).

Evidence for the efficacy of antihypertensive treatment to prevent dementia is still limited. Few of the trials included in the AHRQ review were designed specifically to target dementia or cognitive decline, in that most studies were underpowered, had inadequate outcome measures or were limited in follow-up duration (Downey et al. 2017). Targeting dementia risk with antihypertensive treatment requires that treatment is started early in life and that careful cognitive follow-up later in life remains part of the study (Qiu 2012). Other relevant questions for the future are the potential mediating effect of genetic factors (ApoE genotype) and environmental factors (e.g. education, lifestyle) on the relationship between hypertension and dementia, the optimal BP levels to protect cognitive function in older individuals and whether the effect of antihypertensive treatment is age-dependent (Qiu et al. 2005).

Conclusion

The evidence for the association of most of these disease-based risk factors and dementia ranges from modest to substantial. The co-occurrence of these primarily vascular risk factors for dementia is considerably high. They can act synergistically and thereby magnify dementia risk. The prevalence of comorbidity in people with dementia is also high (Browne et al. 2017; Bunn et al. 2014), which complicates treatment and can accelerate the progression of dementia, making preventive strategies even more salient. In times of increased life expectancy in our ageing population, the absence of a disease-modifying drug for dementia and the low public awareness on the relation between lifestyle and long-term brain health, personalized dementia risk reduction strategies should become the main strategy in the fight against dementia.

References

Afshin, A., Forouzanfar, M. H., Reitsma, M. B., Sur, P., Estep, K., Lee, A., Marczak, L., Mokdad, A. H., Moradi-Lakeh, M., Naghavi, M., Salama, J. S., Vos, T., Abate, K. H., Abbafati, C., Ahmed, M. B., Al-Aly, Z., Alkerwi, A., Al-Raddadi, R., Amare, A. T., Amberbir, A., Amegah, A. K., Amini, E., Amrock, S. M., Anjana, R. M., Arnlov, J., Asayesh, H., Banerjee, A., Barac, A., Baye, E., Bennett, D. A., Beyene, A. S., Biadgilign, S., Biryukov, S., Bjertness, E., Boneya,

D. J., Campos-Nonato, I., Carrero, J. J., Cecilio, P., Cercy, K., Ciobanu, L. G., Cornaby, L., Damtew, S. A., Dandona, L., Dandona, R., Dharmaratne, S. D., Duncan, B. B., Eshrati, B., Esteghamati, A., Feigin, V. L., Fernandes, J. C., Furst, T., Gebrehiwot, T. T., Gold, A., Gona, P. N., Goto, A., Habtewold, T. D., Hadush, K. T., Hafezi-Nejad, N., Hay, S. I., Horino, M., Islami, F., Kamal, R., Kasaeian, A., Katikireddi, S.V., Kengne, A. P., Kesavachandran, C. N., Khader, Y. S., Khang, Y. H., Khubchandani, J., Kim, D., Kim, Y. J., Kinfu, Y., Kosen, S., Ku, T., Defo, B. K., Kumar, G. A., Larson, H. J., Leinsalu, M., Liang, X., Lim, S. S., Liu, P., Lopez, A. D., Lozano, R., Majeed, A., Malekzadeh, R., Malta, D. C., Mazidi, M., McAlinden, C., McGarvey, S. T., Mengistu, D. T., Mensah, G. A., Mensink, G. B. M., Mezgebe, H. B., Mirrakhimov, E. M., Mueller, U. O., Noubiap, J. J., Obermeyer, C. M., Ogbo, F. A., Owolabi, M. O., Patton, G. C., *et al.* (2017). Health effects of overweight and obesity in 195 countries over 25 years. *The New England Journal of Medicine*, 377(1), 13–27.

Akomolafe, A., Beiser, A., Meigs, J. B., Au, R., Green, R. C., Farrer, L. A., Wolf, P. A. & Seshadri, S. (2006). Diabetes mellitus and risk of developing Alzheimer disease: Results from the Framingham study. *Archives of Neurology*, 63(11), 1551–1555.

Albanese, E., Davis, B., Jonsson, P.V., Chang, M., Aspelund, T., Garcia, M., Harris, T., Gudnason, V. & Launer, L. J. (2015). Overweight and obesity in midlife and brain structure and Dementia 26 years later: The AGES-Reykjavik study. *American Journal of Epidemiology*, 181(9), 672–679.

Albanese, E., Launer, L. J., Egger, M., Prince, M. J., Giannakopoulos, P., Wolters, F. J. & Egan, K. (2017). Body mass index in midlife and dementia: Systematic review and meta-regression analysis of 589,649 men and women followed in longitudinal studies. *Alzheimers Dement*, 8, 165–178.

Anstey, K. J., Ashby-Mitchell, K. & Peters, R. (2017). Updating the evidence on the association between serum cholesterol and risk of late-life Dementia: Review and meta-analysis. *Journal of Alzheimers Diseases*, 56(1), 215–228.

Anstey, K. J., Cherbuin, N., Budge, M. & Young, J. (2011). Body mass index in midlife and late-life as a risk factor for dementia: A meta-analysis of prospective studies. *Obesity Reviews*, 12(5), e426–437.

Anstey, K. J., Lipnicki, D. M. & Low, L. F. (2008). Cholesterol as a risk factor for dementia and cognitive decline: A systematic review of prospective studies with meta-analysis. *American Journal of Geriatric Psychiatry*, 16(5), 343–354.

Areosa Sastre, A., Vernooij, R. W., Gonzalez-Colaco Harmand, M. & Martinez, G. (2017). Effect of the treatment of Type 2 diabetes mellitus on the development of cognitive impairment and dementia. *Cochrane Database of Systematic Reviews*, 6, CD003804.

Barnes, D. E. & Yaffe, K. (2011). The projected effect of risk factor reduction on Alzheimer's disease prevalence. *The Lancet Neurology*, 10(9), 819–828.

Beydoun, M. A., Beydoun, H. A. & Wang, Y. (2008). Obesity and central obesity as risk factors for incident dementia and its subtypes: A systematic review and meta-analysis. *Obesity Reviews*, 9(3), 204–218.

Biessels, G. J., Deary, I. J. & Ryan, C. M. (2008). Cognition and diabetes: A lifespan perspective. *The Lancet Neurology*, 7(2), 184–190.

Biessels, G. J., Kerssen, A., de Haan, E. H. & Kappelle, L. J. (2007). Cognitive dysfunction and diabetes: Implications for primary care. *Prim Care Diabetes*, 1(4), 187–193.

Brady, C. B., Gaziano, J. M., Cxypoliski, R. A., Guarino, P. D., Kaufman, J. S., Warren, S. R., Hartigan, P., Goldfarb, D. S. & Jamison, R. L. (2009). Homocysteine lowering and cognition in CKD: The Veterans Affairs homocysteine study. *American Journal of Kidney Diseases*, 54(3), 440–449.

Browne, J., Edwards, D. A., Rhodes, K. M., Brimicombe, D. J. & Payne, R. A. (2017). Association of comorbidity and health service usage among patients with dementia in the UK: A population-based study. *BMJ Open*, 7(3).

Bugnicourt, J. M., Godefroy, O., Chillon, J. M., Choukroun, G. & Massy, Z. A. (2013). Cognitive disorders and dementia in CKD: The neglected kidney-brain axis. *Journal of the American Society of Nephrology*, 24(3), 353–363.

Bunn, F., Burn, A-M., Goodman, C., Rait, G., Norton, S., Robinson, L., Schoeman, J. & Brayne, C. (2014). Comorbidity and dementia: A scoping review of the literature. *BMC Medicine*, 12, 192.

Chang-Quan, H., Hui, W., Chao-Min, W., Zheng-Rong, W., Jun-Wen, G., Yong-Hong, L., Yan-You, L. & Qing-Xiu, L. (2011). The association of antihypertensive medication use with risk of cognitive decline and dementia: A meta-analysis of longitudinal studies. *International Journal of Clinical Practice*, 65(12), 1295–1305.

Cheng, G., Huang, C., Deng, H. & Wang, H. (2012). Diabetes as a risk factor for dementia and mild cognitive impairment: A meta-analysis of longitudinal studies. *Internal Medicine Journal*, 42(5), 484–491.

Chertow, G. M., Levin, N. W., Beck, G. J., Depner, T. A., Eggers, P. W., Gassman, J. J., Gorodetskaya, I., Greene, T., James, S., Larive, B., Lindsay, R. M., Mehta, R. L., Miller, B., Ornt, D. B., Rajagopalan, S., Rastogi, A., Rocco, M. V., Schiller, B., Sergeyeva, O., Schulman, G., Ting, G. O., Unruh, M. L., Star, R. A. & Kliger, A. S. (2010). In-center hemodialysis six times per week versus three times per week. *The New England Journal of Medicine*, 363(24), 2287–2300.

Cole, A. R., Astell, A., Green, C. & Sutherland, C. (2007). Molecular connexions between dementia and diabetes. *Neuroscience & Biobehavioral Reviews*, 31(7), 1046–1063.

de Bruijn, R. F., Bos, M. J., Portegies, M. L., Hofman, A., Franco, O. H., Koudstaal, P. J. & Ikram, M. A. (2015). The potential for prevention of dementia across two decades: The prospective, population-based Rotterdam Study. *BMC Medicine*, 13, 132.

De Deyn, P. P., Vanholder, R., Eloot, S. & Glorieux, G. (2009). Guanidino compounds as uremic (neuro)toxins. *Seminar in Dialysis*, 22(4), 340–345.

Deckers, K., Camerino, I., van Boxtel, M. P., Verhey, F. R., Irving, K., Brayne, C., Kivipelto, M., Starr, J. M., Yaffe, K., de Leeuw, P. W. & Kohler, S. (2017a). Dementia risk in renal dysfunction: A systematic review and meta-analysis of prospective studies. *Neurology*, 88(2), 198–208.

Deckers, K., Schievink, S. H. J., Rodriquez, M. M. F., van Oostenbrugge, R. J., van Boxtel, M. P. J., Verhey, F. R. J. & Kohler, S. (2017b). Coronary heart disease and risk for cognitive impairment or dementia: Systematic review and meta-analysis. *PLoS One*, 12(9), e0184244.

Deckers, K., van Boxtel, M. P., Schiepers, O. J., de Vugt, M., Munoz Sanchez, J. L., Anstey, K. J., Brayne, C., Dartigues, J. F., Engedal, K., Kivipelto, M., Ritchie, K., Starr, J. M., Yaffe, K., Irving, K., Verhey, F. R. & Kohler, S. (2015). Target risk factors for dementia prevention: A systematic review and Delphi consensus study on the evidence from observational studies. *International Journal of Geriatric Psychiatry*, 30(3), 234–246.

Downey, A., Stroud, C., Landis, S. & Leshner, A. I. eds. (2017). *Preventing Cognitive Decline and Dementia: A Way Forward.*, Washington, DC: National Academy of Sciences.

Emmerzaal, T. L., Kiliaan, A. J. & Gustafson, D. R. (2015). 2003–2013: A decade of body mass index, Alzheimer's disease, and dementia. *Journal of Alzheimers Diseases*, 43(3), 739–755.

Etgen, T., Chonchol, M., Forstl, H. & Sander, D. (2012). Chronic kidney disease and cognitive impairment: A systematic review and meta-analysis. *Americna Journal of Nephrology*, 35(5), 474–482.

Exalto, L. G., Biessels, G. J., Karter, A. J., Huang, E. S., Katon, W. J., Minkoff, J. R. & Whitmer, R. A. (2013). Risk score for prediction of 10 year dementia risk in individuals with type 2 diabetes: A cohort study. *The Lancet Diabetes Endocrinology*, 1(3), 183–190.

Georgakis, M. K., Dimitriou, N. G., Karalexi, M. A., Mihas, C., Nasothimiou, E. G., Tousoulis, D., Tsivgoulis, G. & Petridou, E. T. (2017). Albuminuria in association with cognitive function and Dementia: A systematic review and meta-analysis. *Journal of the American Geriatrics Society*, 65(6), 1190–1198.

Gorelick, P. B., Scuteri, A., Black, S. E., Decarli, C., Greenberg, S. M., Iadecola, C., Launer, L. J., Laurent, S., Lopez, O. L., Nyenhuis, D., Petersen, R. C., Schneider, J. A., Tzourio, C., Arnett, D. K., Bennett, D. A., Chui, H. C., Higashida, R. T., Lindquist, R., Nilsson, P. M., Roman, G. C., Sellke, F. W. & Seshadri, S. (2011). Vascular contributions to cognitive impairment and dementia: A statement for healthcare professionals from the American heart association/American stroke association. *Stroke*, 42(9), 2672–2713.

Grimm, M. O., Zimmer, V. C., Lehmann, J., Grimm, H. S. & Hartmann, T. (2013). The impact of cholesterol, DHA, and sphingolipids on Alzheimer's disease. *BioMed Research International*, 814390.

Gudala, K., Bansal, D., Schifano, F. & Bhansali, A. (2013). Diabetes mellitus and risk of dementia: A meta-analysis of prospective observational studies. *Journal of Diabetes Investigation*, 4(6), 640–650.

Gustafson, D. (2006). Adiposity indices and dementia. *The Lancet Neurology*, 5(8), 713–720.

Helzner, E. P., Luchsinger, J. A., Scarmeas, N., Cosentino, S., Brickman, A. M., Glymour, M. M. & Stern, Y. (2009). Contribution of vascular risk factors to the progression in Alzheimer disease. *Archives of Neurology*, 66(3), 343–348.

Hill, N. R., Fatoba, S. T., Oke, J. L., Hirst, J. A., O'Callaghan, C. A., Lasserson, D. S. & Hobbs, F. D. (2016). Global prevalence of chronic kidney disease – a systematic review and meta-analysis. *PLoS One*, 11(7), e0158765.

Jha, V., Garcia-Garcia, G., Iseki, K., Li, Z., Naicker, S., Plattner, B., Saran, R., Wang, A. Y. & Yang, C. W. (2013). Chronic kidney disease: Global dimension and perspectives. *The Lancet*, 382(9888), 260–272.

Justin, B. N., Turek, M. & Hakim, A. M. (2013). Heart disease as a risk factor for dementia. *Clinical Epidemiology*, 5, 135–145.

Kalantarian, S., Stern, T. A., Mansour, M. & Ruskin, J. N. (2013). Cognitive impairment associated with atrial fibrillation: A meta-analysis. *Annals of Internal Medicine*, 158(5 Pt 1), 338–346.

Kane, R. L., Butler, M., Fink, H. A., Brasure, M., Davila, H., Desai, P., Jutkowitz, E., McCreedy, E., Nelson, V. A., McCarten, J. R., Calvert, C., Ratner, E., Hemmy, L. S. & Barclay, T. (2017). *Interventions to Prevent Age-Related Cognitive Decline, Mild Cognitive Impairment, and Clinical Alzheimer's-Type Dementia*. Rockville, MD: Agency for Healthcare Research and Quality (US).

Kiliaan, A. J., Arnoldussen, I. A. & Gustafson, D. R. (2014). Adipokines: A link between obesity and dementia? *The Lancet Neurology*, 13(9), 913–923.

Knopman, D. S., Edland, S. D., Cha, R. H., Petersen, R. C. & Rocca, W. A. (2007). Incident dementia in women is preceded by weight loss by at least a decade. *Neurology*, 69(8), 739–746.

Kwok, C. S., Loke, Y. K., Hale, R., Potter, J. F. & Myint, P. K. (2011). Atrial fibrillation and incidence of dementia: A systematic review and meta-analysis. *Neurology*, 76(10), 914–922.

Levi Marpillat, N., Macquin-Mavier, I., Tropeano, A. I., Bachoud-Levi, A. C. & Maison, P. (2013). Antihypertensive classes, cognitive decline and incidence of dementia: A network meta-analysis. *Journal of Hypertension*, 31(6), 1073–1082.

Li, J., Shao, Y. H., Gong, Y. P., Lu, Y. H., Liu, Y. & Li, C. L. (2014). Diabetes mellitus and dementia – a systematic review and meta-analysis. *European Review for Medical and Pharmacological Sciences*, 18(12), 1778–1789.

Lipska, K. J. & Montori, V. M. (2013). Glucose control in older adults with diabetes mellitus – more harm than good? *JAMA Internal Medicine*, 173(14), 1306–1307.

Livingston, G., Sommerlad, A., Orgeta, V., Costafreda, S. G., Huntley, J., Ames, D., Ballard, C., Banerjee, S., Burns, A., Cohen-Mansfield, J., Cooper, C., Fox, N., Gitlin, L. N., Howard, R., Kales, H. C., Larson, E. B., Ritchie, K., Rockwood, K., Sampson, E. L., Samus, Q., Schneider, L. S., Selbaek, G., Teri, L. & Mukadam, N. (2017). Dementia prevention, intervention, and care. *The Lancet*, 390(10113), 2673–2734.

Loef, M. & Walach, H. (2013). Midlife obesity and dementia: Meta-analysis and adjusted forecast of dementia prevalence in the United States and China. *Obesity (Silver Spring)*, 21(1), E51–E55.

Madero, M., Gul, A. & Sarnak, M. J. (2008). Cognitive function in chronic kidney disease. *Seminars in Dialysis*, 21(1), 29–37.

McGuinness, B., Craig, D., Bullock, R. & Passmore, P. (2016). Statins for the prevention of dementia. *Cochrane Database of Systematic Review*, (1), CD003160.

Mozaffarian, D., Benjamin, E. J., Go, A. S., Arnett, D. K., Blaha, M. J., Cushman, M., Das, S. R., de Ferranti, S., Despres, J. P., Fullerton, H. J., Howard, V. J., Huffman, M. D., Isasi, C. R., Jimenez, M. C., Judd, S. E., Kissela, B. M., Lichtman, J. H., Lisabeth, L. D., Liu, S., Mackey, R. H., Magid, D. J., McGuire, D. K., Mohler, E. R., 3rd, Moy, C. S., Muntner, P., Mussolino, M. E., Nasir, K., Neumar, R. W., Nichol, G., Palaniappan, L., Pandey, D. K., Reeves, M. J., Rodriguez, C. J., Rosamond, W., Sorlie, P. D., Stein, J., Towfighi, A., Turan, T. N., Virani, S. S., Woo, D., Yeh, R. W. & Turner, M. B. (2016). Executive summary: Heart disease and stroke statistics – 2016 update: A report from the American heart association. *Circulation*, 133(4), 447–454.

Mukherjee, S., Walter, S., Kauwe, J. S. K., Saykin, A. J., Bennett, D. A., Larson, E. B., Crane, P. K. & Glymour, M. M. (2015). Genetically predicted body mass index and Alzheimer's disease-related phenotypes in three large samples: Mendelian randomization analyses. *Alzheimers Dement*, 11(12), 1439–1451.

Murray, A. M., Hsu, F. C., Williamson, J. D., Bryan, R. N., Gerstein, H. C., Sullivan, M. D., Miller, M. E., Leng, I., Lovato, L. L. & Launer, L. J. (2017). ACCORDION MIND: Results of the observational extension of the ACCORD MIND randomised trial. *Diabetologia*, 60(1), 69–80.

NCD Risk Factor Collaboration. (2016). Trends in adult body-mass index in 200 countries from 1975 to 2014: A pooled analysis of 1698 population-based measurement studies with 19.2 million participants. *The Lancet*, 387(10026), 1377–1396.

Norton, S., Matthews, F. E., Barnes, D. E., Yaffe, K. & Brayne, C. (2014). Potential for primary prevention of Alzheimer's disease: An analysis of population-based data. *The Lancet Neurology*, 13(8), 788–794.

Ostergaard, S. D., Mukherjee, S., Sharp, S. J., Proitsi, P., Lotta, L. A., Day, F., Perry, J. R., Boehme, K. L., Walter, S., Kauwe, J. S., Gibbons, L. E., Larson, E. B., Powell, J. F., Langenberg, C., Crane, P. K., Wareham, N. J. & Scott, R. A. (2015). Associations between potentially modifiable risk factors and Alzheimer disease: A mendelian randomization study. *PLoS Medicine*, 12(6), e1001841.

Panza, F., D'Introno, A., Colacicco, A. M., Capurso, C., Pichichero, G., Capurso, S. A., Capurso, A. & Solfrizzi, V. (2006). Lipid metabolism in cognitive decline and dementia. *Brain Research Reviews*, 51(2), 275–292.

Panza, F., Solfrizzi, V., D'Introno, A., Colacicco, A. M., Santamato, A., Seripa, D., Pilotto, A., Capurso, A. & Capurso, C. (2009). Higher total cholesterol, cognitive decline, and dementia. *Neurobiology of Aging*, 30(4), 546–548.

Pedditizi, E., Peters, R. & Beckett, N. (2016). The risk of overweight/obesity in mid-life and late life for the development of dementia: A systematic review and meta-analysis of longitudinal studies. *Age Ageing*, 45(1), 14–21.

Peters, R., Booth, A. & Peters, J. (2014). A systematic review of calcium channel blocker use and cognitive decline/dementia in the elderly. *Journal of Hypertension*, 32(10), 1945–1957.

Power, M. C., Weuve, J., Gagne, J. J., McQueen, M. B., Viswanathan, A. & Blacker, D. (2011). The association between blood pressure and incident Alzheimer disease: A systematic review and meta-analysis. *Epidemiology*, 22(5), 646–659.

Qiu, C. (2012). Preventing Alzheimer's disease by targeting vascular risk factors: Hope and gap. *Journal of Alzheimers Diseases*, 32(3), 721–731.

Qiu, C., Winblad, B. & Fratiglioni, L. (2005). The age-dependent relation of blood pressure to cognitive function and dementia. *The Lancet Neurology*, 4(8), 487–499.

Qizilbash, N., Gregson, J., Johnson, M. E., Pearce, N., Douglas, I., Wing, K., Evans, S. J. W. & Pocock, S. J. (2015). BMI and risk of dementia in two million people over two decades: A retrospective cohort study. *The Lancet Diabetes Endocrinology*, 3(6), 431–436.

Rouch, L., Cestac, P., Hanon, O., Cool, C., Helmer, C., Bouhanick, B., Chamontin, B., Dartigues, J. F., Vellas, B. & Andrieu, S. (2015). Antihypertensive drugs, prevention of cognitive decline and dementia: A systematic review of observational studies, randomized controlled trials and meta-analyses, with discussion of potential mechanisms. *CNS Drugs*, 29(2), 113–130.

Santangeli, P., Di Biase, L., Bai, R., Mohanty, S., Pump, A., Cereceda Brantes, M., Horton, R., Burkhardt, J. D., Lakkireddy, D., Reddy, Y. M., Casella, M., Dello Russo, A., Tondo, C. & Natale, A. (2012). Atrial fibrillation and the risk of incident dementia: A meta-analysis. *Heart Rhythm*, 9(11), 1761–1768.

Santos, C. Y., Snyder, P. J., Wu, W. C., Zhang, M., Echeverria, A. & Alber, J. (2017). Pathophysiologic relationship between Alzheimer's disease, cerebrovascular disease, and cardiovascular risk: A review and synthesis. *Alzheimers Dement*, 7, 69–87.

Siervo, M., Arnold, R., Wells, J. C., Tagliabue, A., Colantuoni, A., Albanese, E., Brayne, C. & Stephan, B. C. (2011). Intentional weight loss in overweight and obese individuals and cognitive function: A systematic review and meta-analysis. *Obesity Reviews*, 12(11), 968–983.

Singh-Manoux, A., Dugravot, A., Shipley, M., Brunner, E. J., Elbaz, A., Sabia, S. & Kivimaki, M. (2017). Obesity trajectories and risk of dementia: 28 years of follow-up in the Whitehall II Study. *Alzheimers Dement*, 14(2), 178–186.

Stefanidis, K. B., Askew, C. D., Greaves, K. & Summers, M. J. (2017). The effect of non-stroke cardiovascular disease states on risk for cognitive decline and Dementia: A systematic and meta-analytic review. *Neuropsychology Review*, 28(1), 1–15.

Tully, P. J., Hanon, O., Cosh, S. & Tzourio, C. (2016). Diuretic antihypertensive drugs and incident dementia risk: A systematic review, meta-analysis and meta-regression of prospective studies. *Journal of Hypertension*, 34(6), 1027–1035.

van Buchem, M. A., Biessels, G. J., Brunner la Rocca, H. P., de Craen, A. J., van der Flier, W. M., Ikram, M. A., Kappelle, L. J., Koudstaal, P. J., Mooijaart, S. P., Niessen, W., van Oostenbrugge, R., de Roos, A., van Rossum, A. C. & Daemen, M. J. (2014). The heart-brain connection: A multidisciplinary approach targeting a missing link in the pathophysiology of vascular cognitive impairment. *Journal of Alzheimers Diseases*, 42(Suppl 4), S443–451.

van Vliet, P. (2012). Cholesterol and late-life cognitive decline. *Journal of Alzheimers Diseases*, 30(Suppl 2), S147–162.

Veronese, N., Facchini, S., Stubbs, B., Luchini, C., Solmi, M., Manzato, E., Sergi, G., Maggi, S., Cosco, T. & Fontana, L. (2017). Weight loss is associated with improvements in cognitive function among overweight and obese people: A systematic review and meta-analysis. *Neuroscience & Biobehavioral Reviews*, 72, 87–94.

Wang, H., Naghavi, M., Allen, C., *et al.* (2016). GBD 2015 Mortality and causes of death collaborators. Global, regional, and national life expectancy, all-cause mortality, and cause-specific mortality for 249 causes of death, 1980–2015: A systematic analysis for the Global Burden of Disease Study 2015. *Lancet*, 388, 1459–1544.

Wexler, R. & Aukerman, G. (2006). Nonpharmacologic strategies for managing hypertension. *American Family Physician*, 73(11), 1953–1956.

Whitworth, J. A. (2003). 2003 World Health Organization (WHO)/International Society of Hypertension (ISH) statement on management of hypertension. *Journal of Hypertension*, 21(11), 1983–1992.

Wild, S., Roglic, G., Green, A., Sicree, R. & King, H. (2004). Global prevalence of diabetes: Estimates for the year 2000 and projections for 2030. *Diabetes Care*, 27(5), 1047–1053.

Zlokovic, B.V. (2011). Neurovascular pathways to neurodegeneration in Alzheimer's disease and other disorders. *Nature Reviews Neuroscience*, 12(12), 723–738.

Chapter 5

Mood and other psychiatric factors

Sebastian Köhler and Alan Thomas

Introduction

Psychiatric symptoms of depression, anxiety or psychosis (delusions or hallucinations) are common in the prodromal and subsequent stages of dementia (Bos et al. 2017). In some forms of dementia, such as the behavioural variant of frontotemporal dementia or dementia with Lewy bodies, psychiatric symptoms are the main features of the disorder, may sometimes precede the cognitive symptoms by years and often lead to misdiagnosis and wrong treatment decisions. On the other hand, concentration difficulties and indecisiveness are often part of the symptom complex of major depressive disorder and part of its diagnostic criteria. Besides subjective cognitive complaints, objective impairments on neuropsychological tests are common in older patients with depression and do not appear to resolve after remission of mood symptoms (Alexopoulos 2005). Both clinical and population-based studies suggest that depression and anxiety is associated with a higher risk for dementia. Tentative evidence for psychosis and other psychiatric factors exists but is more limited. Yet, whether mood and other psychiatric symptoms represent a causal risk factor, a prodromal symptom of underlying pathology or a psychological reaction is still questionable because both the temporality of effects and the biological pathways have not been established. In this chapter, we will review the current evidence for mental health factors, with a focus on depression, anxiety and psychotic symptoms for risk and prevention of dementia.

Depression

Terms, prevalence/incidence

Depression is a prevalent mental disorder that may cause serious suffering for the person affected and their environment. The World Health Organization estimated that more than 300 million people suffer from depression worldwide (World Health Organization 2017). Depression is a heterogeneous disorder including differences in severity, clinical presentation, age of onset, treatment response and course (Comijs et al. 2015; Licht-Strunk et al. 2007; Driscoll et al. 2005; Hardeveld et al. 2013; Trivedi et al. 2006; Souery et al. 2006). Major depressive disorder as defined according the fifth edition of the Diagnostic and Statistical Manual of Mental Disorders (DSM5) includes the presence of at least five from nine symptoms of which one has to be either sad mood or loss of interest or pleasure in addition to accompanying symptoms, such as difficulties sleeping, loss of appetite, lack of energy, concentration problems or suicidal thoughts. These symptoms need to be present most of the time for at least two weeks and to interfere with social or occupational functioning. A minor depressive disorder is present if someone experiences two, three or four symptoms. Most epidemiological studies rely on self-report questionnaires that assess symptom severity such as the Centre for Epidemiological Studies Depression Scale (CES-D) (Radloff 1977) or the Patient Health Questionnaire (PHQ) (Kroenke et al. 2001), rather than clinical diagnosis, and participants are usually classified as having 'high depressive symptoms' based on commonly accepted cut-offs. In late-life depression (after age 60 or 65 years), new episodes may arise from a lifetime history of depression or de novo (late-onset depression). In older adults, the prevalence of major depression is estimated to be 1%–4% and 4%–13% for minor depression, with a higher prevalence in women than men (Alexopoulos 2005).

Evidence from observational studies

In patients with late life depression, cognitive impairment is common and includes deficits in episodic memory, executive functioning and processing speed (Thomas and O'brien 2008). In some patients, low cognitive performance seems to be transient, i.e. secondary to the depressive episode, because depressive thoughts and anhedonic and apathetic symptoms interfered with neuropsychological testing. However, in more than half of patients, cognitive deficits have been shown to persist despite remission of depressive symptoms, and they appear to be independent from current symptom severity and antidepressant use (Lee et al. 2007; Bhalla et al. 2009; Köhler et al. 2009). The cognitive deficits have been linked to structural brain changes, including hippocampus volume reductions (Hendricksen et al. 2004) and white matter lesions (Köhler et al. 2010b).

Meta-analyses of both clinical and community-based studies found that people with major depressive disorders or those who score highly on depressive symptoms have twice the risk for all-type dementia, (Diniz et al. 2013) and that this risk increases as the latency period between assessment of depression and diagnosis of dementia widens (Ownby et al. 2006). An umbrella review of meta-analysis of risk factors for dementia reported that, among a total of 76 unique associations, seven showed convincing evidence. Of these, three associations related to depression as a putative risk factor for all-type dementia (depression assessed at any age, depression assessed in late life) and as a risk factor for Alzheimer's disease (AD) dementia (depression assessed in late life) (Bellou et al. 2017). As the authors stress, these associations are not necessarily causal. Similarly, epidemiological studies have found older people with depression or high depressive symptoms to show faster decline on repeated measures of memory and other cognitive domains (Köhler et al. 2009; Yaffe et al. 1999; Comijs et al. 2004; Köhler et al. 2010c).

Only a few studies have looked at the relationship with different forms of dementia. There appears to be a general consistency that depression is more strongly associated with vascular dementia than AD dementia (Diniz et al. 2013; Gao et al. 2013). In a retrospective cohort study of >13,000 members of the Kaiser Permanente Medical Care Program, the hazard for vascular dementia was highest in individuals with depression starting in midlife and continuing (or re-occurring) in late life, while the risk for AD dementia was highest in people with late-onset depression (Barnes et al. 2012). Using population attributable fractions, it has been suggested that 8% (Norton et al. 2014) to 10% of cases of AD dementia or all-type dementia, respectively, can be attributed to depression. In the Baltimore Longitudinal Ageing Study with 1,239 older adults followed for a median of 24.7 years, an increase in the risk for all-type and AD dementia was observed with increasing numbers of depressive episode (measured every two years). Each additional episode conveyed a 14% increase in the risk for all-type dementia, suggesting a cumulative exposure effect during the life course (Dotson et al. 2010). In the retrospective study from the Kaiser Permanente Medical Care Program mentioned already, the presence of depressive episodes in midlife (30–45 years before dementia outcome ascertainment) and late life (3–15 years before dementia outcome ascertainment) was investigated. The risk for all-type dementia was 19% higher in those with midlife depressive symptoms only, 72% in those with late-onset depression and 80% for those with episodes in both midlife and late life. Intriguingly, the risk for vascular dementia in the latter group was increase by 251% compared to only 24% in those with midlife depression only and 47% in those with late life depression only (Barnes et al. 2012).

While these studies seem to suggest that an earlier onset of depression, through cumulative exposure, leads to a higher risk for dementia, especially in vascular forms, other studies found more support for depression being a prodromal symptom. For instance, the Whitehall II prospective cohort study of >10,000 individuals and a mean follow-up of 28 years found no statistically significant association between high depressive symptoms assessed at age 35–55 years and risk for all-type dementia in later life (HR = 1.21, 95% CI 0.95–91.54). At later waves, when the same participants were aged 50–74 years, high depressive symptoms were associated with an increased risk (HR = 1.72, 95% CI = 1.21–22.44) (Singh-Manoux et al. 2017). In the Rotterdam Study, all-type dementia risk was only increased in two groups of depressed elderly. One group showed increasing levels of depressive symptoms over time, and the other had permanent high symptoms. The latter group was small (< 2% of the total sample), and the association became non-significant after controlling for the contribution of vascular factors to the risk, possibly indicating a shared vascular mechanism (see the following). For the 'increasing group', the association remained unchanged, suggesting that depressive symptoms became more severe as the underlying dementia process evolved (Mirza et al. 2016).

Some studies found bipolar disorder (mania or manic-depressive disorder) to increase risk for dementia, but a recent meta-analysis of 22 prospective study found no evidence of accelerated cognitive decline (Bora and Ozerdem 2017).

Evidence from RCTs

Pharmacological treatment for depression in older adults follows the same regime as in younger patients. Usually, selective serotonin reuptake inhibitors are the first-line treatment because they have fewer side effects, although they cause more drug-by-drug interactions in older adults (Kok et al. 2017). No RCTs exist that have tested whether treatment of depressive symptoms with antidepressants slows cognitive decline or prevents dementia. However, one randomized augmentation trial in late-life depression found that addition of donepezil to antidepressants worsened the rate of depression recurrence, especially in those with MCI and produced no lasting benefits on cognition (Reynolds et al. 2011). Clinical studies have noted a small improvement in some cognitive domains with treatment, but patients on average still performed far below normal levels (Nebes et al. 2000; Köhler et al. 2010a). A meta-analysis of five prospective cohort studies reported a higher risk for AD dementia and all-cause dementia in generic antidepressant users, with higher odds in users aged younger than 65 years (Moraros et al. 2017). The authors noted that there might be confounding by indication, meaning that it was not possible to separate possible effects of antidepressant use from effects of depression itself. In a prospective study of 8,732 participants with normal cognition, depression increased the risk for dementia, but antidepressant medication use did not. In addition, depression did not convey higher risk among antidepressant users (Burke et al. 2017). However, long-term treatment with antidepressants with known anticholinergic properties (tricyclic antidepressants) has been associated with an increased risk for all-cause dementia and AD dementia (Gray et al. 2015). In addition, in a nationwide study from Taiwan, antidepressant use was associated with an increased risk for dementia among depressed as well as non-depressed users and was irrespective of drug class (e.g. tricyclic antidepressants, selective serotonin reuptake inhibitors), although the risk was highest for tricyclic antidepressants (Then et al. 2017).

Plausible biological pathways

Theories explaining the association between depression and dementia risk can be divided into theories, suggesting that depression is a (causal) risk factor and theories linking both to a common underlying pathology in which depression is a prodromal symptom.

Depression as a risk factor

Most research has focussed on the role of cortisol and inflammation. Cortisol is the major human glucocorticoid best known for its importance in the stress response mediated by the hypothalamic-pituitary-adrenal (HPA) axis. High cortisol levels, hippocampal atrophy and neuropsychiatric symptoms are common in Cushing's syndrome, a condition caused by excessive exposure to cortisol-like drugs or tumour, most often pituitary adenoma (Sapolsky 2000). Animal studies have shown that chronic exposure to high levels of glucocorticoids can induce hippocampus atrophy by causing glucocorticoid receptor-linked excitotoxicity of glutamatergic neurons (Sapolsky et al. 1986; Sapolsky 2000). In humans, people with high cortisol levels have been reported to have worse memory and smaller hippocampal volumes (Lupien et al. 1998). Patients with late-life depression have indeed commonly been observed to have lower hippocampal volume than controls (O'brien 1997; Sexton et al. 2013). Hippocampal volume in depression has been related to lifetime exposure to depression (Sheline et al. 1996), and memory deficits after 6 months (Hendricksen et al. 2004), but not 18 months (Köhler et al. 2010b). Direct evidence linking high cortisol to the cognitive deficits seen in depression is lacking (Köhler et al. 2010b). In addition, studies on hippocampus volume in depression have largely been cross-sectional, making it impossible to disentangle whether depression is a cause or consequence of hippocampus damage. In fact, some studies found that a shorter duration of depression predicted hippocampus volume (Andreescu et al. 2007). The hippocampus serves an important function in contributing to the negative feedback loop that ultimately signals to the adrenal glands to stop glucocorticoid release. Smaller hippocampal volumes might therefore mark stress-vulnerability rather than being due to prolonged cortisol excretion.

Stress also increases *immune activity* and may lead to changes in pro- and anti-inflammatory markers. Higher levels of pro-inflammatory cytokines have been commonly reported in depression (Howren et al. 2009) and have been suggested to cause changes to neurotransmitters, neurotrophic factor and oxidative stress (Miller et al. 2009). In a meta-analysis of 24 studies, higher levels of TNF-α and interleukin 6 have been found (Dowlati et al. 2010). Higher levels of C-reactive protein are also common in people with depression (Dinan 2009). Depression has been characterized as a pro-inflammatory state that carries a high risk for cardiovascular disease (Dinan 2009) and dementia (Leonard 2007). In a recent meta-analysis, levels of inflammatory markers (*e.g.* TNF-α) were lower in antidepressant treatment responders than non-responders. Treatment resistance was associated with persistently elevated inflammation markers (Strawbridge 2015). On the other hand, an acute inflammatory response such as induced by treatment of hepatitis C with interferon-gamma often causes depression, suggesting that depression might also be a consequence rather than a stress-related cause of inflammation (Wichers et al. 2006). Inflammation can modulate metabolism of tryptophan, an essential amino and precursor of the neurotransmitters serotonin and melatonin. More than 90% of bioavailable tryptophan is metabolized via the *kynurenine pathway* into L-kynurenine and its downstream metabolites. Some of these metabolites appear neuroprotective while others are neurotoxic, and they play a role in moderating neuronal plasticity (Lemieux et al. 2015), glial (Guillemin et al. 2005), neuronal (Wu et al. 2013) and epithelial apoptosis (Wang et al. 2014), and might cause blood-brain-barrier damage (Gold et al. 2011) and neurodegenerative diseases (Vecsei et al. 2013). Pro-inflammatory markers (e.g. TNF-α, interferon-γ) stimulate the tryptophan-to-kynurenine turnover, which is hypothesized to happen at the expense of serotonin and melatonin, thereby inducing a relative serotonin depletion causing depression. However, only small and mostly cross-sectional studies in patients with dementia exist. Direct evidence in cognitively normal participants and follow-up studies in depression are lacking.

Depression as a prodromal symptom

Hippocampal atrophy is also a sign of Alzheimer's disease dementia and hence might also signal evolving AD pathology in the brains of people with depression. The parahippocampal gyrus and other limbic structures are affected in the earlier clinical stages of AD, and might give rise to depressive symptoms by disconnecting frontal and limbic brain regions involved in affect regulation. Depression and cognitive impairment might thus both be symptoms of underlying neurodegenerative changes causing them independently, without a direct path between them (Gudmundsson et al. 2015). Few studies have looked at AD pathology, i.e. β-amyloid$_{1-42}$ or tau protein aggregation, in depression. A study by Pomera et al. found lower levels of β-amyloid$_{1-42}$ in the cerebrospinal fluid of 28 patients with late-life depression compared to a control group, indicating higher retention levels in the brain and, thus, more severe AD pathology (Pomara et al. 2012). The study also found higher levels of oxidative stress markers in the depressed group. Both groups had normal cognition. On the contrary, another study found higher levels of cerebrospinal fluid β-amyloid in a sample of 14 women with any depression (11 major depression) but no differences in tau relative to controls. A small pilot study used positron emission tomography to study β-amyloid receptor occupancy in the brains of eight remitted patients, of which seven met criteria for mild cognitive impairment. The two cognitively normal patients had normal β-amyloid levels, three of the cognitively impaired patients had levels indicative of AD and the other three patients scored in-between (Butters et al. 2008). Likewise, one study in 55 patients with major depression found that those with amnestic mild cognitive impairment showed higher β-amyloid levels on positron emission tomography, although differences were significant for parietal regions only. Patients with non-amnestic or without mild cognitive impairment had levels similar to controls (Wu et al. 2016). Other studies did not find overall higher β-amyloid binding in depressed patients relative to controls (Madsen et al. 2012). A recent study among 46 patients with late-life depression showed lower hippocampal volume compared with 54 controls, but no differences in cortical β-amyloid binding levels. Moreover, β-amyloid levels correlated with APOE genotype, but not with hippocampal volume in depression (De Winter et al. 2016). In addition, autopsy studies generally failed to find evidence for more-than-average AD pathology in depressed cases (Thomas et al. 2001; Tsopelas et al. 2011).

According to the '*vascular depression hypothesis*', strategic ischemic lesions in fronto-limbic neuronal networks underlying mood regulation result in depressive symptoms and cognitive deficits, especially executive dysfunctions (Krishnan et al. 1997; Alexopoulos et al. 1997). According to this theory, depression, again, is a marker of cerebral damage and not a causal risk factor. Cerebral small vessel disease in the brains of depressed patients, such as white matter hyperintensities (Herrmann et al. 2008) and ischemic lesions (Thomas et al. 2002; Thomas et al. 2003), are common in late-life depression and have been related to the severity of cognitive deficits (Köhler et al. 2010b). Connectivity changes at the microstructural and functional level have been observed too (Colloby et al. 2011). In line with these observations, evidence is accumulating that depression carries a higher risk for vascular dementia than for AD dementia (Diniz et al. 2013; Barnes et al. 2012). Depression further has strong bidirectional relations with vascular disease, both as a consequence (Pan et al. 2010; Kivimäki et al. 2012) and a predictor of vascular events, such as coronary heart disease and stroke (Wulsin and Singal 2003; Van Der Kooy et al. 2007; Surtees et al. 2008; Pan et al. 2011). Next, patients with late-life depression often show evidence of atherosclerosis (Tiemeier et al. 2004; Agatisa et al. 2005) and endothelial damage (Van Agtmaal et al. 2017). Cerebral small vessel disease can predate the onset of depression (Teodorczuk et al. 2007; Godin et al. 2008) and progresses over time in subjects with prevalent depression (Godin et al. 2008). In addition, more severe white matter changes have been associated with the worsening prognosis of depression, including poor response to antidepressant treatment (Hickie et al. 1995; Alexopoulos et al. 2008), chronic and relapsing course (O'brien et al. 1998) and an increased risk for dementia and higher mortality (Baldwin et al. 2000).

Future directions

The question whether depression is a risk factor or prodromal symptom of dementia has not been fully resolved. While these prospective studies provide strong and consistent evidence that depression in midlife and late life is associated with a higher risk for dementia, the biological pathways as well as temporality of effects have not been established, which questions whether the relationship is causal in nature or due to shared mechanisms. It is therefore important to have studies with long follow-up durations and repeated assessments of cognitive function or dementia diagnosis that can clarify the trajectory of depression and cognitive changes. Even studies with more extended follow-up durations might not have been able to capture the very earliest pathological brain changes that precede the onset of cognitive impairment by decades (Jansen et al. 2015). The large heterogeneity in findings, with evidence both for and against each biological mechanism, sometimes refined to specific subgroups, points towards different operating mechanisms. Depression might be a marker of underlying vascular disease or possibly neurodegenerative changes in some late-onset depression, leading to different neuropsychological dysfunctions (amnestic or non-amnestic impairment), while it might be a risk factor due to prolonged cortisol exposure or lifestyle changes in others. As the risk for dementia in general is unlikely to be mono-causal, more complex approaches should be embraced more often to study different disease trajectories and population mixtures, biological pathways and their interactions, timing of depression and cognitive changes and the way depression interacts and clusters with other dementia risk factors, such as inactivity, smoking, poor diets and social isolation. Population-based studies with extensive phenotyping would be desirable to study the direct and mediating effects of biomarkers of AD pathology and markers of cerebral small vessel disease, microvascular changes and brain connectivity, to dementia risk. It is also unclear, whether treatment of depression restores dementia risk or whether prevention of depression itself translates into lower dementia risk in the long run.

In observational studies, having a purpose in life has been suggested to protect against the development of mild cognitive impairment and dementia in a seven-year, follow-up study of community-dwelling older adults (Boyle et al. 2010b). Also, low social participation, less frequent social contact and more loneliness, but not low satisfaction with social networks, have been associated with incident dementia (Kuiper et al. 2015). A positive attitude towards ageing has also been related to lower dementia risk, even in those with high-risk genes (Levy et al. 2018). These factors highlight the complexity surrounding depression, dementia and related risk and protective factors such as psychosocial resilience and support.

Anxiety

Terms, prevalence/incidence

Anxiety disorders according to DSM5 include conditions such as panic disorder with and without agoraphobia, specific phobias and generalized anxiety disorder. Post-traumatic stress disorders are related to anxiety disorders but now are under a separate category. Severity of anxiety symptoms can be assessed using clinical or self-report questionnaires, e.g. the Hospital Anxiety and Depression Scale (HADS) or the Hamilton Anxiety Rating Scale (HAM-A). In the US

National Comorbidity Survey, the one-year prevalence of any anxiety disorder after age 55 years was 7.6% in men and 14.7 in women, with the highest estimates in age 55–64 years (Byers et al. 2010).

Evidence from observational studies

Compared to depression, the literature on anxiety is much less extensive and mostly focussed on anxiety symptoms rather than anxiety disorders. Prospective studies in post-traumatic stress disorder (PTSD) have mostly been done in veterans because prevalence is high. For instance, 22% of soldiers in the Iraq and Afghanistan wars admitted to the Veterans Affairs health care system between 2002 and 2008 had PTSD (Weiner et al. 2013). In a retrospective cohort study comparing 181,093 veterans with PTSD to 127,938 veterans without PTDS, the adjusted hazard ratio for all-type dementia was 1.77 and remained after excluding comorbid depression (Yaffe et al. 2010). In another report by the same group, that risk was further increased (the hazard ratio was 2.24 in veterans who were prisoners of war (Meziab et al. 2014)). In another retrospective cohort study of ca 500,000 health care recipients of the Kaiser Permanente Northern California, PTSD diagnoses in males and females were linked to future dementia during an average follow-up of eight years (Flatt et al., 2018). PTSD was associated with a 57% increased risk in women and a 92% increased risk in men, compared to those without PTSD. The risk was further increased in those with comorbid depression. In a meta-analysis on high levels of anxiety symptoms, evidence from 20 prospective cohort studies suggested a 77% higher risk for cognitive impairment and a 57% higher risk for dementia in the general population. The latter association was only present in studies with a mean age of 80 years and older. The risk was not increased in people with existing mild cognitive impairment (Gulpers et al. 2016). In the Rotterdam Study, anxiety was cross-sectionally associated with worse cognitive performance, but neither anxiety symptoms nor anxiety disorder predicted later dementia (De Bruijn et al. 2014).

Evidence from RCTs

Benzodiazepines are the most common pharmacological treatment for anxiety. Clinical trials on the effect of benzodiazepines for dementia risk are lacking. In general, benzodiazepines have been criticized for being addictive and their detrimental effect on cognition and their use is discouraged in adults aged 65 years and older. As for the effect of antidepressants in depression (which is often comorbid with anxiety), it is difficult to exclude the possibility of confounding by indication. In a case-control study, long-term benzodiazepine use was associated with an increased risk for AD dementia, which was not affected by adjusting for reasons for prescription (anxiety, depression or insomnia). The authors conclude that there might be a direct association (Billioti De Gage et al. 2014).

Directionality of effects and plausible biological pathways

Biological changes seen in PTSD and anxiety largely resemble those for depression. Structural brain abnormalities include reductions in hippocampus volume (Karl et al. 2006, Woon et al. 2010) and white matter (Villarreal et al. 2002), as well as a change in the amygdala and other fronto-limbic structures (Karl et al. 2006). For PTSD, a review and meta-analysis found higher levels of inflammatory markers (C-reactive protein, interleukins 1 and 6, tumour necrosis factor α-TNF-α) (Lohr et al. 2015). A prospective study in 524 women from the Nurses' Health Survey II found higher levels of inflammatory markers (C-reactive protein, TNF-α), as well as higher or increasing levels over time for markers of endothelial dysfunction (intercellular adhesion molecule-1, vascular adhesion molecule-1) (Sumner et al. 2017). In addition, reduced leukocyte telomere lengths and higher oxidative stress levels have been found in PTSD, suggesting accelerated ageing (Lohr et al. 2015). In functional imaging studies, PTSD has been associated with impairments in the medial prefrontal cortex, amygdala and hippocampus (Shin et al. 2006). Higher severity of PTSD symptoms has been shown to predict more brain atrophy (Weiner et al. 2013). Hippocampal volume reductions in PTSD and anxiety are often thought to be due to stress-induced HPA-axis dysregulation and glucocorticoid actions similar to the mechanisms proposed for depression. Analogously to depression, people with smaller hippocampi might, however, also be more vulnerable to develop anxiety/PTSD more because of an overactive stress system (Greenberg et al. 2014). In addition, higher prevalence of shared health and lifestyle-related risk factors might contribute to the development of dementia, such as such as cardiovascular disease and type 2 diabetes mellitus, physical inactivity, poor diet or smoking and alcohol abuse (Yaffe et al. 2014; Lohr et al. 2015). In a co-twin study, the risk for dementia increased with increasing anxiety levels, but the association was stronger for dizygotic than for monozygotic twins. Since genetic differences are controlled for in the latter, results suggested that genetic factors common to both anxiety and dementia partly explain the higher risk (Petkus et al. 2016). Finally, the meta-analysis of Gulpers et al. found that stronger associations between risk for dementia and anxiety increases with age. This suggests that anxiety might be a prodromal symptom, rather than causal risk factor (Gulpers et al. 2016).

Future directions

The high co-occurrence between depression and anxiety warrants further research into their independent effects. In older adults, some differences have been noted with a linear relationship between depression and cognitive decline (more symptoms predicted more decline), but a curvilinear relation for anxiety (only severe anxiety symptoms predicted more decline) (Bierman et al. 2005). Again, research into the underlying pathology, multimodal imaging studies and timing of effects would help to shed light on the putative mechanisms underlying the association.

Psychosis

Terms, prevalence/incidence

Psychotic disorders according to DSM5 range from brief psychotic disorder to schizophrenia. Schizophrenia and related non-affective psychotic disorders have predominantly been studied in adolescence and young adulthood, where incidence peaks (Van Der Werf et al. 2014). Some individuals, however, experience psychotic symptoms for the first time after the age of 40 or 60 years, i.e. late-onset schizophrenia and very-late-onset, schizophrenia-like psychosis (Howard et al. 2000). Especially in the latter, the question has been raised whether the incident psychotic symptoms (mostly paranoid delusions and visual hallucinations) are prodromal signs of dementia.

Evidence from observational studies

For patients with chronic schizophrenia that started in early life, cognitive deficits have traditionally been reported drop in the first five years and then level of into a 'stable cognitive encephalopathy' (Goldberg et al. 1993; Rund 1998). Most studies report similar age-related decline in cognitive abilities in schizophrenic patients compared to healthy controls, although faster decline in isolated executive functions have been sometimes reported (Fucetola et al. 2000). Very few studies into cognitive ability in patients with a late or very late onset of psychotic disorders are available, but findings generally find no evidence of accelerated decline or more severe impairment than in early onset disorders (Heaton et al. 1994; Hanssen et al. 2014).

However, in a population-based study of 2.8 million people aged 50 years and older, where 20,683 individuals had schizophrenia, the presence of schizophrenia conferred a circa two-times higher risk for all-cause dementia during an 18-year follow-up. The risk was independent from other major dementia risk factors and was higher in those younger than 65 years. A handful of studies examined whether presence of psychotic symptoms (delusions or hallucinations) predicted dementia risk in older adults, finding evidence for an increased risk (Östling et al. 2007; Fischer and Agüera-Ortiz 2017). In a study of 2,025 adults 65 years and older, psychotic symptoms were present in 13%, and were related to a 2.73 times higher risk for all-cause dementia during a 10-year follow-up. The risk was independent of age, gender and education, comorbid depression and anxiety, as well as differences in baseline cognitive ability, and was equal in size for paranoid symptoms and visual hallucinations and after exclusion of participants with suggestive cognitive impairment at baseline (Köhler et al. 2013). However, it cannot be ruled out that symptoms were due to impeding dementia, e.g. visual hallucinations can be an early symptom in dementia with Lewy bodies.

Directionality of effects and plausible biological pathways

Neuroimaging studies report brain changes comparable to those seen in younger patients (including increased ventricle-to-brain ratios and temporal lobe reductions) or no abnormalities compared to a healthy comparison group (Walterfang et al. 2005). Yet, differences with early onset psychosis have also been reported to include atrophic changes (Förstl et al. 1994), reduced cerebral blood flow in temporal cortices (Sachdev et al. 1997) and increased white matter changes (Tonkonogy and Geller 1999; Sachdev et al. 1999; Rivkin et al. 2000; Casanova and Lindzen 2003). In addition, Casanova et al. report that women with late-onset psychosis and no diagnosis of dementia do have higher Alzheimer pathology load as indicated by high prevalence of Braak stages III and IV in post-mortem brain tissue (Casanova and Lindzen 2003). Whether the latter finding represents a subgroup with progressive brain changes or whether findings are due to misclassification of some patients with other aetiologies is unknown.

Future directions

More studies, particularly in late and very late onset of psychotic disorders, are needed to study whether these are prodromal stages of dementia or true expressions of psychotic disorders at later age. Clinical studies have largely been small because sampling of patients, who usually suffer from paranoid delusions and are care avoiders, is very difficult to undertake. Imaging studies and studies collecting cerebrospinal fluid markers in these patients are especially challenging, and will require collaborative, multi-centre efforts. Assessment of psychotic symptoms in epidemiological studies also imposes challenges. A comprehensive psychiatric assessment using clinical rating scales by an expert are time consuming and usually unfeasible, or they need intensive training of lay interviewers. Some shorter instruments such as the Mini Neuropsychiatric Interview could be used (Sheehan et al. 1998). Also, self-report questionnaires on psychotic experiences can be used (Hanssen et al. 2003).

Other psychiatric factors

Other predisposing or related mental health factors have been related to an increased risk for dementia. Neuroticism, denoting a personality trait characterized by higher sensitivity to daily stress, have been shown to be related to worse cognition (Boyle et al. 2010a) and to predict a higher risk for mild cognitive impairment (Wilson et al. 2007). Both associations were independent from comorbid depression. On the other hand, as said, having a purpose in life has been suggested to protect against development of mild cognitive impairment and dementia in a seven-year follow-up study of community-dwelling older adults. The association was independent from depressive symptoms, neuroticism, social network size and number of chronic medical conditions (Boyle et al. 2010b). Also, low social participation, less frequent social contact and more loneliness, but not low satisfaction with social networks, have been associated with incident dementia (Kuiper et al. 2015). These findings could lead to psychosocial interventions to promote resilience and reduce stress sensitivity, to help find meaning in life (e.g. by engaging with charity work or having a late life second career) and to feel less lonely and isolated. Whether such activities could result in reduced risk for late life poor mental health and dementia remains to be further investigated. Finally, some studies found bipolar disorder (mania or manic-depressive disorder) to increase risk for dementia, but a recent meta-analysis of 22 prospective study found no evidence of accelerated cognitive decline (Bora and Ozerdem 2017).

Overall summary

There is a large evidence base that psychiatric factors, such as depression, anxiety and, albeit to a lesser degree, psychotic symptoms, are associated with a higher risk for dementia. Future studies should focus on explaining inter-individual differences in risks and identify putative pathways and timing of effects. Psychosocial factors such as having a purpose in life and intact social network need more intensive study as they might carry protective effects for dementia either directly or by lowering risk for psychiatric disorders.

References

Agatisa, P. K., *et al.* (2005). Coronary and aortic calcification in women with a history of major depression. *Archives of Internal Medicine*, 165(11), 1229–1236.

Alexopoulos, G. S. (2005). Depression in the elderly. *The Lancet*, 365(9475), 1961–1970.

Alexopoulos, G. S., *et al.* (1997). 'Vascular depression' hypothesis. *Archives of General Psychiatry*, 54.

Alexopoulos, G. S., *et al.* (2008). Microstructural white matter abnormalities and remission of geriatric depression. *American Journal of Psychiatry*, 165(2), 238–244.

Andreescu, C., *et al.* (2007). Gray matter changes in late life depression-a structural mri analysis. *Neuropsychopharmacology*, 33(11), 2566–2572.

Baldwin, R. C., *et al.* (2000). The prognostic significance of abnormalities seen on magnetic resonance imaging in late life depression: Clinical outcome, mortality and progression to dementia at three years. *International Journal of Geriatric Psychiatry*, 15(12), 1097–1104.

Barnes, D. E., *et al.* (2012). Midlife vs late-life depressive symptoms and risk of dementia: Differential effects for Alzheimer disease and vascular dementia. *Archives of General Psychiatry*, 69(5), 493–498.

Bellou, V., *et al.* (2017). Systematic evaluation of the associations between environmental risk factors and dementia: An umbrella review of systematic reviews and meta-analyses. *Alzheimer's & Dementia*, 13(4), 406–418.

Bhalla, R. K., *et al.* (2009). Patterns of mild cognitive impairment after treatment of depression in the elderly. *American Journal of Geriatric Psychiatry*, 17(4), 308–316.

Bierman, E. J. M., *et al.* (2005). Effects of anxiety versus depression on cognition in later life. *American Journal of Geriatric Psychiatry*, 13(8), 686–693.

Billioti De Gage, S., *et al.* (2014). Benzodiazepine use and risk of Alzheimer's disease: Case-control study. *BMJ*, 349.

Bora, E. & Ozerdem, A. (2017). Meta-analysis of longitudinal studies of cognition in bipolar disorder: Comparison with healthy controls and schizophrenia. *Psychological Medicine*, 47(16), 2753–2766.

Bos, I., *et al.* (2017). The frequency and influence of dementia risk factors in prodromal Alzheimer's disease. *Neurobiology of Aging*, 56, 33–40.

Boyle, L. L., *et al.* (2010a). Trait neuroticism, depression, and cognitive function in older primary care patients. *American Journal of Geriatric Psychiatry*, 18(4), 305–312.

Boyle, P. A., *et al.* (2010b). Effect of a purpose in life on risk of incident Alzheimer disease and mild cognitive impairment in community-dwelling older persons. *Archives of General Psychiatry*, 67(3), 304–310.

Burke, S. L., *et al.* (2017). Decreasing hazards of Alzheimer's disease with the use of antidepressants: Mitigating the risk of depression and apolipoprotein E. *International Journal of Geriatrics Psychiatry*, 33(1), 200–211.

Butters, M. A., *et al.* (2008). Imaging Alzheimer pathology in late-life depression with pet and pittsburgh compound-b. *Alzheimer Disease and Associated Disorders*, 22(3), 261–268.

Byers, A. L., *et al.* (2010). High occurrence of mood and anxiety disorders among older adults: The national comorbidity survey replication. *Archives of General Psychiatry*, 67(5), 489–496.

Casanova, M. F. & Lindzen, E. C. (2003). Changes in gray-/white-matter ratios in the parahippocampal gyri of late-onset schizophrenia patients. *American Journal of Geriatric Psychiatry*, 11(6), 605–609.

Colloby, S. J., *et al.* (2011). White matter changes in late-life depression: A diffusion tensor imaging study. *Journal of Affective Disorders*, 135(1–3), 216–220.

Comijs, H. C., *et al.* (2004). Do severity and duration of depressive symptoms predict cognitive decline in older persons? Results of the longitudinal aging study amsterdam. *Aging Clinical and Experimental Research*, 16(3), 226–232.

Comijs, H. C., *et al.* (2015). The two-year course of late-life depression: Results from the Netherlands study of depression in older persons. *BMC Psychiatry*, 15(1), 20.

De Bruijn, R. F., *et al.* (2014). Anxiety is not associated with the risk of dementia or cognitive decline: The rotterdam study. *American Journal of Geriatric Psychiatry*, 22(12), 1382–1390.

De Winter, F-L., *et al.* (2016). No association of lower hippocampal volume with Alzheimer's disease pathology in late-life depression. *American Journal of Psychiatry*, 174(3), 237–245.

Dinan, T. G. (2009). Inflammatory markers in depression. *Current Opinion in Psychiatry*, 22(1), 32–36.

Diniz, B. S., *et al.* (2013). Late-life depression and risk of vascular dementia and Alzheimer's disease: Systematic review and meta-analysis of community-based cohort studies. *The British Journal of Psychiatry*, 202(5), 329–335.

Dotson, V. M., Beydoun, M. A. & Zonderman, A. B. (2010). Recurrent depressive symptoms and the incidence of dementia and mild cognitive impairment. *Neurology*, 75(1), 27–34.

Dowlati, Y., *et al.* (2010). A meta-analysis of cytokines in major depression. *Biological Psychiatry*, 67(5), 446–457.

Driscoll, H. C., *et al.* (2005). Late-onset major depression: Clinical and treatment-response variability. *International Journal of Geriatric Psychiatry*, 20(7), 661–667.

Fischer, C. E. & Agüera-Ortiz, L. (2017). Psychosis and dementia: Risk factor, prodrome, or cause? *International Psychogeriatrics*, 1–11.

Flatt, J. D., *et al.* (2018). Post-traumatic stress disorder and risk of dementia among members of a health care delivery system. *Alzheimer's & Dementia: The Journal of the Alzheimer's Association*, 14(1), 28–34.

Förstl, H., *et al.* (1994). Organic factors and the clinical features of late paranoid psychosis: A comparison with Alzheimer's disease and normal ageing. *Acta Psychiatrica Scandinavica*, 89(5), 335–340.

Fucetola, R., *et al.* (2000). Age and neuropsychologic function in schizophrenia: A decline in executive abilities beyond that observed in healthy volunteers. *Biological Psychiatry*, 48(2), 137–146.

Gao, Y., *et al.* (2013). Depression as a risk factor for dementia and mild cognitive impairment: A meta-analysis of longitudinal studies. *International Journal of Geriatric Psychiatry*, 28(5), 441–449.

Godin, O., *et al.* (2008). White matter lesions as a predictor of depression in the elderly: The 3c-dijon study. *Biological Psychiatry*, 63.

Gold, A. B., *et al.* (2011). The relationship between indoleamine 2,3-dioxygenase activity and post-stroke cognitive impairment. *Journal of Neuroinflammation*, 8, 17.

Goldberg, T. E., *et al.* (1993). Course of schizophrenia: Neuropsychological evidence for a static encephalopathy. *Schizophr Bull*, 19(4), 797–804.

Gray, S. L., *et al.* (2015). Cumulative use of strong anticholinergic medications and incident dementia. *JAMA Internal Medicine*, 175(3), 401–407.

Greenberg, M. S., *et al.* (2014). Stress, ptsd, and dementia. *Alzheimer's & Dementia*, 10(3), S155–S165.

Gudmundsson, P., *et al.* (2015). White matter lesions and temporal lobe atrophy related to incidence of both dementia and major depression in 70-year-olds followed over 10 years. *European Journal of Neurology*, 22.

Guillemin, G. J., Wang, L. & Brew, B. J. (2005). Quinolinic acid selectively induces apoptosis of human astrocytes: Potential role in aids dementia complex. *Journal of Neuroinflammation*, 2, 16.

Gulpers, B., *et al.* (2016). Anxiety as a predictor for cognitive decline and dementia: A systematic review and meta-analysis. *The American Journal of Geriatric Psychiatry*, 24(10), 823–842.

Hanssen, M. S. S., *et al.* (2003). Self-reported psychotic experiences in the general population: A valid screening tool for dsm-iii-r psychotic disorders? *Acta Psychiatr Scand*, 107(5), 369–377.

Hanssen, M. S. S., *et al.* (2014). Comparative study of clinical and neuropsychological characteristics between early- late and very-late-onset schizophrenia-spectrum disorders. *American Journal of Geriatric Psychiatry*, 23(8), 852–862.

Hardeveld, F., *et al.* (2013). Recurrence of major depressive disorder across different treatment settings: Results from the nesda study. *Journal of Affective Disorders*, 147(1), 225–231.

Heaton, R., *et al.* (1994). Neuropsychological deficits in schizophrenics. Relationship to age, chronicity, and dementia. *Archives of General Psychiatry*, 51(6), 469–476.

Hendricksen, M., *et al.* (2004). Neuropathological study of the dorsal raphe nuclei in late-life depression and Alzheimer's disease with and without depression. *American Journal of Psychiatry*, 161.

Herrmann, L.L., Le Masurier, M. & Ebmeier, K. P. (2008). White matter hyperintensities in late life depression: A systematic review. *Journal of Neurology, Neurosurgery and Psychiatry*, 79(6), 619–624.

Hickie, I., *et al.* (1995). Subcortical hyperintensities on magnetic resonance imaging: Clinical correlates and prognostic significance in patients with severe depression. *Biological Psychiatry*, 37(3), 151–160.

Howard, R., *et al.* (2000). Late-onset schizophrenia and very-late-onset schizophrenia-like psychosis: An international consensus. *American Journal of Psychiatry*, 157, 172–178.

Howren, M. B., Lamkin, D. M. & Suls, J. (2009). Associations of depression with c-reactive protein, il-1, and il-6: A meta-analysis. *Psychosomatic Medicine*, 71(2), 171–186.

Jansen, W. J., *et al.* (2015). Prevalence of cerebral amyloid pathology in persons without dementia: A meta-analysis. *JAMA*, 313(19), 1924–1938.

Karl, A., *et al.* (2006). A meta-analysis of structural brain abnormalities in ptsd. *Neuroscience & Biobehavioral Reviews*, 30(7), 1004–1031.

Kivimäki, M., *et al.* (2012). Vascular risk status as a predictor of later-life depressive symptoms: A cohort study. *Biological Psychiatry*, 72(4), 324–330.

Köhler, S., *et al.* (2009). Evidence that better outcome of psychosis in women is reversed with increasing age of onset: A population-based 5-year follow-up study. *Schizophrenia Research*, 113(2–3), 226–232.

Köhler, S., *et al.* (2010a). The pattern and course of cognitive impairment in late-life depression. *Psychological Medicine*, 40(4), 591–602.

Köhler, S., *et al.* (2010b). White matter hyperintensities, cortisol levels, brain atrophy and continuing cognitive deficits in late-life depression. *The British Journal of Psychiatry*, 196(2), 143–149.

Köhler, S., *et al.* (2010c). Depressive symptoms and cognitive decline in community-dwelling older adults. *Journal of the American Geriatrics Society*, 58(5), 873–879.

Köhler, S., *et al.* (2013). Cognitive decline and dementia risk in older adults with psychotic symptoms: A prospective cohort study. *American Journal of Geriatric Psychiatry*, 21(2), 119–128.

Kok, R. M. & Reynolds, C. F. (2017). Management of depression in older adults: A review. *JAMA*, 317(20), 2114–2122.

Krishnan, K., Hays, J. & Blazer, D. (1997). Mri-defined vascular depression. *American Journal of Psychiatry*, 154(4), 497–501.

Kroenke, K., Spitzer Robert, L. & Williams Janet, B. W. (2001). The phq-9: Validity of a brief depression severity measure. *Journal of General Internal Medicine*, 16(9), 606–613.

Kuiper, J. S., *et al.* (2015). Social relationships and risk of dementia: A systematic review and meta-analysis of longitudinal cohort studies. *Ageing Research Reviews*, 22, 39–57.

Lee, J. S., *et al.* (2007). Persistent mild cognitive impairment in geriatric depression. *International Psychogeriatrics*, 19(1), 125–135.

Lemieux, George a., *et al.* (2015). Kynurenic acid is a nutritional cue that enables behavioral plasticity. *Cell*, 160(1), 119–131.

Leonard, B. E. (2007). Inflammation, depression and dementia: Are they connected? *Neurochemical Research*, 32(10), 1749–1756.

Levy, B. R., *et al.* (2018). Positive age beliefs protect against dementia even among elders with high-risk gene. *PLOS One*, 13(2), e0191004.

Licht-Strunk, E., *et al.* (2007). The prognosis of depression in older patients in general practice and the community. A systematic review. *Family Practice*, 24(2), 168–180.

Lohr, J. B., *et al.* (2015). Is post-traumatic stress disorder associated with premature senescence? A review of the literature. *The American Journal of Geriatric Psychiatry*, 23(7), 709–725.

Lupien, S. J., *et al.* (1998). Cortisol levels during human aging predict hippocampal atrophy and memory deficits. *Nature Neuroscience*, 1(1), 69–73.

Madsen, K., *et al.* (2012). Lack of association between prior depressive episodes and cerebral [11c]pib binding. *Neurobiology of Aging*, 33(10), 2334–2342.

Meziab, O., *et al.* (2014). Prisoner of war status, posttraumatic stress disorder, and dementia in older veterans. *Alzheimer's & Dementia*, 10(3), S236–S241.

Miller, A. H., Maletic, V. & Raison, C. L. (2009). Inflammation and its discontents: The role of cytokines in the pathophysiology of major depression. *Biological Psychiatry*, 65(9), 732–741.

Mirza, S. S., *et al.* (2016). 10-year trajectories of depressive symptoms and risk of dementia: A population-based study. *The Lancet Psychiatry*, 3(7), 628–635.

Moraros, J., *et al.* (2017). The association of antidepressant drug usage with cognitive impairment or dementia, including Alzheimer disease: A systematic review and meta-analysis. *Depression and Anxiety*, 34(3), 217–226.

Nebes, R. D., *et al.* (2000). Decreased working memory and processing speed mediate cognitive impairment in geriatric depression. *Psychological Medicine*, 30(3), 679–691.

Norton, S., *et al.* (2014). Potential for primary prevention of Alzheimer's disease: An analysis of population-based data. *The Lancet Neurology*, 13(8), 788–794.

O'brien, J. T. (1997). The "glucocorticoid cascade" hypothesis in man. *British Journal of Psychiatry*, 170, 199–201.

O'brien, J. T., *et al.* (1998). Severe deep white matter lesions and outcome in elderly patients with major depressive disorder: Follow up study. *BMJ*, 317(7164), 982–984.

Östling, S., Pálsson, S. P. & Skoog, I. (2007). The incidence of first-onset psychotic symptoms and paranoid ideation in a representative population sample followed from age 70–90 years. Relation to mortality and later development of dementia. *International Journal of Geriatric Psychiatry*, 22(6), 520–528.

Ownby, R. L., *et al.* (2006). Depression and risk for Alzheimer disease: Systematic review, meta-analysis, and metaregression analysis. *Archives of General Psychiatry*, 63(5), 530–538.

Pan, A., *et al.* (2010). Bidirectional association between depression and type 2 diabetes mellitus in women. *Archives of Internal Medicine*, 170(21), 1884–1891.

Pan, A., *et al.* (2011). Depression and risk of stroke morbidity and mortality. *JAMA*, 306(11), 1241–1249.

Petkus, A. J., *et al.* (2016). Anxiety is associated with increased risk of dementia in older swedish twins. *Alzheimer's & Dementia*, 12(4), 399–406.

Pomara, N., *et al.* (2012). Lower csf amyloid beta peptides and higher f2-isoprostanes in cognitively intact elderly individuals with major depressive disorder. *American Journal of Psychiatry*, 169(5), 523–530.

Radloff, L. S. (1977). The ces-d scale: A self-report depression scale for research in the general population. *Applied Psychological Measurement*, 1(3), 385–401.

Reynolds, C. F., Iii, *et al.* (2011). Maintenance treatment of depression in old age: A randomized, double-blind, placebo-controlled evaluation of the efficacy and safety of donepezil combined with antidepressant pharmacotherapy. *Archives of General Psychiatry*, 68(1), 51–60.

Rivkin, P., *et al.* (2000). White matter hyperintensity volume in late-onset and early-onset schizophrenia. *International Journal of Geriatric Psychiatry*, 15(12), 1085–1089.

Rund, B. R. (1998). A review of longitudinal studies of cognitive functions in schizophrenia patients. *Schizophrenia Bulletin*, 24(3), 425–435.

Sachdev, P., *et al.* (1997). Regional cerebral blood flow in late-onset schizophrenia: A spect study using 99mtc-hmpao. *Schizophrenia Research*, 27(2–3), 105–117.

Sachdev, P., *et al.* (1999). Schizophrenia with onset after age 50 years. 2: Neurological, neuropsychological and mri investigation. *British Journal of Psychiatry*, 175, 416–421.

Sapolsky, R. M. (2000). Glucocorticoids and hippocampal atrophy in neuropsychiatric disorders. *Archives of General Psychiatry*, 57(10), 925–935.
Sapolsky, R. M., Krey, L. C. & Mcewen, B. S. (1986). The neuroendocrinology of stress and aging: The glucocorticoid cascade hypothesis. *Endocrine Reviews*, 7(3), 284–301.
Sexton, C. E., Mackay, C. E. & Ebmeier, K. P. (2013). A systematic review and meta-analysis of magnetic resonance imaging studies in late-life depression. *American Journal of Geriatric Psychiatry*, 21(2), 184–195.
Sheehan, D. V., *et al.* (1998). The mini-international neuropsychiatric interview (m.I.N.I.): The development and validation of a structured diagnostic psychiatric interview for dsm-iv and icd-10. *Journal of Clinical Psychiatry*, 59(Suppl 20), 22–33.
Sheline, Y. I., *et al.* (1996). Hippocampal atrophy in recurrent major depression. *PNAS*, 93(9), 3908–3913.
Shin, L. M., Rauch, S. L. & Pitman, R. K. (2006). Amygdala, medial prefrontal cortex, and hippocampal function in ptsd. *Annals of the New York Academy of Sciences*, 1071(1), 67–79.
Singh-Manoux, A., *et al.* (2017). Trajectories of depressive symptoms before diagnosis of dementia: A 28-year follow-up study. *JAMA Psychiatry*, 74(7), 712–718.
Strawbridge, R., *et al.* (2015). Inflammation and clinical response to treatment in depression: A meta-analysis. *Eur Neuropsychopharmacol*, 25(10), 1532–1543.
Souery, D., Papakostas, G. I. & Trivedi, M. H. (2006). Treatment-resistant depression. *The Journal of Clinical Psychiatry*, 67, 16–22.
Sumner, J. A., *et al.* (2017). Cross-sectional and longitudinal associations of chronic post-traumatic stress disorder with inflammatory and endothelial function markers in women. *Biological Psychiatry*, 82(12), 875–884.
Surtees, P. G., *et al.* (2008). Depression and ischemic heart disease mortality: Evidence from the epic-norfolk united kingdom prospective cohort study. *American Journal of Psychiatry*, 165(4), 515–523.
Teodorczuk, A., *et al.* (2007). White matter changes and late-life depressive symptoms: Longitudinal study. *The British Journal of Psychiatry*, 191(3), 212–217.
Then, C. K., *et al.* (2017). Risk analysis of use of different classes of antidepressants on subsequent dementia: A nationwide cohort study in taiwan. *PLOS One*, 12(4), e0175187.
Thomas, A. J. & O'brien, J. T. (2008). Depression and cognition in older adults. *Current Opinion in Psychiatry*, 21(1), 8–13.
Thomas, A. J., *et al.* (2001). A neuropathological study of vascular factors in late-life depression. *Journal of Neurology, Neurosurgery & Psychiatry*, 70(1), 83–87.
Thomas, A. J., *et al.* (2002). Ischemic basis for deep white matter hyperintensities in major depression: A neuropathological study. *Archives of General Psychiatry*, 59(9), 785–792.
Thomas, A. J., *et al.* (2003). Neuropathological evidence for ischemia in the white matter of the dorsolateral prefrontal cortex in late-life depression. *International Journal of Geriatric Psychiatry*, 18(1), 7–13.
Tiemeier, H., *et al.* (2004). Relationship between atherosclerosis and late-life depression: The rotterdam study. *Archives of General Psychiatry*, 61(4), 369–376.
Tonkonogy, J. M. & Geller, J. L. (1999). Late-onset paranoid psychosis as a distinct clinicopathologic entity: Magnetic resonance imaging data in elderly patients with paranoid psychosis of late onset and schizophrenia of early onset. *Neuropsychiatry Neuropsychology, and Behavioral Neurology*, 12(4), 230–235.
Trivedi, M. H., *et al.* (2006). Evaluation of outcomes with citalopram for depression using measurement-based care in star* d: Implications for clinical practice. *American Journal of Psychiatry*, 163(1), 28–40.

Tsopelas, C., *et al.* (2011). Neuropathological correlates of late-life depression in older people. *British Journal of Psychiatry*, 198, 109–114.
Van Agtmaal, M. J. M., *et al.* (2017). Association of microvascular dysfunction with late-life depression: A systematic review and meta-analysis. *JAMA Psychiatry*, 74(7), 729–739.
Van Der Kooy, K., *et al.* (2007). Depression and the risk for cardiovascular diseases: Systematic review and meta analysis. *International Journal of Geriatric Psychiatry*, 22(7), 613–626.
Van Der Werf, M., *et al.* (2014). Systematic review and collaborative recalculation of 133,693 incident cases of schizophrenia. *Psychological Medicine*, 44(1), 9–16.
Vecsei, L., *et al.* (2013). Kynurenines in the cns: Recent advances and new questions. *Natural Reviews Drug Discovery*, 12(1), 64–82.
Villarreal, G., *et al.* (2002). Reduced hippocampal volume and total white matter volume in posttraumatic stress disorder. *Biological Psychiatry*, 52(2), 119–125.
Walterfang, M., *et al.* (2005). Neuroimaging in late-onset schizophrenia. *In:* Hasset, A., Ames, D. & Chiu, E. eds. *Psychosis in the Eldery*. London: Taylor & Francis, 37–58.
Wang, Q., *et al.* (2014). Activation of nad(p)h oxidase by tryptophan-derived 3-hydroxykynurenine accelerates endothelial apoptosis and dysfunction in vivo. *Circulation Research*, 114(3), 480–492.
Weiner, M.W., *et al.* (2013). Military risk factors for Alzheimer's disease. *Alzheimer's & Dementia*, 9(4), 445–451.
Wichers, M. C., *et al.* (2006). Baseline immune activation as a risk factor for the onset of depression during interferon-alpha treatment. *Biological Psychiatry*, 60(1), 77–79.
Wilson, R. S., *et al.* (2007). Chronic distress and incidence of mild cognitive impairment. *Neurology*, 68(24), 2085–2092.
Woon, F. L., Sood, S. & Hedges, D. W. (2010). Hippocampal volume deficits associated with exposure to psychological trauma and posttraumatic stress disorder in adults: A meta-analysis. *Progress in Neuro-Psychopharmacoly & Biological Psychiatry*, 34(7), 1181–1188.
World Health Organization. (2017). *Depression and Other Common Mental Disorders: Global Health Estimates*. Geneve: World Health Organization.
Wu, K.Y., *et al.* (2016). Beta-amyloid deposition and cognitive function in patients with major depressive disorder with different subtypes of mild cognitive impairment: (18)f-florbetapir (av-45/amyvid) pet study. *European Journal of Nuclear Medicine and Molecular Imaging*, 43.
Wu, W., *et al.* (2013). Expression of tryptophan 2,3-dioxygenase and production of kynurenine pathway metabolites in triple transgenic mice and human Alzheimer's disease brain. *PLOS One*, 8(4), e59749.
Wulsin, L. R. & Singal, B. M. (2003). Do depressive symptoms increase the risk for the onset of coronary disease? A systematic quantitative review. *Psychosomatic Medicine*, 65(2), 201–210.
Yaffe, K., *et al.* (1999). Depressive symptoms and cognitive decline in nondemented elderly women: A prospective study. *Archives of General Psychiatry*, 56(5), 425–430.
Yaffe, K., *et al.* (2010). Posttraumatic stress disorder and risk of dementia among us veterans. *Archives of General Psychiatry*, 67(6), 608–613.
Yaffe, K., *et al.* (2014). Lifestyle and health-related risk factors and risk of cognitive aging among older veterans. *Alzheimer's & Dementia*, 10(3), S111–S121.

Chapter 6

Cognitive activity within a dementia prevention hierarchy

The potential roles of cognitive reserve in detecting, modifying and managing disease expression

Lisa McGarrigle and Lorraine Boran

Introduction

The concept of protection against the clinical manifestation of acquired and progressive disease processes in the brain is known as "cognitive reserve" (CR). CR is commonly defined as the hypothesised capacity of the brain to cope with brain damage in order to minimise the clinical symptoms of that damage (Stern 2009), and there is a growing body of literature that points to an important role played by CR in moderating the expression of progressive and often multiple disease processes in dementia (Chapko et al. 2017). The protective effects of an individual's degree of engagement in cognitive activities throughout the lifespan can be characterised as CR, and measures of cognitive enrichment, such as education level, level of occupational complexity and participation in cognitively stimulating leisure activities, are frequently used as proxy measures of CR (Valenzuela and Sachdev 2006). We argue that CR can be considered from the point of view of a three-tiered dementia prevention hierarchy – primary prevention, secondary prevention and tertiary prevention (Thal 2006; Mowszowski et al. 2010). Within this hierarchy, CR may prevent the initial occurrence of dementia in healthy older adults (primary prevention), delay disease expression in "at-risk" or prodromal populations (secondary prevention) and may also moderate (or "manage") disease progression in individuals with diagnosed dementia (tertiary prevention). This chapter examines the usefulness of the CR concept with regard to dementia prevention at all levels of this hierarchy by firstly outlining the evidence for the preventive effects of cognitive activity across the lifespan. Theoretical approaches to CR are then reviewed and the mechanisms by which protection operates are addressed within a CR framework. Questions regarding the interactions between cognitive protective factors and higher-order cognitive functions are addressed, with particular focus on the role of cognitive control in CR capacity and its potential role in prevention. Finally, this chapter reviews the evidence for the modifiability of control processes implicated in CR and the significance of this in relation to prevention of dementia. Future directions for both population and personalised approaches to dementia prevention are also suggested.

Cognitive reserve: characterising the preventive effects of cognitive activity

The concept of cognitive reserve was proposed following the observation that the severity of neuropathological symptoms did not always correlate with brain damage severity (Solé-Padullés et al. 2009). For instance, post-mortem examinations have found high rates of Alzheimer's disease neurodegeneration in individuals who did not display neurocognitive clinical symptoms of the disease (Katzman et al. 1988). The theory of CR posits that this may be due to the buffering effect of protective factors, such as lifestyle and cognitive activity. This was demonstrated by a pivotal longitudinal study investigating the onset of Alzheimer's disease, the Nun Study, which found that linguistic ability in nuns at a mean age of 22 years was a significant predictor of the development of Alzheimer's disease in older age (Riley et al. 2005). This suggests that certain cognitive activities across the lifespan may have a preventive effect on the development of dementia. Further epidemiological research supports this finding and suggests that CR not only protects against dementia (primary prevention) but also helps to maximise performance in prodromal populations and in those with established dementia (secondary and tertiary prevention) (see Stern 2009; Stern 2012 for literature overview). Research has consistently demonstrated a significant protective effect of cognitive leisure activities and findings suggest that early as well as late-life activity have the potential to significantly moderate the risk of Alzheimer's Disease (AD) by increasing CR (Karp et al. 2006; Scarmeas et al. 2001; Verghese et al. 2003; Wilson et al. 2002). Related to dementia is the concept of cognitive decline in healthy ageing, or normative cognitive decline. Objective cognitive decline can be viewed as reduced information processing capacity and efficiency as a result of healthy ageing (Ramscar et al. 2014). Subjective cognitive decline, on the other hand, can be viewed as memory concerns, or other cognitive concerns, experienced by an individual despite having intact cognitive performance (Jessen 2014). Distinguishing between decline as a result of pathology and decline as a result of healthy ageing is not always straightforward as brain changes due to dementia are often found in healthy older adults, and many of the risk factors implicated in dementia have also been found to increase the risk of cognitive decline in healthy ageing (Deary et al. 2009). There is also mounting evidence for a shared set of protective factors that can moderate both dementia and cognitive decline (Hanna-Pladdy and MacKay 2011; Mitchell, Cimino, et al. 2012). As follows, CR can be broadly viewed as a protective mechanism against the development of dementia and cognitive decline, as well as a moderator of disease expression in the face of pathology.

Cognitive protective factors in dementia: a framework for primary, secondary and tertiary prevention

Epidemiological and longitudinal research, as well as systematic reviews, provide strong evidence for the role of cognitive activity in primary prevention, as a number of studies have demonstrated that participation in cognitively stimulating activities across the lifespan is associated with reduced incident dementia in later life (Bosma et al. 2002; Crowe et al. 2003; Scarmeas et al. 2001; Wilson et al. 2013). Activities that require cognitive effort, such as reading, doing crosswords or puzzles or learning a new language, have been linked with protection against developing dementia in later life (Crowe et al. 2003; Helzner et al. 2007; Hughes 2010; Sattler et al. 2012; Valenzuela et al. 2011; Wilson et al. 2002). Large-scale epidemiological studies have also indicated that high levels of education and occupational complexity, as well as cognitively stimulating leisure activities, are protective against dementia (Valenzuela and Sachdev 2006). Education level, in particular, is a widely acknowledged protective factor for dementia and cognitive decline. While evidence for the protective effects of education has been mixed (Alley et al. 2007; van Dijk et al. 2008), a recent systematic review on the life-course determinants of CR, concluded that the evidence for the protective effects of education on cognition in the face of a number of brain burden measures was consistent (Chapko et al. 2017).

Participation in stimulating leisure activities also impacts on primary prevention. A longitudinal cohort study by Wilson et al. (2002), with a mean follow-up of 4.5 years, was conducted on 801 cognitively healthy older catholic nuns, priests and brothers in the United States. Frequency of participation in common cognitive leisure activities (such as reading a newspaper) were rated at baseline. A proportional hazards model controlling for age, sex and education found that a one-point increase in cognitive activity score was associated with a 33% reduction in risk of AD. A systematic review investigating the role of cognitive leisure activities examined 13 observational studies, the majority of which were cohort design. Meta-analysis was deemed inappropriate due to a number of factors, including the heterogeneity of interventions, the study design, participant groupings and the different stages of life at which they were measured. It was found that five out of six studies demonstrated a positive association between participation in cognitive activities and a reduced risk of developing AD and other dementias when interventions occurred in midlife. Moreover, six out of seven studies indicated a positive association for late-life participation. There was some evidence to suggest that certain activities may be more beneficial than others (such as reading). However, this must be interpreted cautiously due to the subjective nature of activity inclusion across studies and the absence of RCTs in the review (Stern and Munn 2010). A more recent systematic review investigated the effects of late-life cognitive activity on delaying or preventing dementia (Sajeev et al. 2016). The review focused on cohort or case-control studies that had been explicit in their definition of cognitive activity and their criteria for evaluating dementia. It was concluded that late-life cognitive activity offers some protection against dementia. However, more data are required to clarify the type of activities and levels of engagement that appear to be most effective.

More recently, the Lancet Commission on Dementia prevention, intervention and care (Livingston et al. 2017) have highlighted hearing loss as a potentially modifiable risk factor, suggesting that the management of hearing loss in midlife, amongst other lifestyle risk factors, could result in the prevention or delay of dementia. Based on a meta-analysis of three studies, the commission found that hearing loss has a high relative risk and due to its high prevalence in the population should be considered for inclusion in models of dementia risk. According to WHO 2012 data accessed online, of 42 population-based studies, 5.3% has disabled hearing loss, with one-third of people over 65 being affected. As the association between hearing loss and dementia is relatively new, little research has been done on the mechanisms underlying this risk. One study investigating the relationship between word recall and hearing loss suggested that individuals with impaired hearing are investing more processing resources in verbal memory encoding compared to non-hearing-impaired individuals, which can have negative effects on subsequent memory performance (McCoy et al. 2005). Similarly, it has been suggested that hearing loss depletes cognitive reserve in that greater cognitive resources are expended on auditory processing at the expense of other cognitive processes such as working memory (Lin et al. 2011). It is possible that preservation of hearing through the use of hearing aids or other devices may mitigate this risk, however, further research in this area is necessary.

Whereas primary prevention measures have the potential to prevent the initial occurrence of dementia, secondary prevention aims to reduce disease prevalence through the early identification of markers of dementia in people who are not yet symptomatic (Fratiglioni et al. 2007). This aims to delay the disease expression by modifying the pathological process. On the other hand, tertiary prevention seeks to slow or manage dementia progression in individuals with a dementia diagnosis. There is evidence in the form of systematic reviews, RCT's and case-controlled intervention studies suggesting that cognitive training interventions can improve cognition, therefore modifying disease expression, in populations experiencing mild cognitive impairment (MCI) and dementia. With regard to secondary prevention, a review of cognitive training interventions in MCI found that cognitive training can have beneficial effects on a broad range of cognitive functions, including memory performance, executive functioning, processing speed, attention and fluid intelligence (Reijnders et al. 2013). A systematic review on cognitive training in MCI populations found that cognitive exercises can result in moderate-to-large positive effects on measures of memory. However, high-quality RCT's are lacking and further trails are recommended (Gates et al. 2011). A more recent systematic review and meta-analysis investigated the impact of computerised cognitive training in MCI and found a moderate effect on global cognition, attention and working memory, as well as psychosocial functioning (Hill et al. 2016). A pilot RCT was conducted with 47 individuals with MCI where participants performed computer-based cognitive training exercises. A pattern was observed whereby the intervention group outperformed the control group on measures of verbal learning and memory. However, the authors acknowledge that further large-scale research is necessary (Barnes et al. 2009).

With regard to tertiary prevention, a review investigating the impact of non-pharmacological interventions to improve cognitive and functional symptoms of dementia found that RCT evidence supported modest benefits from cognitive training, cognitive rehabilitation and cognitive stimulation therapy (CST) in dementia, with the strongest evidence relating to CST (Ballard et al. 2011). CST is a multifaceted psychosocial intervention aimed at targeting cognition in the form of stimulating reasoning (increasing novel associative, implicit and integrative thinking), memory (through use of reminiscence, and recall triggers) and language and other relationship building exercises (Yates et al. 2017). An RCT investigating the impact of CST in individuals with dementia found that CST improved language function, which may result in generalised benefits for the person with dementia (Spector et al. 2010). Furthermore, a study investigating the efficacy of CST in dementia found that CST improves cognitive abilities as well as quality of life, even in individuals already taking medication (Aguirre et al. 2013).

Overall, there is a broad evidence base for primary, secondary and tertiary preventive measures to address dementia. With regard to primary prevention, some of the evidence is mixed, particularly in relation to the protective effects of education. However, in general, there is strong evidence in the form of epidemiological and longitudinal research, as well as systematic reviews and meta-analyses, for a number of cognitive protective factors in dementia. Primary protective factors related to cognitive activity can be considered modifiable and therefore subject to targeted interventions aimed at increasing protection by preventing or delayed symptom expression. With regards to secondary and tertiary prevention, there is moderate evidence from systematic reviews and intervention studies for the modifying effects of cognitive training interventions on disease expression in MCI and the rehabilitative effects of CST interventions in populations already affected by dementia (Richie et al., 2016). What is unclear from the literature on cognitive protective factors is the nature of the underlying cognitive mechanisms that facilitate protection from dementia. However, this can be addressed within a CR framework.

Theoretical approaches to cognitive reserve: implications for a prevention hierarchy

Theoretical approaches to CR differ in terms of whether they view CR as a passive process, or view the brain as actively attempting to compensate for pathology (Stern 2002). Passive models define reserve in terms of the amount of brain damage that can be sustained before reaching a clinical expression threshold. The brain reserve capacity (BRC) construct depends on a passive threshold model of reserve (Katzman 1993). It asserts that reserve derives from brain size or number of synapses. Under this model, it is hypothesised that larger brains can sustain more neuropathology before clinical deficit can be observed. Thus, more BRC can be considered a protective factor, while less BRC would leave an individual more vulnerable to the effects of pathology (Stern 2002). This view is problematic with regard to normal age-associated decline as the cognitive effects of ageing are continuous across the lifespan, rather than abrupt (Salthouse et al. 2004). Threshold models, such as the BRC model, also fail to account for individual differences in how brains are affected by neurodegeneration process of cognitive or functional tasks (Stern 2009).

In contrast, active models of CR propose that the brain actively attempts to cope with brain damage and age-related decline by using pre-existing cognitive processes or by recruiting compensatory processes (Stern 2002). An active model differs from a passive model as it does not assume that there is a fixed threshold at which functional impairment will be observed. Stern (2009) proposes two subtypes of active CR, neural reserve and neural compensation, which may have implications for understanding how interventions based on boosting CR can reduce dementia risk in both healthy people and people with dementia. Neural *reserve* refers to cognitive processing differences between healthy brains. Neural *compensation* refers to variability in the ability to compensate for brain pathology's disruption of standard processing networks by recruiting alternative brain structures or networks not normally used by individuals with healthy brains. There is a general consensus that active and passive models are not mutually exclusive and both may play a role in how the brain protects itself when faced with neurodegeneration (Stern et al. 2005).

The mechanisms underlying the association between cognitive activity and effects on cognition are not clearly understood (Marioni et al. 2012; Wilson et al. 2013). Two proposed mechanisms to explain how cognitive activity protects brain function from neuropathology include disease modification and compensation. Disease modification suggests a decreased risk for developing neuropathology (primary prevention), or a slower rate of the expression of pathology (secondary prevention), while compensation indicates a better ability to cope with underlying brain damage (secondary and tertiary prevention) (Marioni et al. 2012).

A tale of two reserve systems: cognitive enrichment and cognitive control and the implications of both in dementia prevention

Traditionally, the candidate indicators of CR are cognitive enrichment measures, such as education level (Scarmeas et al. 2003; Stern et al. 1994; Tucker-Drob et al. 2009) and crystallised abilities that are acquired over the lifespan. In this sense, CR is viewed as a "cumulative" process, whereby protection is built up over the lifespan. However, Barulli and Stern (2013) note that one of the outstanding questions in CR research is the extent to which CR is based on acquired knowledge (e.g., crystallised abilities) versus cognitive processes (e.g. fluid abilities). Addressing the mechanisms of cognitive change across the lifespan, Craik and Bialystok (2006) propose a framework whereby crystallised and fluid abilities are viewed as two interactive systems. Representations of the world (crystallised schema that evolve through cognitive enrichment) are selected based on needs and desires, and in turn, these representations demonstrate control (fluid ability) through their influence on further selection of schema-relevant information across the lifespan. Under this framework, traditional CR proxy measures of cognitive enrichment may reflect a representational system, while fluid abilities may reflect a cognitive control system. Stern's theory of neural reserve posits that more efficient cognitive networks can protect against the impact of brain changes as a result of ageing or pathology. This highlights the potential role of higher-order cognitive control processes in CR, as neural reserve operates by allowing greater flexibility in network selection, an ability believed to be captured by executive function (EF) tasks (Tucker and Stern 2011). From this perspective, both cognitive enrichment and cognitive control can be viewed as two arms of CR, with cognitive enrichment measures representing "cumulative" CR and cognitive control measures representing "current" CR, which has the potential to be modified at any time point across the lifespan. This has implications for interventions targeting CR. As cumulative CR proxies reflect lifetime experience, they are not suitable targets for a short-term intervention. However, if modifiable cognitive abilities are implicated in current CR, targeted cognitive training could potentially provide a means of boosting CR in a timely and accessible manner.

There is evidence to suggest that traditional CR proxies are highly related to cognitive control measures, such as executive function (EF), which refers to the ability to inhibit impulsive responses, update and monitor incoming information and exhibit mental flexibility (Miyake et al. 2000). Mitchell, Shaughnessy, Shirk, Yang and Atri (2012) examined the factor structure of typical proxy CR indicators (years of education and premorbid IQ) in relation to other cognitive functions in order to validate a model of cognitive domains and cognitive reserve (CDCR model). A priori, CR was considered distinct from other cognitive domains in the model. The four-factor model comprised measures of memory/language, processing speed/EF, attention and CR (years of education and the American version of the National Adult Reading Test). The model was tested using confirmatory factor analysis in a group of cognitively healthy older adults and a group of older individuals with memory impairment along the spectrum of amnestic mild cognitive impairment to Alzheimer's disease (aMCI-AD). Results supported the construct validity of a CR factor as distinct from indicators of processing speed/EF. However, there was a moderate positive correlation between the two factors in both healthy adults and those with aMCI-AD. Similar results were found in a study by Siedlecki et al. (2009) in which the construct validity of CR (education level, vocabulary, literacy) was evaluated using four structural equation models that represented progressively more stringent tests of construct validity. The latent variable models comprised constructs of memory, processing speed and EF, as well as CR. In general, findings supported CR as a construct distinct from measures of memory and processing speed based on convergent validity and moderate discriminant validity. However, the results from the most demanding model suggested a strong relationship between the CR and EF constructs, which calls into question the discriminant validity of the traditional CR construct in relation to EF. Although Siedlecki and colleagues conclude that, based on their overall findings, it is reasonable to describe CR as a distinct construct, they advise that the relationship between CR and EF must also be acknowledged, and go on to suggest that the CR construct should be revised to include EF indicators, as CR may be highly related to fluid executive abilities.

Further empirical research is necessary to clarify the nature of the relationship between EF and traditional CR proxy measures. However, the apparent overlap between these constructs may have implications for dementia prevention by broadening the range of the potentially modifiable factors involved in CR. The relationship between traditional proxy CR measures and measures of cognitive function, such as EF, offers a promising approach to modifying certain protective factors in dementia and cognitive decline. For instance, research has suggested that cognitive control processes such as EF may be modifiable through cognitive training interventions. Furthermore, healthy ageing can lead to deficits in EF, which is strongly correlated with other cognitive abilities, such as fluid intelligence, mental capacity and memory (Verhaeghen and Salthouse 1997). Craik and Bialystok (2006) point out that cognitive control peaks in the early 20s and then declines with age, while crystallised abilities remain relatively stable across the lifespan. The authors view cognitive change across the lifespan in terms of an interaction between these systems. This lends support to the idea that an intervention based on EF training may in turn impact on CR in terms of a positive change in current CR status, thus strengthening the brain's capacity to sustain cognitive abilities in the face of healthy ageing and/or neuropathology.

Training interventions targeting cognitive control at all levels of the prevention hierarchy

The concept of neuroplasticity, the brain's ability to change neural structure and function in response to experiences or environmental stimulation, is fundamental to cognitive training interventions (Rabipour and Raz 2012), and can be applied to primary, secondary and tertiary prevention measures. There has been evidence to suggest that the adult brain is neuroplastic, with the greatest brain changes occurring through repeated practice of a skill over a prolonged period of time (Cannonieri et al. 2007; Maguire et al. 2006). Recent systematic reviews of RCTs and clinical studies investigating cognitive interventions in healthy elderly (primary prevention) and MCI (secondary prevention) have generally reported positive effects of training on cognitive control abilities, suggestive of nascent CR modification. Kelly et al. (2014) conducted a meta-analysis on 31 RCTs involving cognitively healthy older adults and found that cognitive training improved performance on measures of EF compared to active controls, and improved performance on measures of memory compared to no-contact controls. The authors found that effects of training were maintained for longer when the difficulty level of the training adapted to the individual's performance, and participants engaged in at least ten training sessions. Similarly, a systematic review of RCTs and clinical studies involving both healthy elderly and individuals with MCI found that cognitive training can be effective in improving memory performance, EF, processing speed, attention and fluid intelligence (Reijnders et al. 2013). A more recent systematic review and meta-analysis focused on RCTs conducted in participants with MCI (secondary prevention) or dementia (tertiary prevention) (Hill et al. 2016). The authors found that computerised cognitive training improved performance on measures of global cognition, memory, working memory and attention in individuals with MCI. However, the authors found little evidence for the efficacy of training in individuals with dementia, calling into question the impact of cognitive control training with regard to tertiary prevention.

A selective review of the brain training literature focusing on healthy elderly concluded that plasticity is key to the long-term retention and transferability of training gains (Buitenweg et al. 2012). The authors suggest that maximal benefit can be achieved if not just one, but multiple cognitive functions are engaged during training tasks. Targeting higher-order cognitive abilities such as EF may potentially meet these criteria. There has been evidence to suggest that age effects diminish after extensive training on a cognitive switching task (Kramer et al. 1999). It has also been suggested that training in task switching[1] might potentially have transfer gains as a study found that elderly people who grew up as bilinguals, thus constantly needing to switch between the two languages during their lifetime, were found to have greater inhibitory control compared to monolingual elderly (Bialystok et al. 2006). A systematic review investigating the efficacy of brain training interventions in individuals with MCI focused on 10 studies (five RCTs) and found moderate-sized effects on memory performance and global cognition measures following cognitive training (Gates et al. 2011). The effect sizes and generalisability of benefits were stronger for computer-based cognitive exercise interventions compared to memory strategy training. Cognitive exercise involving multiple cognitive domains also demonstrated greater efficacy than unimodal memory strategy training.

Overall the evidence for the benefits of cognitive control training in primary and secondary prevention, in particular, is compelling, although further longitudinal research is necessary to investigate hypotheses relating to the delaying of dementia onset. Boosting current CR through cognitive control training may also help to modify disease expression in at-risk populations.

Future directions

The existing body of evidence suggests there is great potential for both population and personalised approaches in the future of dementia prevention. The Lancet Commission on Dementia Prevention, Intervention, and Care (Livingston et al. 2017) have calculated that over a third of dementia cases are theoretically preventable through population approaches targeting a variety of lifestyle factors. These include increasing childhood education and managing hearing loss, both of which have the potential to increase cognitive reserve. The Commission also advocate for personalised approaches to modify dementia risk, such as cognitive training. Research into the potential protective effects of computerised cognitive training has demonstrated some promising results. However, findings are often mixed and limited to the specific ability being trained. Additionally, participants often report that cognitive training tasks are not very engaging, which may be a contributing factor to some of the null findings in the field as engagement typically promotes motivation to train with potentially deeper training transfer effects (Mishra et al. 2016). A new and gamified innovative approach to cognitive training seeks to combine the strengths of training tasks designed to enhance cognition (e.g., adaptive mechanisms, training that targets a neural deficit) and promote engagement and entertainment (e.g., fun, engaging and motivating, high-quality graphics) (Anguera and Gazzaley 2015). The authors, in collaboration with Lucas Arts, developed a game targeting cognitive control abilities in older adults and found that following 12 hours of gameplay over a 4-week period, participants demonstrated improved performance on untrained tasks. Although further research is needed to validate the findings, the authors suggest that the novel hybrid design of the game contributed to the positive results and may provide a basis for a new generation of cognitive training tools, co-designed by video game industry professionals and cognitive neuroscientists.

Conclusion

In conclusion, there are a number of factors to consider when assessing the protective effects of cognitive activity in dementia and cognitive decline. Findings from observational and epidemiological studies, systematic reviews and meta-analyses, provide strong evidence for the protective effects of cognitive activity, the mechanisms of which can be explained within a CR framework. Clarification of the multidimensional factors involved in CR, and a greater understanding of how these factors interact with each other in both dementia and healthy ageing, could inform the development of simple and clear public messages about what kinds of activities are likely to make a difference to cognitive health in an ageing population. While evidence for the efficacy of cognitive training interventions is mixed, a number of RCTs have demonstrated positive findings. Personalised and engaging training programs that can be easily integrated with an individual's lifestyle have the potential to provide cognitive benefits for both healthy older adults and those with cognitive deficits (Mishra et al. 2016). Greater emphasis on population approaches, such as increased childhood education, together with further research on the benefits of cognitive training, could help in the development of primary and secondary prevention programmes aimed at boosting current CR in healthy and prodromal populations, as well as tertiary prevention by improving cognition in those affected by pathology.

Note

1 Task switching is an executive function that involves shifting back and forth between multiple tasks and mental sets (Miyake et al. 2000).

References

Aguirre, E., Hoare, Z., Streater, A., Spector, A., Woods, B., Hoe, J. & Orrell, M. (2013). Cognitive Stimulation Therapy (CST) for people with dementia – who benefits most? *International Journal of Geriatric Psychiatry*, 28(3), 284–290.

Alley, D., Suthers, K. & Crimmins, E. (2007). Education and cognitive decline in older Americans: Results from the AHEAD sample. *Research on Aging*, 29(1), 73–94.

Anguera, J. A. & Gazzaley, A. (2015). Video games, cognitive exercises, and the enhancement of cognitive abilities. *Current Opinion in Behavioral Sciences*, 4, 160–165.

Ballard, C., Khan, Z., Clack, H. & Corbett, A. (2011). Nonpharmacological treatment of Alzheimer disease. *The Canadian Journal of Psychiatry*, 56(10), 589–595.

Barnes, D. E., Yaffe, K., Belfor, N., Jagust, W. J., DeCarli, C., Reed, B. R. & Kramer, J. H. (2009). Computer-based cognitive training for mild cognitive impairment: Results from a pilot randomized, controlled trial. *Alzheimer Disease and Associated Disorders*, 23(3), 205–210.

Barulli, D. & Stern, Y. (2013). Efficiency, capacity, compensation, maintenance, plasticity: Emerging concepts in cognitive reserve. *Trends in Cognitive Sciences*, 17(10), 502–509.

Bialystok, E., Craik, F. I. M. & Ryan, J. (2006). Executive control in a modified antisaccade task: Effects of aging and bilingualism. *Journal of Experimental Psychology: Learning, Memory, and Cognition*, 32(6), 1341–1354.

Bosma, H., Van Boxtel, M. P. J., Ponds, R. W. H. M., Jelicic, M., Houx, P., Metsemakers, J. & Jolles, J. (2002). Engaged lifestyle and cognitive function in middle and old-aged, non-demented persons: A reciprocal association? *Zeitschrift Für Gerontologie Und Geriatrie*, 35(6), 575–581.

Buitenweg, J. I. V., Murre, J. M. J. & Ridderinkhof, K. R. (2012). Brain training in progress: A review of trainability in healthy seniors. *Frontiers in Human Neuroscience*, 6(183), 1–11.

Cannonieri, G. C., Bonilha, L., Fernandes, P. T., Cendes, F. & Li, L. M. (2007). Practice and perfect: Length of training and structural brain changes in experienced typists. *Neuroreport*, 18(10), 1063–1066.

Chapko, D., McCormack, R., Black, C., Staff, R. & Murray, A. (2017). Life-course determinants of Cognitive Reserve (CR) in cognitive aging and dementia – a systematic literature review. *Aging & Mental Health*, 1–12.

Craik, F. I. M. & Bialystok, E. (2006). Cognition through the lifespan: Mechanisms of change. *Trends in Cognitive Sciences*, 10(3), 131–138.

Crowe, M., Andel, R., Pedersen, N. L., Johansson, B. & Gatz, M. (2003). Does participation in leisure activities lead to reduced risk of Alzheimer's disease? A prospective study of Swedish twins. *The Journals of Gerontology. Series B, Psychological Sciences and Social Sciences*, 58(5), 249–255.

Deary, I. J., Corley, J., Gow, A. J., Harris, S. E., Houlihan, L. M., Marioni, R. E., Penke, L., Rafnsson, S. B. & Starr, J. M. (2009). Age-associated cognitive decline. *British Medical Bulletin*, 92(1), 135–152.

Fratiglioni, L., Winblad, B. & von Strauss, E. (2007). Prevention of Alzheimer's disease and dementia: Major findings from the Kungsholmen Project. *Physiology & Behavior*, 92(1), 98–104.

Gates, N. J., Sachdev, P. S., Fiatarone Singh, M. A. & Valenzuela, M. (2011). Cognitive and memory training in adults at risk of dementia: A systematic review. *BMC Geriatrics*, 11(55), 1–14.

Hanna-Pladdy, B. & MacKay, A. (2011). The relation between instrumental musical activity and cognitive aging. *Neuropsychology*, 25(3), 378–386.

Helzner, E. P., Scarmeas, N., Cosentino, S., Portet, F. & Stern, Y. (2007). Leisure activity and cognitive decline in incident Alzheimer disease. *Archives of Neurology*, 64(12), 1749–1754.

Hill, N. T. M., Mowszowski, L., Naismith, S. L., Chadwick, V. L., Valenzuela, M. & Lampit, A. (2016). Computerized cognitive training in older adults with mild cognitive impairment or Dementia: A systematic review and meta-analysis. *American Journal of Psychiatry*, 174(4), 329–340.

Hughes, T. F. (2010). Promotion of cognitive health through cognitive activity in the aging population. *Aging Health*, 6(1), 111–121.

Jessen, F. (2014). Subjective and objective cognitive decline at the pre-dementia stage of Alzheimer's disease. *European Archives of Psychiatry and Clinical Neuroscience*, 264(1), 3–7.

Karp, A., Paillard-Borg, S., Wang, H-X., Silverstein, M., Winblad, B. & Fratiglioni, L. (2006). Mental, physical and social components in leisure activities equally contribute to decrease dementia risk. *Dementia and Geriatric Cognitive Disorders*, 21(2), 65–73.

Katzman, R. (1993). Education and the prevalence of dementia and Alzheimer's disease. *Neurology*, 43(1), 13–20.

Katzman, R., Terry, R., DeTeresa, R., Brown, T., Davies, P., Fuld, P., Renbing, X. & Peck, A. (1988). Clinical, pathological, and neurochemical changes in dementia: A subgroup with preserved mental status and numerous neocortical plaques. *Annals of Neurology*, 23(2), 138–144.

Kelly, M. E., Loughrey, D., Lawlor, B. A., Robertson, I. H., Walsh, C. & Brennan, S. (2014). The impact of cognitive training and mental stimulation on cognitive and everyday functioning of healthy older adults: A systematic review and meta-analysis. *Ageing Research Reviews*, 15, 28–43.

Kramer, A. F., Hahn, S. & Gopher, D. (1999). Task coordination and aging: Explorations of executive control processes in the task switching paradigm. *Acta Psychologica*, 101(2–3), 339–378.

Lin, F. R., Metter, E. J., O'Brien, R. J., Resnick, S. M., Zonderman, A. B. & Ferrucci, L. (2011). Hearing loss and incident dementia. *Archives of Neurology*, 68(2), 214–220.

Livingston, G., Sommerlad, A., Orgeta, V., Costafreda, S. G., Huntley, J., Ames, D., Ballard, C., Banerjee, S., Burns, A., Cohen-Mansfield, J., Cooper, C., Fox, N., Gitlin, L. N., Howard, R., Kales, H. C., Larson, E. B., Ritchie, K., Rockwood, K., Sampson, E. L., Samus, Q.,

Schneider, L. S., Selbæk, G., Teri, L. & Mukadam, N. (2017). Dementia prevention, intervention, and care. *The Lancet*, 390(10113), 2673–2734.

Maguire, E. A., Woollett, K. & Spiers, H. J. (2006). London taxi drivers and bus drivers: A structural MRI and neuropsychological analysis. *Hippocampus*, 16(12), 1091–1101.

Marioni, R. E., van den Hout, A., Valenzuela, M. J., Brayne, C., Matthews, F. E. & MRC Cognitive Function and Ageing Study. (2012). Active cognitive lifestyle associates with cognitive recovery and a reduced risk of cognitive decline. *Journal of Alzheimer's Disease*, 28(1), 223–230.

McCoy, S. L., Tun, P., Cox, L. C., Colangelo, M., Stewart, R. A. & Wingfield, A. (2005). Hearing loss and perceptual effort: Downstream effects on older adults' memory for speech. *Quarterly Journal of Experimental Psychology: Section A*, 58(1), 22–33.

Mishra, J., Anguera, J. A. & Gazzaley, A. (2016). Video games for neuro-cognitive optimization. *Neuron*, 90(2), 214–218.

Mitchell, M. B., Cimino, C. R., Benitez, A., Brown, C. L., Gibbons, L. E., Kennison, R. F., Shirk, S. D., Atri, A., Robitaille, A., MacDonald, S. W. S., Lindwall, M., Zelinski, E. M., Willis, S. L., Schaie, K. W., Johansson, B., Dixon, R. A., Mungas, D. M., Hofer, S. M. & Piccinin, A. M. (2012). Cognitively stimulating activities: Effects on cognition across four studies with up to 21 years of longitudinal data. *Journal of Aging Research*, 2012(e461592), 1–12.

Mitchell, M. B., Shaughnessy, L. W., Shirk, S. D., Yang, F. M. & Atri, A. (2012). Neuropsychological test performance and cognitive reserve in healthy aging and the Alzheimer's disease spectrum: A theoretically-driven factor analysis. *Journal of the International Neuropsychological Society : JINS*, 18(6), 1071–1080.

Miyake, A., Friedman, N. P., Emerson, M. J., Witzki, A. H., Howerter, A. & Wager, T. D. (2000). The unity and diversity of executive functions and their contributions to complex 'frontal lobe' tasks: A latent variable analysis. *Cognitive Psychology*, 41(1), 49–100.

Mowszowski, L., Batchelor, J. & Naismith, S. L. (2010). Early intervention for cognitive decline: Can cognitive training be used as a selective prevention technique? *International Psychogeriatrics*, 22(4), 537–548.

Rabipour, S. & Raz, A. (2012). Training the brain: Fact and fad in cognitive and behavioral remediation. *Brain and Cognition*, 79(2), 159–179.

Ramscar, M., Hendrix, P., Shaoul, C., Milin, P. & Baayen, H. (2014). The myth of cognitive decline: Non-linear dynamics of lifelong learning. *Topics in Cognitive Science*, 6(1), 5–42.

Reijnders, J., van Heugten, C. & van Boxtel, M. P. J. (2013). Cognitive interventions in healthy older adults and people with mild cognitive impairment: A systematic review. *Ageing Research Reviews*, 12(1), 263–275.

Riley, K. P., Snowdon, D. A., Desrosiers, M. F. & Markesbery, W. R. (2005). Early life linguistic ability, late life cognitive function, and neuropathology: Findings from the Nun Study. *Neurobiology of Aging*, 26(3), 341–347.

Ritchie, C. W., Molinuevo, J. L., Truyen, L., Satlin, A., Van der Geyten, S. & Lovestone, S. (2016). Development of interventions for the secondary prevention of Alzheimer's Dementia: The European prevention of Alzheimer's Dementia (EPAD) project. *The Lancet Psychiatry*, 3(2), 179–186.

Sajeev, G., Weuve, J., Jackson, J. W., VanderWeele, T. J., Bennett, D. A., Grodstein, F. & Blacker, D. (2016). Late-life cognitive activity and Dementia: A systematic review and bias analysis. *Epidemiology*, 27(5), 732–742.

Salthouse, T. A., Berish, D. E. & Siedlecki, K. L. (2004). Construct validity and age sensitivity of prospective memory. *Memory & Cognition*, 32(7), 1133–1148.

Sattler, C., Toro, P., Schönknecht, P. & Schröder, J. (2012). Cognitive activity, education and socioeconomic status as preventive factors for mild cognitive impairment and Alzheimer's disease. *Psychiatry Research*, 196(1), 90–95.

Scarmeas, N., Levy, G., Tang, M. X., Manly, J. & Stern, Y. (2001). Influence of leisure activity on the incidence of Alzheimer's disease. *Neurology*, 57(12), 2236–2242.

Scarmeas, N., Zarahn, E., Anderson, K. E., Hilton, J., Flynn, J., Van Heertum, R. L., Sackeim, H. A. & Stern, Y. (2003). Cognitive reserve modulates functional brain responses during memory tasks: A PET study in healthy young and elderly subjects. *Neuroimage*, 19(3), 1215–1227.

Siedlecki, K. L., Stern, Y., Reuben, A., Sacco, R. L., Elkind, M. S.V. & Wright, C. B. (2009). Construct validity of cognitive reserve in a multiethnic cohort: The Northern Manhattan study. *Journal of the International Neuropsychological Society*, 15(4), 558–569.

Solé-Padullés, C., Bartrés-Faz, D., Junqué, C., Vendrell, P., Rami, L., Clemente, I. C., Bosch, B., Villar, A., Bargalló, N., Jurado, M. A., Barrios, M. & Molinuevo, J. L. (2009). Brain structure and function related to cognitive reserve variables in normal aging, mild cognitive impairment and Alzheimer's disease. *Neurobiology of Aging*, 30(7), 1114–1124.

Spector, A., Orrell, M. & Woods, B. (2010). Cognitive Stimulation Therapy (CST): Effects on different areas of cognitive function for people with dementia. *International Journal of Geriatric Psychiatry*, 25(12), 1253–1258.

Stern, C. & Munn, Z. (2010). Cognitive leisure activities and their role in preventing dementia: A systematic review. *International Journal of Evidence-Based Healthcare*, 8(1), 2–17.

Stern, Y. (2002). What is cognitive reserve? Theory and research application of the reserve concept. *Journal of the International Neuropsychological Society*, 8(3), 448–460.

Stern, Y. (2009). Cognitive reserve. *Neuropsychologia*, 47(10), 2015–2028.

Stern, Y. (2012). Cognitive reserve in ageing and Alzheimer's disease. *The Lancet Neurology*, 11(11), 1006–1012.

Stern, Y., Gurland, B., Tatemichi, T. K., Tang, M. X., Wilder, D. & Mayeux, R. (1994). Influence of education and occupation on the incidence of Alzheimer's disease. *JAMA*, 271(13), 1004–1010.

Stern, Y., Habeck, C., Moeller, J., Scarmeas, N., Anderson, K. E., Hilton, H. J., Flynn, J., Sackeim, H. & van Heertum, R. (2005). Brain networks associated with cognitive reserve in healthy young and old adults. *Cerebral Cortex*, 15(4), 394–402.

Thal, L. J. (2006). Prevention of Alzheimer disease. *Alzheimer Disease & Associated Disorders*, 20, S97–S99.

Tucker, A. M. & Stern, Y. (2011). Cognitive reserve in aging. *Current Alzheimer Research*, 8(4), 354–360.

Tucker-Drob, E. M., Johnson, K. E. & Jones, R. N. (2009). The cognitive reserve hypothesis: A longitudinal examination of age-associated declines in reasoning and processing speed. *Developmental Psychology*, 45(2), 431–446.

Valenzuela, M. J., Brayne, C., Sachdev, P., Wilcock, G., Matthews, F. & Medical Research Council Cognitive Function and Ageing Study. (2011). Cognitive lifestyle and long-term risk of dementia and survival after diagnosis in a multicenter population-based cohort. *American Journal of Epidemiology*, 173(9), 1004–1012.

Valenzuela, M. J. & Sachdev, P. (2006). Brain reserve and dementia: A systematic review. *Psychological Medicine*, 36(4), 441–454.

van Dijk, K. R., van Gerven, P. W., van Boxtel, M. P. J., van der Elst, W. & Jolles, J. (2008). No protective effects of education during normal cognitive aging: Results from the 6-year follow-up of the Maastricht Aging Study. *Psychology and Aging*, 23(1), 119–130.

Verghese, J., Lipton, R. B., Katz, M. J., Hall, C. B., Derby, C. A., Kuslansky, G., Ambrose, A. F., Sliwinski, M. & Buschke, H. (2003). Leisure activities and the risk of dementia in the elderly. *New England Journal of Medicine*, 348(25), 2508–2516.

Verhaeghen, P. & Salthouse, T. A. (1997). Meta-analyses of age-cognition relations in adulthood: Estimates of linear and nonlinear age effects and structural models. *Psychological Bulletin*, 122(3), 231–249.

Wilson, R. S., Boyle, P. A., Yu, L., Barnes, L. L., Schneider, J. A. & Bennett, D. A. (2013). Life-span cognitive activity, neuropathologic burden, and cognitive aging. *Neurology*, 81(4), 314–321.

Wilson, R. S., Mendes De Leon, C. F., Barnes, L. L., Schneider, J. A., Bienias, J. L., Evans, D. A. & Bennett, D. A. (2002). Participation in cognitively stimulating activities and risk of incident Alzheimer disease. *JAMA*, 287(6), 742–748.

Yates, L. A., Yates, J., Orrell, M., Spector, A. & Woods, B. (2017). *Cognitive Stimulation Therapy for Dementia: History, Evolution and Internationalism*. London: Routledge.

Chapter 7

Sleep problems

Yue Leng and Kristine Yaffe

Introduction

Older adults experience major changes in sleep patterns, including decreased sleep duration and efficiency, increased sleep fragmentation and decreased time spent in slow wave sleep and rapid eye movement (REM) sleep (Ohayon et al. 2004; Pace-Schott and Spencer 2011; Wolkove et al. 2007). People with Alzheimer disease (AD) and other dementias are particularly affected by sleep disturbances (Bliwise 1993). This is caused partially by degeneration of key brain regions, such as the suprachiasmatic nucleus (SCN), which is critical in the homeostatic maintenance of circadian rhythms (Swaab et al. 1985). Sleep disturbances in these individuals are often characterized by poor nocturnal sleep, excessive day napping and disrupted circadian rhythms (Deschenes and Mccurry 2009), which in turn reduce individual quality of life, increase carer burden and increase the risk for premature institutionalization (Lim et al. 2014; Pollak et al. 1990). Importantly, a bi-directional relationship has been suggested: sleep disturbances could be both a result and a trigger of amyloid beta (Aβ) accumulation, a key pathological feature of AD (Ju et al. 2014). A growing number of epidemiologic studies also suggest that sleep disorders contribute to increased risk of AD, in addition to commonly occurring after disease onset (De Almondes et al. 2016; Blackwell et al. 2014; Johar et al. 2016; Yaffe et al. 2011; Tranah et al. 2011). Therefore, sleep disturbances are increasingly recognized as an important risk factor for AD (Yaffe et al. 2014).

The aim of this chapter is to provide an overview of the link between sleep disorders and dementia, including AD. We summarize evidence from observational studies that examined the risk of dementia associated with sleep disturbances, including studies of sleep duration, sleep quality, insomnia, sleep-disordered breathing (SDB), circadian rhythm disorders and excessive daytime sleepiness (EDS) or daytime napping. We also discuss underlying physiological mechanisms of these associations, as well as future study directions, including results from clinical trials that examine potential cognitive benefits of sleep interventions.

Observational epidemiologic studies of sleep and risk of dementia in the elderly

Sleep duration

Over a third of adults aged 45 and older report short or long sleep duration, other than the typical 7–9h of sleep per day (Liu et al. 2013). Growing evidence suggests that both short and long sleep duration are associated with an increased risk of dementia (Chen et al. 2016; Benito-Leon et al. 2009; Hahn et al. 2014; Lutsey et al. 2017). One meta-analysis (Bubu et al. 2017) summarized results from six studies and concluded that the long sleepers (>8h/day) were twice as likely to develop cognitive decline or AD, and the short sleepers (<7h/day) were 63% more likely than the normal sleepers (7–8h/day). Lo et al. (Lo et al. 2016) found in their meta-analysis of 11 cross-sectional studies and 7 prospective studies that self-reported short and long sleep increased the odds for poor cognitive function by 1.40 (95% CI 1.27–21.56) and 1.58 (95% CI 1.43–41.74) times, respectively. More recently, a few prospective studies have examined the effects of sleep duration on the risk of developing dementia (Chen et al. 2016; Lutsey et al. 2017). The Women's Health Initiative Memory Study found a v-shaped association between self-reported sleep duration and risk of mild cognitive impairment (MCI)/dementia, showing a 35%–36% increased risk in both short and long sleepers (Chen et al. 2016). The Atherosclerosis Risk in Communities (ARIC) Study (Lutsey et al. 2017) conducted in-home polysomnography (PSG) among 1,667 older adults (mean age 63 years) and reported that the 15-year risk of developing dementia almost doubled among those with a short sleep duration (<7h/night), compared to those with 8 to <9 h/night, while the association was not statistically significant for long sleep duration (≥9h/night). While reviews generally concluded that long sleep duration is related to worse cognition than normal or short sleep duration (Bubu et al. 2017); (Devore et al. 2016), it is also recognized that more studies with objective measures of sleep duration and prospective designs are needed to help understand the association. Table 7.1 summarizes the prospective studies that have examined the association between sleep duration and risk of dementia.

Insomnia and sleep quality

Insomnia is characterized by chronic complaints of difficulty falling or staying asleep, or poor sleep quality that lasts for one month or longer, causes significant functional impairment, does not occur solely in the context of another sleep or mental disorder and is not a result of substance use or a medical comorbidity (Association 2000; Medicine 2005). Chronic insomnia is common among older adults, with a prevalence ranging from 12% to 41% (Wolkove et al. 2007; Crowley 2011; Liu and Liu 2005). One systematic review with meta-analysis identified five prospective studies (Osorio et al. 2011; Chen et al. 2012; Jaussent

Table 7.1 Prospective studies of sleep duration and risk of dementia

First author, year	*Sample, mean age*	*Follow-up length*	*Sleep assessment*	*Identification of dementia*	*Results*
Lutsey et al. 2017	1,667 adults aged 63 years	15 years	Unattended polysomnography	Various diagnostic sources	Adjusted RR for <7h: 1.89 (1.01, 3.51); 7 to <8h: 1.42 (0.75, 2.70); ≥9h: 1.53 (0.69, 3.39)
Bokenberger et al. 2017	11,247 men aged ≥65 years	17 years	Telephone screening interview	National health registers	Adjusted HR for ≤6h: 1.40 (1.06–1.85); >9h: 1.11 (1.00–1.24)
Chen et al. 2016	7,444 women aged 70 years	7 years	Self-report	Validated four-phase protocols	Adjusted HR for ≤6h: 1.36 (1.09–1.71); ≥8h: 1.27 (0.98–1.64)
Hahn et al. 2014	214 adults aged 83 years	9 years	Self-report	Thorough clinical examination	Adjusted HR for reduced sleep duration: 1.75 (1.04–2.93)
Benito-Leon et al. 2009	3,286 adults aged 73 years	3 years	Self-report	DSM-IV diagnostic criteria	Adjusted RR for ≤5h: 1.87 (0.85–4.15); 6h: 1.13 (0.48–2.69); 8h: 2.05 (0.97–4.31); ≥9h: 2.18 (1.09–4.37)

et al. 2012; Benedict et al. 2015; Foley et al. 2001) that examined the association between insomnia and dementia risk, and suggested that individuals with insomnia have a 53% increased risk of incident all-cause dementia (De Almondes et al. 2016). Another meta-analysis (Shi et al. 2017) included four more prospective studies (Yaffe et al. 2015; Elwood et al. 2011; Tsapanou et al. 2015; Morgan and Lilley 1994) in addition to the studies noted earlier and showed that insomnia alone was not a risk factor for dementia. The discrepancy among these results could be due to the heterogeneity among the included studies (Table 7.2). Specifically, studies have used various instruments to assess and diagnose insomnia or dementia, many of which were not standardized or did not include structural interviews. Moreover, the study populations have come from different sources and have been followed up for different length periods. Given the high prevalence of insomnia in the elderly, it is important for future studies to use standardized measures of insomnia and dementia and long duration of follow-up to determine whether insomnia is a risk factor for dementia.

Increasing numbers of studies have also examined dementia risk associated with other non-specific sleep disturbances, sleep fragmentations or general sleep quality (Lim et al. 2013; Virta et al. 2013; Bokenberger et al. 2017; Luojus et al. 2017). Findings from the Swedish Twin Registry suggested that a sleep quality index, which covers difficulty falling asleep, disturbed sleep, repeated awakenings and premature awakenings, was not significantly associated with risk of dementia over 17 years (Bokenberger et al. 2017). Another recent longitudinal study suggested that middle-aged Finnish men with frequent self-reported sleep disturbances had ~1.5-fold increased risk of physician-diagnosed dementia in later life (Luojus et al. 2017). In addition, the Rush Memory and Aging Project reported that individuals with high sleep fragmentation as assessed by actigraphy had a 1.5-fold risk of developing AD. Overall, very few studies have examined the effects of objective sleep disturbances on subsequent dementia risk. More studies are needed to clarify this association, and those that incorporate a life course perspective can be particularly useful.

Sleep-disordered breathing

Sleep-disordered breathing (SDB) or sleep apnea is a condition characterized by abnormal respiratory patterns during sleep, often including repeated episodes of apneas (cessation of breathing) and hypopneas (reduced breathing). SDB is very common in the population and is believed to increase with age. It is estimated that 17% of older-aged (50–70 year olds) men and 9% older-aged women have moderate-to-severe SDB (Peppard et al. 2013). This rate is also expected to keep rising as a result of the ongoing obesity epidemic. Growing evidence has suggested a link between SDB and cognitive decline in the elderly (Ayalon et al. 2010; Zimmerman and Aloia 2012; Bliwise 2002). However, the majority of studies have used cross-sectional study designs, or have focused on specific

Table 7.2 Prospective studies of insomnia and risk of dementia

First author, year	*Sample, mean age or age range*	*Follow-up length*	*Insomnia assessment*	*Identification of dementia*	*Results*
Tsapanou et al. 2015	1041 adults aged 79 years	3 years	Self-report	DSM-IIIR	Insomnia was not associated with risk of dementia
Yaffe et al. 2015	179,738 men aged ≥55 years	8 years	Diagnosis by ICD-9	ICD-9	Insomnia was associated with risk of dementia (HR = 1.29, 1.20–1.39)
Benedict et al. 2015	1,574 men aged 50 years	40 years	Self-report	DSM-IV	Sleep disturbances were associated with risk of dementia (HR = 1.33, 1.01–1.75)
Jaussent et al. 2012	4,894 adults ≥65 years	8 years	Self-report	DSM-IV	Number of insomnia complaints was not associated with risk of dementia
Chen et al. 2012	34,158 adults aged ≥50 years	3 years	Diagnosis by ICD-9	ICD-9	Long-term insomnia was significantly associated with risk of dementia (HR = 2.34, 1.92–2.85)
Osorio et al. 2011	346 adults aged 76 years	7.7 years	Hamilton Depression Rating Scale	DSM-IV	Insomnia was significantly associated with AD (OR = 2.39, 1.03–5.55) and faster progression to dementia
Elwood et al. 2011	1,986 men aged 55–69 years	10 years	Self-report	Clinical assessment of vascular dementia	Insomnia was not associated with incident vascular dementia
Foley et al. 2001	2,346 men aged 77 years	3 years	Self-report	DSM-IIIR	Insomnia was not associated with the risk of dementia
Morgan and Lilley 1994	84 adults aged ≥65 years	4 years	Self-report	DSM-IIIR	Insomnia was not associated with the risk of dementia

cognitive tasks rather than the development of dementia itself. The Study of Osteoporotic Fractures (SOF) was one of the first longitudinal study to report a doubled risk of dementia among older women with SDB (Yaffe et al. 2011). One recent meta-analysis (Leng et al. 2017a) covering over four million adults showed that individuals with SDB were 26% more likely to develop cognitive impairment. Of the included prospective studies, three (Yaffe et al. 2015; Yaffe et al. 2011; Chang et al. 2013) specifically examined the effects of SDB on the risk of dementia (Table 7.3) and suggested a 23%–86% increase in the risk of dementia among those with SDB (determined either by clinical diagnosis or a apnea-hypopnea index (AHI) of ≥15). Another meta-analysis (Shi et al. 2017) also included studies that used self-reported apnea or snoring rather than standardized measures and showed a 18% increase in the risk of dementia associated with sleep apnea. Results from these studies suggested that SDB might be an important modifiable risk factor for dementia, and hypoxemia might play a key role in the relationship between SDB and dementia.

Excessive daytime sleepiness/daytime napping

Excessive daytime sleepiness or day napping is very common in older adults, affecting 20%–30% of the population (Young 2004; Slater and Steier 2012). Findings from the SOF showed that older women with dementia were more than three times as likely to be day nappers compared to those without dementia (Leng et al. 2017b). It has also been increasingly recognized that EDS could not only be a symptom resulted from other health problems in the elderly, but it could also be an independent predictor of future dementia risk (Tsapanou et al. 2015; Foley et al. 2001; Jaussent et al. 2012; Elwood et al. 2011). The Honolulu-Asia Aging Study suggested that older Japanese-American Men who reported EDS at baseline were twice as likely to be diagnosed with incident dementia after three years (Foley et al. 2001). The Caerphily Cohort Study showed that older men who reported 'severe' daytime sleepiness had a more than fourfold increased risk of vascular dementia (Elwood et al. 2011). Table 7.4 summarizes prospective studies on the association between EDS or daytime sleep and risk of dementia. As it can be seen, no study to date has objectively examined the relationship between measured daytime napping and future risk of developing dementia. Objective measures of napping are particularly important, given the difficulty in reporting daytime sleep among older adults (Leng et al. 2017b). Additional longitudinal studies using both subjective and objective measures of daytime sleepiness and napping are required to help understand the relationship between daytime sleep and development of dementia and underlying mechanisms.

Circadian rhythm disorders

Circadian rhythms are biological processes that oscillate within 24-hour cycles and help regulate our sleep patterns (Dijk and Czeisler 1995; Rosenwasser

Table 7.3 Prospective studies of sleep-disordered breathing and risk of dementia

First author, year	*Sample, mean age or age range*	*Follow-up length*	*Sleep apnea measure*	*Identification of dementia*	*Results*
Yaffe et al. 2015	200,000, men aged ≥55 years	8 years	Clinical diagnosis	ICD-9	Adjusted RR for sleep apnea: 1.23 (1.14–1.33)
Chang et al. 2013	8,484 adults aged ≥40	5 years	Clinical diagnosis	ICD-9	Adjusted RR for sleep apnea: 1.70 (1.24–2.32)
Yaffe et al. 2011	298 women aged 82 years	4.7 years	Unattended polysomnography	DSM-IV	Adjusted RR for sleep apnea: 1.86 (1.12–3.09)

Table 7.4 Prospective studies of excessive daytime sleepiness and risk of dementia

First author, year	*Sample, mean age or age range*	*Follow-up length*	*Measure of daytime sleepiness*	*Identification of dementia*	*Results*
Tsapanou et al. 2015	1,041 adults aged 79 years	3 years	Self-report	DSM-IIIR	Adjusted HR for EDS: 1.24 (1.00–1.54)
Jaussent et al. 2012	4,894 adults ≥65 years	8 years	Self-report	DSM-IV	Adjusted OR for EDS: 1.39 (1.00–1.97)
Elwood et al. 2011	1,986 men aged 55–69 years	10 years	Self-report	Clinical assessment of vascular dementia	Adjusted OR for EDS: 4.44 (2.05–9.61)
Foley et al. 2001	2,346 men aged 77 years	3 years	Self-report	DSM-IIIR	Adjusted OR for EDS: 2.19 (1.37–3.50)

2009). Circadian rhythm disorders are common in older adults, especially among patients with neurodegenerative diseases, such as AD (Kondratova and Kondratov 2012; Wu and Swaab 2007). Only one prospective study reported on the association between objectively measured circadian rhythm disorders and future risk of dementia, and showed an increased risk of MCI/dementia among older women with decreased activity rhythms or delayed timing of peak activity during the day (Tranah et al. 2011). Since circadian rhythms are regulated by the SCN of the brain, the link between circadian rhythm disorders and dementia is of particular interest and warrants further investigations (Swaab et al. 1985).

Potential biological mechanisms

Sleep disturbances might contribute to dementia through several mechanisms (Figure 7.1). Growing evidence suggests a potential bi-directional association between poor sleep and Aβ accumulation (Ju et al. 2014; Brown et al. 2016). Accumulation of Aβ could lead to disrupted sleep and increased wakefulness (Ju et al. 2014). Furthermore, disruption of sleep architecture, poor sleep quality and reports of short sleep duration have been shown to increase Aβ levels in the elderly (Spira et al. 2013; Ju et al. 2017; Sprecher et al. 2017). Both chronic and acute sleep deprivation also increases amyloid plaque deposition (Ooms et al. 2014; Kang et al. 2009). It is generally recognized that sleep is crucial for memory consolidation and normal brain function (Diekelmann and Born 2010; Stickgold 2005). Poor sleep is believed to interfere with neuronal pathways, especially those of GABA and cAMP, which subsequently cause impaired synaptic plasticity (Havekes et al. 2012). Sleep disturbances also lead to neuroinflammation and disrupt neurogenesis, especially in hippocampal areas, which

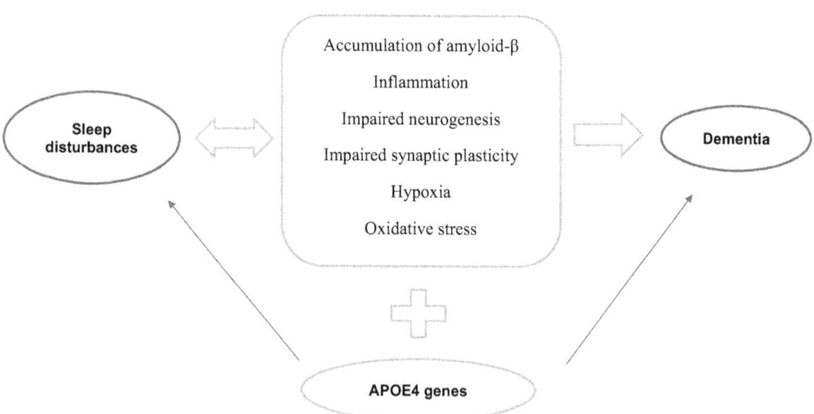

Figure 7.1 Potential biological mechanisms for sleep disturbances and dementia

plays a critical role in the process of learning and memory (Zhu et al. 2012; Meerlo et al. 2009).

Potential mechanisms for the relationship between SDB and dementia include hypoxemia, daytime sleepiness, sleep fragmentation and oxidative stress (Engleman and Joffe 1999; Lim and Veasey 2010). Findings from several epidemiologic studies, including the HypnoLaus study (Haba-Rubio et al. 2017), the Sleep Heart Health Study (Quan et al. 2006), the Apnea Positive Pressure Long-term Efficacy Study (Quan et al. 2011) and the SOF (Yaffe et al. 2011) all suggested significant effects of hypoxemia or oxygen desaturation, rather than sleep fragmentation, on cognition in middle-aged to elderly adults. Hypoxia has been linked to increased apoptosis and hippocampal atrophy in animal models (Gozal et al. 2003) and could lead to increased amyloid-β levels (Li et al. 2009). Regular intermittent hypoxia may also cause vascular dysfunction and impair the blood-brain barrier, leading to long-term disruption of the brain's microenvironment and synaptic plasticity (Zimmerman and Aloia 2012; Lim and Pack 2014). These ongoing cerebrovascular problems might eventually lead to cognitive impairment in the elderly. Besides, a few studies showed that the effects of SDB on cognition were more pronounced in the APOE4 carriers (Nikodemova et al. 2013; Spira et al. 2008). Although the exact mechanisms for the interaction between SDB and APOE4 on cognition are unclear, the presence of APOE4 genotype is believed to increase cellular vulnerability to oxidative damage, promote neuroinflammation and increase amyloid-β levels (Nunomura et al. 2006; Fazekas et al. 2006). Future studies are needed to investigate the combined effects of APOE4 and SDB on dementia risk.

Several mechanisms have been proposed linking circadian rhythms and cognition (Kondratova and Kondratov 2012; Schmidt et al. 2012; Wright et al. 2012). Circadian clock genes could also regulate neurogenesis (Kimiwada et al. 2009) and circadian rhythms affect brain activity in a range of regions: frontal, thalamic and hypothalamic regions and the brainstem locus coeruleus (Schmidt et al. 2012). Animal studies suggested that disruptions in circadian rhythms could impair hippocampal function, particularly learning and memory (Kondratova and Kondratov 2012; Stranahan 2012; Craig and Mcdonald 2008). Circadian rhythms dysfunctions could also contribute to cognitive impairment through dysregulated levels of melatonin, which is a hormone generated by the pineal gland in a circadian manner that plays a key role in regulating the sleep-wake cycles (Roth 2012). Melatonin is also known to have neuroprotective effects. Melatonin levels in human beings decrease with age, particularly in older adults with AD, even before the onset of clinical symptoms (Wu and Swaab 2007; Wu and Swaab 2005). Therefore, the important interrelationship between melatonin, circadian rhythms and dementia warrants further investigation and might help inform the role of circadian rhythms disruption as an early marker or risk factor for dementia.

Interventional studies

Since sleep disturbances are common in patients with cognitive impairment and might lead to further cognitive decline, it is important to examine whether interventions which target sleep problems can help prevent or delay dementia onset in the high-risk population. While prior evidence has shown benefits of sleep treatments over sleep quality in older populations, very few studies have examined the cognitive benefits of these treatments. A number of small trials have suggested that acetylcholinesterase inhibitors could improve sleep and cognitive performance both in healthy adults and in those with AD (Schliebs and Arendt 2006; Cooke et al. 2006; Hornung et al. 2009; Moraes Wdos et al. 2006; Mizuno et al. 2004; Ancoli-Israel et al. 2005). However, larger prospective trials are needed to examine the long-term impact of these treatments and benefits should be weighed against potential side effects (Inglis 2002). The effects of melatonin supplementation treatment on sleep and cognition have been more extensively investigated, but findings from these trials are inconsistent (Serfaty et al. 2002; Gehrman et al. 2009; Singer et al. 2003; Xu et al. 2015). Two studies suggested that melatonin treatment could be beneficial in patients with MCI and help prevent progression to dementia (Cardinali et al. 2010; Cardinali et al. 2012), while three other studies failed to show any benefit of one to seven weeks of melatonin treatment for sleep or agitation symptoms in people with dementia (Serfaty et al. 2002; Singer et al. 2003; Gehrman et al. 2009), one meta-analysis summarized seven randomized controlled trials (RCTs) and concluded that melatonin therapy might help increase sleep duration and sleep efficiency in people with dementia, but showed no effects on cognitive function (Xu et al. 2015). Future studies are needed to further explore the application of melatonin therapy in patients with MCI or mild AD.

Given that medications are usually associated with side effects which further disrupt sleep-wake rhythms and cognition (Mccurry et al. 2000), non-pharmacological treatment is particularly attractive. Physical exercise has been shown to improve sleep in older adults (Reid et al. 2010; Benloucif et al. 2004), and exercise might also help improve cognitive performance among older adults with or without cognitive impairment (Ahlskog et al. 2011). Further long-term trials are needed to examine the usefulness of exercise intervention in improving both sleep and cognition in community-dwelling older adults. One small interventional study in older adults with insomnia suggested improved sleep onset latency, sleep efficiency and cognitive performance after eight weeks of use of a computerized cognitive training program (Haimov and Shatil 2013). Bright light therapy (BLT) as a simple and low-risk treatment has also received much attention, especially in the treatment of circadian rhythm disorders (Van Maanen et al. 2016; Rosenthal et al. 1990). While studies on the effects of BLT in people with AD have shown mixed findings (Van Someren et al. 1997; Mishima et al. 1994), a recent meta-analysis concluded an overall small to medium treatment effect size of BLT on sleep problems and recommended that a combination of BLT and other behavioural treatment might have favourable additional effects (Van Maanen et al. 2016).

SDB might be an important modifiable risk factor for dementia and a promising target for intervention. As one of the most common treatments for SDB, continuous positive airway pressure (CPAP) has received increasing attention in interventional trials. One meta-analysis (Kylstra et al. 2013) of 13 trials showed a small improvement in attention after treatment with CPAP, but most of the included trials had small sample sizes and were relatively short-term. In a small study of people with AD and an AHI of ≥10, a six-week CPAP treatment was associated with less cognitive decline (Cooke et al. 2009; Ancoli-Israel et al. 2008). In one small study of people with sleep apnea, treatment by CPAP for three months led to improvements in several domains, including attention, psychomotor speed, executive function and non-verbal delayed recall (Aloia et al. 2003). Another small study suggested that a three-month CPAP treatment particularly improved cognitive function as a result of grey matter volume increases in hippocampal and frontal regions (Canessa et al. 2011). One pilot trial in patients with severe SDB found significant improvements in episodic and short-term memory, as well as executive function, and attenuated cortical thinning following CPAP treatment (Dalmases et al. 2015). Findings from the large APPLES trial showed improved executive function following CPAP treatment over two and six months in people with severe SDB; no effects were observed on attention, psychomotor function or learning and memory (Kushida et al. 2012). Future RCTs with larger sample sizes and longer duration of treatment are needed and might consider targeting high-risk populations, such as people with MCI.

Clinical implications and future directions

Mounting evidences suggests that sleep disturbances are not only common in people with cognitive impairment, but are also associated with increased risk of dementia in cognitively normal older adults. This has significant clinical implications. Many changes in sleep patterns might occur very early during the process of developing dementia and could be observed years before the onset of the clinical symptoms of dementia. Therefore, identification of these sleep disturbances might help with the early detection and diagnosis of dementia. Some of the most common sleep disturbances associated with subsequent risk of dementia include extreme sleep duration, poor sleep quality, SDB, increased daytime sleepiness or naps and disrupted circadian rhythms. Clinicians should be cautious about the presence of sleep problems in their patients and should consider administering full neuropsychological batteries, if necessary. Future longitudinal studies are needed to examine the risk of dementia associated with changes in sleep patterns, measured objectively and repeatedly. Studies also need to explore the added value of using sleep disturbances or change in sleep patterns as a marker for predicting future risk of dementia.

Sleep-wake cycle plays a critical role in the brain ageing process. While it is unclear whether sleep disturbances are merely an early marker of dementia pathology, or if it is also a risk factor that contribute to the initiation or progression of dementia, growing evidence from animal studies suggest that there might exist biological mechanisms through which sleep disturbances could accelerate brain ageing and increase the risk for dementia. Additional population-based research using neuroimaging techniques, such as positron emission tomography brain scan and structural MRI, as well as measures of biomarkers, such as Aβ concentrations in cerebrospinal fluid (CSF), will help further determine physiological pathways. Other underlying mechanisms, such as neuroinflammation, vascular factors and change in specific neurotransmitter systems should also be considered. Large epidemiologic studies with objective measures of sleep parameters, standardized measures of insomnia and validated ascertainment of dementia cases are needed to examine which aspects or symptoms of sleep (e.g. duration, initiation, fragmentation, staging, circadian rhythms) might be most important in the development of dementia and to explore whether the associations could be modified by other factors, such as age, sex, education, APOE4 genotype, depression, or medication use.

If sleep disturbance can be proven to be a risk factor for dementia, then treatment of sleep problems might help slow down the brain ageing process and eventually help prevent or delay dementia onset or progression. To this end, treatment trials targeting improved sleep in older adults and examining the effects of sleep interventions on both sleep quality and cognitive outcomes are particularly valuable. While short-term trials have shown some promise for the improvement of sleep and cognition using melatonin, exercise, BLT or CPAP, findings are largely inconsistent, and the interpretation of these findings are limited by small sample sizes or short length of follow-up. The long-term effects of sleep interventions on the risk of dementia are unknown. The feasibility of other intervention strategies, such as cognitive behavioural therapy for insomnia or a comprehensive approach incorporating different existing techniques, are yet to be evaluated in high-risk populations (e.g. patients with MCI). Given the high prevalence of both sleep disturbances and dementia in older populations, the link between the two has profound public health implications. Eventually, this might help open up new opportunities for the prevention and treatment of dementia in the long run.

References

Ahlskog, J. E., *et al.* (2011). Physical exercise as a preventive or disease-modifying treatment of dementia and brain aging. *Mayo Clinical Proceedings*, 86(9), 876–884.

Aloia, M. S., *et al.* (2003). Neuropsychological changes and treatment compliance in older adults with sleep apnea. *Journal of Psychosomatic Research*, 54(1), 71–76.

Ancoli-Israel, S., *et al.* (2005). Effects of galantamine versus donepezil on sleep in patients with mild to moderate Alzheimer disease and their caregivers: A double-blind, head-to-head, randomized pilot study. *Alzheimer Diseases & Associated Disorders*, 19(4), 240–245.

Ancoli-Israel, S., *et al.* (2008). Cognitive effects of treating obstructive sleep apnea in Alzheimer's disease: A randomized controlled study. *Journal of the American Geriatrics Society*, 56(11), 2076–2081.

Association, A. P. (2000). *Diagnostic and Statistical Manual of Mental Disorders: Dsm-iv-tr*, 4th edn. Washington, DC: American Psychiatric Association.

Ayalon, L., Ancoli-Israel, S. & Drummond, S. P. (2010). Obstructive sleep apnea and age: A double insult to brain function? *American Journal of the Respiratory and Critical Care Medicine*, 182(3), 413–419.

Benedict, C., *et al.* (2015). Self-reported sleep disturbance is associated with Alzheimer's disease risk in men. *Alzheimers Dementia*, 11(9), 1090–1097.

Benito-Leon, J., *et al.* (2009). Total daily sleep duration and the risk of dementia: A prospective population-based study. *European Journal of Neurology*, 16(9), 990–997.

Benloucif, S., *et al.* (2004). Morning or evening activity improves neuropsychological performance and subjective sleep quality in older adults. *Sleep*, 27(8), 1542–1551.

Blackwell, T., *et al.* (2014). Associations of objectively and subjectively measured sleep quality with subsequent cognitive decline in older community-dwelling men: The mros sleep study. *Sleep*, 37(4), 655–663.

Bliwise, D. L. (1993). Sleep in normal aging and dementia. *Sleep*, 16(1), 40–81.

Bliwise, D. L. (2002). Sleep apnea, apoe4 and Alzheimer's disease 20 years and counting? *Journal of Psychosomatic Research*, 53(1), 539–546.

Bokenberger, K., *et al.* (2017). Association between sleep characteristics and incident dementia accounting for baseline cognitive status: A prospective population-based study. *Journal of Gerontology Series A, Biological Sciences and Medical Sciences*, 72(1), 134–139.

Brown, B. M., *et al.* (2016). Exploring the bi-directional relationship between sleep and beta-amyloid. *Current Opinion in Psychiatry*, 29(6), 397–401.

Bubu, O. M., *et al.* (2017). Sleep, cognitive impairment, and Alzheimer's disease: A systematic review and meta-analysis. *Sleep*, 40(1).

Canessa, N., *et al.* (2011). Obstructive sleep apnea: Brain structural changes and neurocognitive function before and after treatment. *American Journal of Respiratory and Critical Care Medicine*, 183(10), 1419–1426.

Cardinali, D. P., Furio, A. M. & Brusco, L. I. (2010). Clinical aspects of melatonin intervention in Alzheimer's disease progression. *Current Neuropharmacology*, 8(3), 218–227.

Cardinali, D. P., *et al.* (2012). Therapeutic application of melatonin in mild cognitive impairment. *American Journal of Neurodegenerative Diseases*, 1(3), 280–291.

Chang, W. P., *et al.* (2013). Sleep apnea and the risk of dementia: A population-based 5-year follow-up study in taiwan. *PLOS One*, 8(10), e78655.

Chen, P. L., *et al.* (2012). Risk of dementia in patients with insomnia and long-term use of hypnotics: A population-based retrospective cohort study. *PLOS One*, 7(11), e49113.

Chen, J. C., *et al.* (2016). Sleep duration, cognitive decline, and dementia risk in older women. *Alzheimers Dement*, 12(1), 21–33.

Cooke, J. R., *et al.* (2006). Acetylcholinesterase inhibitors and sleep architecture in patients with Alzheimer's disease. *Drugs Aging*, 23(6), 503–511.

Cooke, J. R., *et al.* (2009). Sustained use of cpap slows deterioration of cognition, sleep, and mood in patients with Alzheimer's disease and obstructive sleep apnea: A preliminary study. *Journal of Clinical Sleep Medicine*, 5(4), 305–309.

Craig, L. A. & Mcdonald, R. J. (2008). Chronic disruption of circadian rhythms impairs hippocampal memory in the rat. *Brain Research Bulletin*, 76(1–2), 141–151.

Crowley, K. (2011). Sleep and sleep disorders in older adults. *Neuropsychology Review*, 21(1), 41–53.

Dalmases, M., *et al.* (2015). Effect of cpap on cognition, brain function, and structure among elderly patients with osa: A randomized pilot study. *Chest*, 148(5), 1214–1223.

De Almondes, K. M., *et al.* (2016). Insomnia and risk of dementia in older adults: Systematic review and meta-analysis. *Journal of Psychiatric Research*, 77, 109–115.

Deschenes, C. L. & Mccurry, S. M. (2009). Current treatments for sleep disturbances in individuals with dementia. *Current Psychiatry Reports*, 11(1), 20–26.

Devore, E. E., Grodstein, F. & Schernhammer, E. S. (2016). Sleep duration in relation to cognitive function among older adults: A systematic review of observational studies. *Neuroepidemiology*, 46(1), 57–78.

Diekelmann, S. & Born, J. (2010). The memory function of sleep. *Nature Reviews Neurosciences*, 11(2), 114–126.

Dijk, D. J. & Czeisler, C. A. (1995). Contribution of the circadian pacemaker and the sleep homeostat to sleep propensity, sleep structure, electroencephalographic slow waves, and sleep spindle activity in humans. *Journal of Neurosciences*, 15(5 Pt 1), 3526–3538.

Elwood, P. C., *et al.* (2011). Sleep disturbance and daytime sleepiness predict vascular dementia. *Journal of Epidemiology Community Health*, 65(9), 820–824.

Engleman, H. & Joffe, D. (1999). Neuropsychological function in obstructive sleep apnoea. *Sleep Medicine Reviews*, 3(1), 59–78.

Fazekas, F., *et al.* (2006). The impact of our genes: Consequences of the apolipoprotein e polymorphism in Alzheimer disease and multiple sclerosis. *Journal of Neurological Sciences*, 245(1–2), 35–39.

Foley, D., *et al.* (2001). Daytime sleepiness is associated with 3-year incident dementia and cognitive decline in older japanese-american men. *Journal of the American Geriatrics Society*, 49(12), 1628–1632.

Gehrman, P. R., *et al.* (2009). Melatonin fails to improve sleep or agitation in double-blind randomized placebo-controlled trial of institutionalized patients with Alzheimer disease. *American Journal of Geriatrics Psychiatry*, 17(2), 166–169.

Gozal, D., *et al.* (2003). Increased susceptibility to intermittent hypoxia in aging rats: Changes in proteasomal activity, neuronal apoptosis and spatial function. *Journal of Neurochemistry*, 86(6), 1545–1552.

Haba-Rubio, J., *et al.* (2017). Sleep characteristics and cognitive impairment in the general population: The hypnolaus study. *Neurology*, 88(5), 463–469.

Hahn, E. A., *et al.* (2014). A change in sleep pattern may predict Alzheimer disease. *American Journal of Geriatrics Psychiatry*, 22(11), 1262–1271.

Haimov, I. & Shatil, E. (2013). Cognitive training improves sleep quality and cognitive function among older adults with insomnia. *PLOS One*, 8(4), e61390.

Havekes, R., Vecsey, C. G. & Abel, T. (2012). The impact of sleep deprivation on neuronal and glial signaling pathways important for memory and synaptic plasticity. *Cell Signal*, 24(6), 1251–1260.

Hornung, O. P., *et al.* (2009). The effects of donepezil on postlearning sleep eeg of healthy older adults. *Pharmacopsychiatry*, 42(1), 9–13.

Inglis, F. (2002). The tolerability and safety of cholinesterase inhibitors in the treatment of dementia. *International Journal of Clinical Practice Supplement*, (127), 45–63.

Jaussent, I., *et al.* (2012). Excessive sleepiness is predictive of cognitive decline in the elderly. *Sleep*, 35(9), 1201–1207.

Johar, H., *et al.* (2016). Impaired sleep predicts cognitive decline in old people: Findings from the prospective kora age study. *Sleep*, 39(1), 217–226.

Ju, Y. E., Lucey, B. P. & Holtzman, D. M. (2014). Sleep and Alzheimer disease pathology – a bidirectional relationship. *Nature Reviews Neurology*, 10(2), 115–119.

Ju, Y. S., *et al.* (2017). Slow wave sleep disruption increases cerebrospinal fluid amyloid-beta levels. *Brain*, 140(8), 2104–2111.

Kang, J. E., *et al.* (2009). Amyloid-beta dynamics are regulated by orexin and the sleep-wake cycle. *Science*, 326(5955), 1005–1007.

Kimiwada, T., *et al.* (2009). Clock genes regulate neurogenic transcription factors, including neurod, and the neuronal differentiation of adult neural stem/progenitor cells. *Neurochemistry International*, 54(5–6), 277–285.

Kondratova, A. A. & Kondratov, R.V. (2012). The circadian clock and pathology of the ageing brain. *Nature Reviews Neurosciences*, 13(5), 325–335.

Kushida, C. A., *et al.* (2012). Effects of continuous positive airway pressure on neurocognitive function in obstructive sleep apnea patients: The apnea positive pressure long-term efficacy study (apples). *Sleep*, 35(12), 1593–1602.

Kylstra, W. A., *et al.* (2013). Neuropsychological functioning after cpap treatment in obstructive sleep apnea: A meta-analysis. *Sleep Medicine Reviews*, 17(5), 341–347.

Leng, Y., *et al.* (2017a). Association of sleep-disordered breathing with cognitive function and risk of cognitive impairment: A systematic review meta-analysis. *JAMA Neurology*, 75(10), 1237.

Leng, Y., *et al.* (2017b). Who take naps? Self-reported and objectively measured napping in very old women. *Journal of Gerontology Series A Biological Sciences and Medical Sciences*, 73(3), 374–379.

Li, L., *et al.* (2009). Hypoxia increases abeta generation by altering beta- and gamma-cleavage of app. *Neurobiological Aging*, 30(7), 1091–1098.

Lim, A. S., *et al.* (2013). Sleep fragmentation and the risk of incident Alzheimer's disease and cognitive decline in older persons. *Sleep*, 36(7), 1027–1032.

Lim, D. C. & Pack, A. I. (2014). Obstructive sleep apnea and cognitive impairment: Addressing the blood-brain barrier. *Sleep Medicine Reviews*, 18(1), 35–48.

Lim, D. C. & Veasey, S. C. (2010). Neural injury in sleep apnea. *Current Neurology and Neuroscience Reports*, 10(1), 47–52.

Lim, M. M., Gerstner, J. R. & Holtzman, D. M. (2014). The sleep-wake cycle and Alzheimer's disease: What do we know? *Neurodegenerative Diseases Management*, 4(5), 351–362.

Liu, X. & Liu, L. (2005). Sleep habits and insomnia in a sample of elderly persons in china. *Sleep*, 28(12), 1579–1587.

Liu, Y., *et al.* (2013). Sleep duration and chronic diseases among u.S. Adults age 45 years and older: Evidence from the 2010 behavioral risk factor surveillance system. *Sleep*, 36(10), 1421–1427.

Lo, J. C., *et al.* (2016). Self-reported sleep duration and cognitive performance in older adults: A systematic review and meta-analysis. *Sleep Medicine*, 17, 87–98.

Luojus, M. K., *et al.* (2017). Self-reported sleep disturbance and incidence of dementia in ageing men. *Journal of Epidemiology Community Health*, 71(4), 329–335.

Lutsey, P. L., *et al.* (2017). Sleep characteristics and risk of dementia and Alzheimer's disease: The atherosclerosis risk in communities study. *Alzheimers Dementia* 14(2), 157–166.

Mccurry, S. M., *et al.* (2000). Treatment of sleep disturbance in Alzheimer's disease. *Sleep Medicine Reviews*, 4(6), 603–628.

Medicine, A. A. O. S. (2005). *Icsd-2-International Classification of Sleep Disorders, 2nd end. Diagnostic and Coding Manual*. Chicago, IL: American Academy of Sleep Medicine.

Meerlo, P., *et al.* (2009). New neurons in the adult brain: The role of sleep and consequences of sleep loss. *Sleep Medicine Reviews*, 13(3), 187–194.

Mishima, K., *et al.* (1994). Morning bright light therapy for sleep and behavior disorders in elderly patients with dementia. *Acta Psychiatrica Scandinavica*, 89(1), 1–7.

Mizuno, S., *et al.* (2004). Effects of donepezil on Alzheimer's disease: The relationship between cognitive function and rapid eye movement sleep. *Psychiatry and Clinical Neurosciences*, 58(6), 660–665.

Moraes Wdos, S., *et al.* (2006). The effect of donepezil on sleep and rem sleep eeg in patients with Alzheimer disease: A double-blind placebo-controlled study. *Sleep*, 29(2), 199–205.

Morgan, K. & Lilley, J. M. (1994). Risk factors among incident cases of dementia in a representative british sample. *International Journal of Geriatrics Psychiatry*, 9, 11–15.

Nikodemova, M., *et al.* (2013). Association of sleep disordered breathing and cognitive deficit in apoe epsilon4 carriers. *Sleep*, 36(6), 873–880.

Nunomura, A., *et al.* (2006). Involvement of oxidative stress in Alzheimer disease. *Journal of Neuropathology & Experimental Neurology*, 65(7), 631–641.

Ohayon, M. M., *et al.* (2004). Meta-analysis of quantitative sleep parameters from childhood to old age in healthy individuals: Developing normative sleep values across the human lifespan. *Sleep*, 27(7), 1255–1273.

Ooms, S., *et al.* (2014). Effect of 1 night of total sleep deprivation on cerebrospinal fluid beta-amyloid 42 in healthy middle-aged men: A randomized clinical trial. *JAMA Neurology*, 71(8), 971–977.

Osorio, R. S., *et al.* (2011). Greater risk of Alzheimer's disease in older adults with insomnia. *Journal of American Geriatrics Society*, 59(3), 559–562.

Pace-Schott, E. F. & Spencer, R. M. (2011). Age-related changes in the cognitive function of sleep. *Progress in Brain Research*, 191, 75–89.

Peppard, P. E., *et al.* (2013). Increased prevalence of sleep-disordered breathing in adults. *American Journal of Epidemiology*, 177(9), 1006–1014.

Pollak, C. P., *et al.* (1990). Sleep problems in the community elderly as predictors of death and nursing home placement. *Journal of Community Health*, 15(2), 123–135.

Quan, S. F., *et al.* (2006). Obstructive sleep apnea-hypopnea and neurocognitive functioning in the sleep heart health study. *Sleep Medicine*, 7(6), 498–507.

Quan, S. F., *et al.* (2011). The association between obstructive sleep apnea and neurocognitive performance – the apnea positive pressure long-term efficacy study (apples). *Sleep*, 34(3), 303–314B.

Reid, K. J., *et al.* (2010). Aerobic exercise improves self-reported sleep and quality of life in older adults with insomnia. *Sleep Medicine*, 11(9), 934–940.

Rosenthal, N. E., *et al.* (1990). Phase-shifting effects of bright morning light as treatment for delayed sleep phase syndrome. *Sleep*, 13(4), 354–361.

Rosenwasser, A. M. (2009). Functional neuroanatomy of sleep and circadian rhythms. *Brain Research Reviews*, 61(2), 281–306.

Roth, H. L. (2012). Dementia and sleep. *Neurologic Clinics*, 30(4), 1213–1248.

Schliebs, R. & Arendt, T. (2006). The significance of the cholinergic system in the brain during aging and in Alzheimer's disease. *Journal of Neural Transmission (Vienna)*, 113(11), 1625–1644.

Schmidt, C., Peigneux, P. & Cajochen, C. (2012). Age-related changes in sleep and circadian rhythms: Impact on cognitive performance and underlying neuroanatomical networks. *Frontiers in Neurology*, 3, 118.
Serfaty, M., *et al.* (2002). Double blind randomised placebo controlled trial of low dose melatonin for sleep disorders in dementia. *International Journal of Geriatrics Psychiatry*, 17(12), 1120–1127.
Shi, L., *et al.* (2017). Sleep disturbances increase the risk of dementia: A systematic review and meta-analysis. *Sleep Medicine Reviews*. 18, 38
Singer, C., *et al.* (2003). A multicenter, placebo-controlled trial of melatonin for sleep disturbance in Alzheimer's disease. *Sleep*, 26(7), 893–901.
Slater, G. & Steier, J. (2012). Excessive daytime sleepiness in sleep disorders. *Journal of Thoracic Disease*, 4(6), 608–616.
Spira, A. P., *et al.* (2008). Sleep-disordered breathing and cognition in older women. *Journal of the American Geriatrics Society*, 56(1), 45–50.
Spira, A. P., *et al.* (2013). Self-reported sleep and beta-amyloid deposition in community-dwelling older adults. *JAMA Neurology*, 70(12), 1537–1543.
Sprecher, K. E., *et al.* (2017). Poor sleep is associated with csf biomarkers of amyloid pathology in cognitively normal adults. *Neurology*, 89(5), 445–453.
Stickgold, R. (2005). Sleep-dependent memory consolidation. *Nature*, 437(7063), 1272–1278.
Stranahan, A. M. (2012). Chronobiological approaches to Alzheimer's disease. *Current Alzheimer Research*, 9(1), 93–98.
Swaab, D. F., Fliers, E. & Partiman, T. S. (1985). The suprachiasmatic nucleus of the human brain in relation to sex, age and senile dementia. *Brain Research*, 342(1), 37–44.
Tranah, G. J., *et al.* (2011). Circadian activity rhythms and risk of incident dementia and mild cognitive impairment in older women. *Annals of Neurology*, 70(5), 722–732.
Tsapanou, A., *et al.* (2015). Daytime sleepiness and sleep inadequacy as risk factors for dementia. *Dementia and Geriatrics Cognitive Disorders Extra*, 5(2), 286–295.
Van Maanen, A., *et al.* (2016). The effects of light therapy on sleep problems: A systematic review and meta-analysis. *Sleep Medicine Reviews*, 29, 52–62.
Van Someren, E. J., *et al.* (1997). Indirect bright light improves circadian rest-activity rhythm disturbances in demented patients. *Biological Psychiatry*, 41(9), 955–963.
Virta, J. J., *et al.* (2013). Midlife sleep characteristics associated with late life cognitive function. *Sleep*, 36(10), 1533–1541, 1541A.
Wolkove, N., *et al.* (2007). Sleep and aging: 1. Sleep disorders commonly found in older people. *CMAJ*, 176(9), 1299–1304.
Wright, K. P., Lowry, C. A. & Lebourgeois, M. K. (2012). Circadian and wakefulness-sleep modulation of cognition in humans. *Frontiers in Molecular Neuroscience*, 5, 50.
Wu, Y. H. & Swaab, D. F. (2005). The human pineal gland and melatonin in aging and Alzheimer's disease. *Journal of the Pineal Research*, 38(3), 145–152.
Wu, Y. H. & Swaab, D. F. (2007). Disturbance and strategies for reactivation of the circadian rhythm system in aging and Alzheimer's disease. *Sleep Medicine*, 8(6), 623–636.
Xu, J., *et al.* (2015). Melatonin for sleep disorders and cognition in dementia: A meta-analysis of randomized controlled trials. *American Journal of the Alzheimers Disease and Other Dementias*, 30(5), 439–447.
Yaffe, K., Falvey, C. M. & Hoang, T. (2014). Connections between sleep and cognition in older adults. *The Lancet Neurology*, 13(10), 1017–1028.
Yaffe, K., *et al.* (2011). Sleep-disordered breathing, hypoxia, and risk of mild cognitive impairment and dementia in older women. *JAMA*, 306(6), 613–619.

Yaffe, K., *et al.* (2015). Sleep quality and risk of dementia among older male veterans. *American Journal of Geriatrics Psychiatry*, 23(6), 651–654.

Young, T. B. (2004). Epidemiology of daytime sleepiness: Definitions, symptomatology, and prevalence. *Journal of the Clinical Psychiatry*, 65(Suppl 16), 12–16.

Zhu, B., *et al.* (2012). Sleep disturbance induces neuroinflammation and impairment of learning and memory. *Neurobiology of Disease*, 48(3), 348–355.

Zimmerman, M. E. & Aloia, M. S. (2012). Sleep-disordered breathing and cognition in older adults. *Current Neurology and Neuroscience Reports*, 12(5), 537–546.

Chapter 8

Behaviour change for dementia prevention and risk reduction

Aimee Aubeeluck

Introduction

Current understanding of cognitive decline suggests that potentially modifiable lifestyle behaviours such as social contacts, leisure activities, physical exercise, alcohol consumption and diet may delay onset, reduce risk or play a preventative role in the development of dementia. However, study findings in this field are often inconsistent and do not allow us to draw definite conclusions. This chapter will review a number of theoretical perspectives of behaviour change from a Health Psychology perspective. Initially, a review the existing dementia prevention literature will be presented, followed by discussion of how the review might be utilised when developing interventions for dementia prevention and risk reduction.

Theoretical perspectives on behaviour change

Health psychologists are concerned with 'the study of psychological and behavioural processes in health, illness and healthcare' (Johnston 1994). Many behaviour change methods have been developed in the context of Clinical Psychology where a motivation for change is anticipated in relation to behavioural issues. In addition to this, social psychologists have placed focus upon how to modify health-related behaviour and the operationalisation of health promoting and disease preventing activities. However, Health Psychology is concerned with methods of both enhancing motivation in the unmotivated and action in the motivated. In considering how individual's behaviours may be changed, this section will consider the definition of 'health behaviours', how these may be predicted and the underpinning theory that drives behaviour change research.

What are health behaviours and how do we measure them?

The term 'health behaviours' has been defined as overt behavioural patterns actions and habits that relate to health maintenance, to health restoration and to health improvement (Gochman 1997, p. 3). As such, a 'health behaviour' is considered to be any action taken by an individual to maintain, gain or regain good health or, to prevent illness. There are a wide range of behaviours that fall within this definition that include diet, physical activity, smoking, alcohol consumption, adherence to medication/treatment regimes, vaccinations and sexual behaviours.

However, although this definition appears straightforward, it can still be difficult to classify when a behaviour is healthy and when it is not, partly due to the subjective nature by which health behaviours are measured (Connor and Norman 2017). The existing literature would suggest that self-report measures of behaviour lack reliability as they depend on the individual to estimate, for example, their level of physical activity or amount of alcohol consumed (Rhodes et al. 2017). Furthermore, where there are objective measures available, such as blood or breath tests, these are often constrained by a small time frame within which to gather that sample. Nonetheless, such behaviours have been extensively researched within the field of Health Psychology (e.g. Lynch et al. 2015; Cameron et al. 2017) with the view that in the study of both healthy and unhealthy populations, Health Psychology can provide some understanding of how health behaviour may be predicted and improved and illness may be subsequently prevented.

What factors predict health behaviours?

We know that many illnesses have a close to causal relationship with health risk behaviours, such as poor diet, binge/problem drinking, smoking or lack of exercise (Ogden 2012). A common-sense perspective on behaviour change would argue that as rational beings, individuals will respond to such risk through the adoption of health behaviours. By adopting health-enhancing behaviours, such as physical exercise, embracing a healthier diet, quitting smoking, reducing alcohol consumption and eliminating health compromising behaviours through self-regulation, it is anticipated that individuals can control their behaviours and regulate their health risks (Leventhal et al. 2001). However, it is recognised that in the face of poor health, individuals may not make changes to their behaviours in order to reduce this risk, even when they are aware that their behaviour may be compromising their health. This is because behaviour change is complex and encompasses not only cognitive factors, but social and emotional factors as well (Schwarzer 2008) (see Chapter 2 for more details on risk reduction). Moreover, individuals also need to be motivated to change their behaviour and have the self-belief that they can do so (Bandura 1977). Several complex models comprising an integrated pattern of determinants and processes of health behaviour change have previously been developed. These include motivation, self-regulation and self-efficacy in their explanations of what predicts health behaviours. Leventhal et al. (1985) describe a number of factors they would argue predict health behaviours and suggest that a combination of these factors can be used to promote health-related behaviours (Table 8.1).

Table 8.1 Factors that predict health behaviours, proposed by Leventhal et al. (1985)

Social factors	Learning, reinforcement, modelling, social norms
Genetic factors	Evidence base for alcohol/substance abuse
Perceived symptoms	Tiredness, breathlessness, pain
Emotional factors	Anxiety, stress, fear, tension
The beliefs of the patient	Self-efficacy "I can make a change"
The beliefs of the healthcare professional	The patient has capacity/motivation to change their behaviour

Much of the existing research has placed focus on the impact of health beliefs in predicting behaviour as can be evidenced in theories, such as attribution theory, health locus of control, unrealistic optimism and stages of change. These are detailed next.

Attribution theory

Attribution theory was introduced by Heider (1944) and developed into a well-defined theory by Kelley (1967, 1971). Kelley's theory suggests that as individuals are driven by a need to understand causality in their social world, attributions about causality can be structured according to causal schemata (Ogden 2012). As such, the attribution process requires the individual to reason backward from the observation of an event or behaviour to a judgement about its cause. This provides an explanation for an event that has already occurred and why, for example, "I did not adhere to my treatment regimen because my doctor did not give me adequate support". Kelley's original schemata have been redefined over time in to the following dimensions of attribution (Table 8.2).

Health locus of control

The construct of health locus of control takes the internal vs. external aspect of attribution theory and applies it specifically to health. Wallston and Wallston (1982) developed a measure of the health locus of control which identifies whether the individual considers their health to be controllable by them, controllable by others or within the hands of fate. Health locus of control has been shown to predict whether individuals will change health risk behaviours, such as smoking, and the type of communication they may require from their healthcare professional in order to make a change (e.g. Ashford and Rayens 2015). However, there is some debate as to whether health locus of control is stable over time, context specific, whether it is possible to be both internal and external (e.g. that the same individual may make both internal and external attributions about what is controllable by them across time and context) and

Table 8.2 Dimensions of the attribution theory proposed by Kelley (1967, 1971)

1. internal vs. external	"my poor health is due to my behaviour" vs. "my poor health is due to my practitioner's ability"
2. stable vs. unstable	"the cause of my poor health will always be due to my behaviour" vs. "the cause of my poor health was specific to a particular event/ interaction"
3. global vs. specific	"the behaviour that causes my poor health also impact on other areas of my life" vs. "the behaviour that causes my poor health is specific to this health-related aspect of my life only"
4. controllable vs. uncontrollable	"my health is controllable my me" vs. "my health is not controllable by me"

some grey areas within which behaviours, such as seeking medical advice, could be reliably perceived as both internal and/or external.

Unrealistic optimism

In addition to attribution theory and health locus of control, it is also argued that individual's will often continue to practice risky health behaviours due to an inaccurate perception of their risk and susceptibility. Weinsten (1983) found that, when individuals are asked about the likelihood of getting an illness, they believe they are less likely to get ill than someone else. Weinstein (1987) argues this concept of unrealistic optimism comprises four cognitive factors that suggest that the perception of one's own risk is not a rational process (Table 8.3).

Stages of change

Finally, the stages of change model (formally the transtheoretical model; Prochska and DiClemente 1982) suggests that behaviour change comprises five stages that individuals move between when making lifestyle changes to their behaviours (Table 8.4).

These stages do not necessarily occur in a linear fashion and an individual may move between stages at different points in time. For example, an individual may move from precontemplation to action and then back to the precontemplation stage without actualising the maintenance of their desired change. The model also allows for exploration of costs and benefits where individuals may focus on the cost involved to them in giving up a health risk behaviour in the precontemplation/contemplation stages and the benefits once they are in the action/maintenance stages.

Table 8.3 Unrealistic optimist theory, proposed by Weinstein (1987)

1) Lack of personal experience with the problem
2) The belief that the problem is preventable by individual action
3) The belief that if the problem has not yet appeared, it will not in the future
4) The belief that the problem is infrequent

Table 8.4 Transtheoretical model (Prochska & DiClimente), stages of change

1) Precontemplation	No intention of making a change
2) Contemplation	Considering making a change
3) Preparation	Making small changes
4) Action	Actively engaging in changed behaviour
5) Maintenance	Sustaining change over time

Models of behaviour change

By integrating the differing aspects of health beliefs that come from attribution theory, health locus of control, unrealistic optimism and stages of change, a number of social cognition models have been developed that allow us to further understand health beliefs and health behaviours. Two of the most commonly used models are the Health Belief Model (Rosenstock 1966; Becker 1974) and the Theory of Planned Behaviour (Ajzen 1988).

The health belief model (HBM)

Originally utilised to predict preventative health behaviours and behavioural responses to treatment in illness, the HBM (Figure 8.1) is currently most widely used to predict a wide variety of health-related behaviours.

The health belief model predicts that our behaviour stems from an individual's perception of his/her susceptibility to illness, modifying factors and cues to action that will determine the likelihood of whether a behaviour change will occur. Whilst there was much debate and some conflicting findings throughout the 1980s (e.g. Janz and Becker 1984), the empirical support for the HBM is robust, and the model is considered to reliably predict health behaviours. However, it has been criticised for its emphasis on the individual and focus on human beings as rational processors of information.

The theory of planned behaviour (TPB)

The TPB (Figure 8.2) was developed from the Theory of Reasoned Action (Fishbein 1967) and places emphasis on behavioural intentions that are a result of three key beliefs, attitude towards a behaviour, the subjective norm and perceived behavioural control.

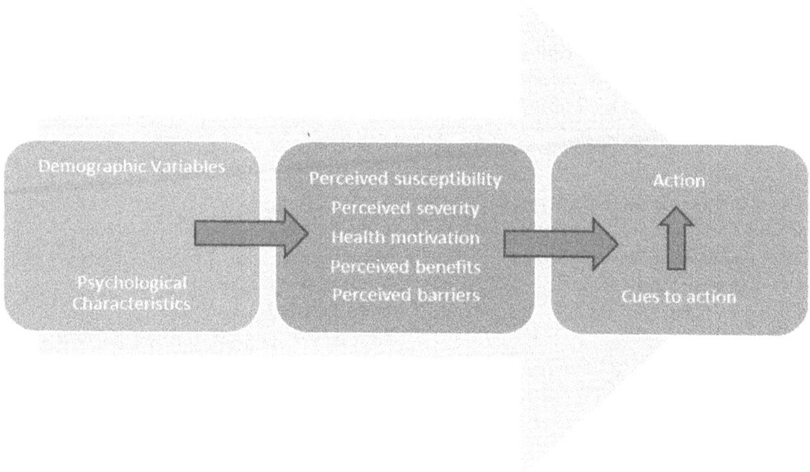

Figure 8.1 The health belief model

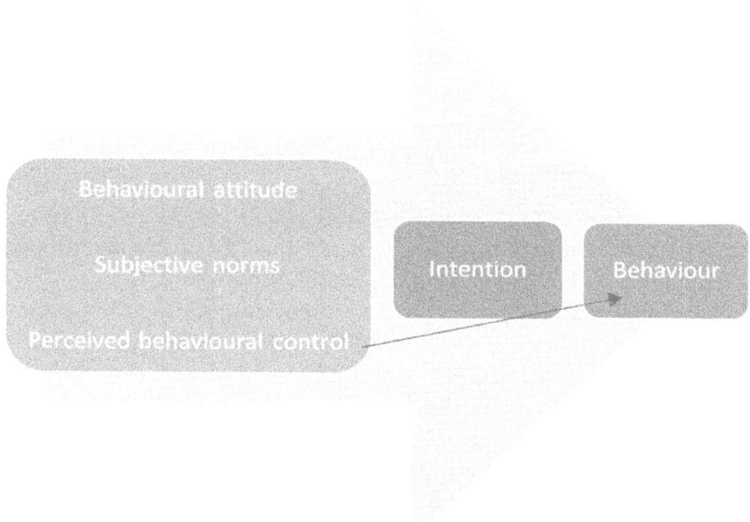

Figure 8.2 The theory of planned behaviour

The TPB suggests that these three key factors predict behavioural intentions, which are in turn linked to behaviour. Furthermore, perceived behavioural control may have a direct effect on behaviour, bypassing the intention stage of the model. The TBP has been the dominant theoretical approach to guiding health-related behaviour research over the last 30 years (Sniehotta et al. 2013).

Whilst intention, perceived behavioural control, attitude and subjective norms all have a role in predicting, understanding and changing health behaviour, the model has not been without its criticism, particularly in terms of its predictive validity (Orbell and Sheeran 1998) and the role of intentions in mediating behaviour (Conner et al. 2013).

Summary

The first part of this chapter has provided a brief overview of behaviour change within the context of Health Psychology. We know that there are many reasons why individuals may take risks with their health and these can be better understood via attribution theory, health locus of control, unrealistic optimism and stages of change. Moreover, there are a number of models that attempt to measure behaviour change with a view to develop interventions that promote change. Although intentions do not predict behaviour all of the time, they do predict behaviour around half of the time. Therefore, such models hold currency with policy makers, practitioners and those concerned with preventative healthcare and may be a useful tool to use in clinical practice.

The role of behavioural factors in dementia prevention

The second part of this chapter will provide a brief overview of a number of dementia prevention trials and discuss their findings within the context of behaviour change methodology. As discussed in previous chapters, modifiable vascular and lifestyle-related risk factors have been associated with higher risk of dementia in a variety of observational studies (e.g. Norton et al. 2014). Previous research on dementia prevention has been focused on assessing the efficacy of multi-domain interventions and their role in the prevention of dementia. The key modifiable risk factors in dementia are considered to be depression, diabetes, physical inactivity, hypertension, obesity, smoking, high cholesterol, coronary heart disease, renal dysfunction and low unsaturated fat intake. Whereas, the key protective factors are considered to be high cognitive activity, low/moderate alcohol consumption and a Mediterranean diet (Deckers et al. 2015). These factors are of significant importance when considering how interventions to reduce risk may be delivered, adhered to and maintained in both the 'at-risk' and the general population.

MAPT (Vellas et al. 2014; Andrieu et al. 2017)

The Multi-domain Alzheimer Preventive trial (MAPT) is a large French clinical trial that includes 1,680 adults aged 70 + who demonstrated early symptoms of memory impairment and cognitive decline, but were at pre-diagnosis. Participants were randomised into 1) an omega-3 supplementation alone group, 2) a multi-domain intervention alone group, 3) an omega-3 plus multi-domain intervention group or 4) a placebo group. Participants underwent cognitive, functional and biological assessments at baseline, and a further four time points (month 6, 12, 24 and 36) and memory function at three years/completion of intervention period was assessed by the Free and Cued Selective Reminding Test. Findings for the primary outcome showed no significant difference in cognition between the four groups. As the mean age of the MAPT population was 75 years, the authors suggest it may have been too late for a preventive intervention of this kind to have an optimal effect. Post-hoc analysis of the MAPT demonstrated that the combination of polyunsaturated fatty acids and multi-domain intervention had potential beneficial effects for individuals in the study. In addition, the intervention intensity used in MAPT was low in terms of content and duration of sessions. Interestingly, but not surprisingly, it was also found that there was reduced adherence to interventions over time, suggesting a potential gap between intentions and actions in this population. Thus, considering ways in which interventions are most easily adhered to may also improve the measurable impact of the intervention.

FINGER (Ngandu 2015)

In the Finnish Geriatric Intervention Study to Prevent Cognitive Impairment and Disability (FINGER), a multi-domain approach intervention was assessed to explore its efficacy in the prevention of cognitive decline in at-risk elderly people taken from the general population (see Chapter 2). This double-blind randomised controlled trial of 2,654 participants aged 60–77 years all with a dementia risk score of at least six points and cognition at mean level or slightly lower than expected for age in the Cardiovascular Risk Factors, Aging and Dementia (CAIDE) scale. Participants were randomly assigned to a two-year, multi-domain intervention, including diet, exercise, cognitive training and vascular risk monitoring, or a control group that received general health advice. A significant between group difference was established suggesting that a multi-domain intervention has the capacity to improve or maintain cognitive functioning in at-risk older adults. As with the MAPT study, there was drop out/non-adherence in 12% of the participant population. Even though this exceptionally low in an intensive intervention of this nature, it does suggest that for some, even where there is intention to take part in the trial and the maintenance of that was difficult to achieve.

PreDIVA (Edo 2009; Charante et al. 2016)

PreDiva is a six-year-long multi-domain vascular care intervention targeting cardiovascular risk factors to prevent dementia (Mollvan et al. 2016). The aim of this study was to establish the impact of the intervention on the prevention of dementia in a population of community-dwelling older people. A total of 3,526 participants were recruited to this open-label, cluster-randomised controlled trial through general practices in the Netherlands. Participants were aged 70–78 years and were randomly assigned to an intervention or control group. Participants in the intervention group visited a practice nurse every four months for a period of six years for an assessment of cardiovascular risk factors, smoking habits, diet, weight, physical activity and blood pressure. Blood glucose and lipid concentrations were assessed every two years. These participants were given tailored advice on the basis of these assessments and supported using motivational interviewing techniques. Participants assigned to the control group received usual care. It was found that the intervention did not result in a reduced incidence of all-cause dementia in this population of older people. The authors argue that absence of any effect may have been caused by modest baseline cardiovascular risks and high standards of usual care. Interestingly, although their overall findings were non-significant, further subgroup analyses did suggest there may be beneficial effects on non-Alzheimer's disease and on all-cause dementia in participants who were adherent to the intervention. This suggests there is an opportunity for dementia prevention where the intention-behaviour gap is minimised and adherence to interventions is realised.

LIBRA model (IN-MINDD study) study (Schiepers et al. 2017)

The 'Lifestyle for Brain Health' (LIBRA) model, was developed to help identify and monitor risk status in dementia prevention programmes, by targeting modifiable, lifestyle-related risk factors. The model, which reflects an individual's potential for dementia prevention, was studied as part of the wider Innovative Midlife Intervention for Dementia Deterrence project (In-MINDD; O'Donnell et al. 2015). The In-MINDD study is a multi-centre, primary care-based, single-blind, randomised controlled feasibility trial currently being conducted in France, Ireland, the Netherlands and the UK. The aim of this wider study is to decrease dementia risk/delay its onset through lifestyle interventions in midlife. Within the LIBRA arm of the trial, Lifestyle for Brain Health was calculated at baseline for a cohort of 949 participants aged 50–81 years. There was a follow-up period of 16 years for dementia and 12 years for incident cognitive impairment and cognitive decline. By using Cox proportional hazard models and testing its relationship with cognitive decline, this study was able to establish a prediction model for late-life risk of dementia based on modifiable risk factors.

What can Health Psychology bring to dementia prevention

Earlier in the chapter, reference to the difference between the behaviour we intend to complete and our actual actions was discussed. This is highlighted in both the existing models of behaviour change and within current dementia research trials that assess the efficacy of multi-domain interventions. Therefore, the existing literature would suggest that there is gap between our intentions and behaviour that would be beneficial to reduce in order to produce the best outcomes possible in dementia prevention/risk reduction. Behavioural intentions can be articulated as self-instructions to perform a particular behaviour or action in order to achieve a particular outcome (e.g. "I intend to exercise three times a week to improve my chances of not developing dementia"). Whilst actions are in part behavioural or situational (e.g. Wood and Neal 2007), forming intentions is also a key aspect of achieving our long-terms goals (e.g. Baumeister and Bargh 2014) and is therefore important to consider when understanding behaviour change theories, models and research.

Despite the shortcoming of the TPB, there is a wealth of evidence that demonstrates that behavioural intentions not only predict behaviour but predict it better than other cognitions, such as attitude, norms and self-efficacy (Sheeran et al. 2017). Hobbs et al. (2013) conducted a systematic review to evaluate the evidence for the effect of behavioural interventions that aim to promote physical activity in adults aged 55–70 years. This review established that such interventions led to long-term improvements in physical activity at 12 months. Albarracin et al. (2005) also found evidence of the effectiveness of behavioural interventions. In conducting an extensive meta-analysis, these authors were able to establish that interventions containing attitudinal arguments, educational information, behavioural skills arguments and behavioural skills training were highly effective in modifying behaviours. Moreover, the impact of the interventions was contingent on the demographics of the target group. As such, it may be useful to situate interventions for dementia prevention within a framework of educational training and to tailor the contents of these to specific age groups, cultures, beliefs and ethnicities in order to see the most benefit.

Although intentions do predict behaviour change with some success, it has been suggested that a medium-to-large intention will only lead to a small to medium sized change in behaviour (Rhodes and Dickau 2012). This may be due to optimistic goal setting, the difficulty of the task to be performed, whether the intention is formed via personal beliefs or from social norms, intention stability ("I am certain I will do this") and stability over time (Sheeran and Webb 2016). As such, intentions only predict behaviours about half of the time suggesting that individuals can find difficulty in initiating, achieving and maintaining their intentions as evidenced in the dementia prevention studies noted earlier. Gollwitzer (1993) suggests that moving an intention into a behaviour requires the development of specific plans as to what an individual will do in a specific environment. Gollwitzer argues that implementation intentions allow individuals to realise their intentions more effectively within a given context. For example, "I intend to eat a balanced diet" is more likely to be translated to "I eat a balanced diet" when implementation intentions are made, e.g. "I intend to start eating a balanced diet tomorrow by adding a banana to my lunchtime meal". Thus, bridging the intention-behaviour gap in dementia prevention may require us to consider the end goal of reducing the risk of dementia as well as making specific plans as to how to achieve this goal, set within the context of a specific time frame and situation.

Encouraging findings are emerging from the Healthy Ageing Throughout Internet Counselling in the Elderly study (HATICE, Richard et al. 2016), an ongoing multinational trial that is due to complete in December 2017. The study has recruited 2,600 participants in the Netherlands, Finland and France aged over 65 years of age and with an increased risk of cardiovascular disease to an 18-month-long internet intervention. Participants who were randomised to the intervention condition have access to a purpose-built interactive internet platform, stimulating self-management of vascular risk factors and remote support from a coach. Participants in the control group have access to a static internet platform that included basic health information only. This type of internet intervention may prove successful in reducing some of the intention-behaviour gap, as it identifies a number of risk factors and allows the participant to view their baseline and set goals and action plans for their own lifestyle. In addition, it includes educational information and a coach to offer support thus addressing many of the issues that individual's may face when attempting to transform intentions into behaviours.

Conclusion

On balance, the existing and ongoing dementia prevention trials have found mixed evidence with regards to the efficacy of multi-domain interventions for use in the prevention of dementia. Although many of these trials include large numbers of participants and are longitudinal in design, they are often confounded by variables, such as good quality care provision in the control condition, identifying the optimal age at which behaviour change may provide optimal results in terms of dementia prevention or non-adherence to the interventions being implemented. However, there are some very positive developments with the FINGER and preDIVA studies as well as the LIBRA model, which has the potential to identify and monitor risk status in dementia prevention programmes and strategies, by targeting modifiable, lifestyle-related risk factors. By combining a model such as LIBRA with behaviour change interventions that target the intention-behaviour gap, there appears to be much potential to reduce the risk of dementia by prioritising lifestyle changes in the middle-aged population.

References

Albarracín, D., Gillette, J. C., Earl, A. N., Glasman, L. R., Durantini, M. R. & Ho, M-H. (2005). A test of major assumptions about behavior change: A comprehensive look at the effects of passive and active HIV-prevention interventions since the beginning of the epidemic. *Psychological Bulletin*, 131(6), 856–897. http://dx.doi.org/10.1037/0033-2909.131.6.856.

Andrieu, Guyonnet, Coley, Cantet, Bonnefoy, Bordes, Bories, Cufi, Dantoine, Dartigues, Desclaux, Gabelle, Gasnier, Pesce, Sudres, Touchon, Robert, Rouaud, Legrand, Payoux, Caubere, Weiner, Carrié, Ousset, Vellas; MAPT Study Group.for the MAPT Study Group. (2017). Effect of long-term omega-3 polyunsaturated fatty acid supplementation with or without multidomain intervention on cognitive function in elderly adults with memory complaints (MAPT): A randomised, placebo-controlled trial. *The Lancet Neurology*, 16(5), 377–389. doi:10.1016/S1474-4422(17)30040-6.

Ashford, K. B. & Rayens, M. K. (2015). Ethnicity, smoking status, and preterm birth as predictors of maternal locus of control, 24(2), 172–187,

Ajzen, I. (1988). Theory of planned behaviour. *Organisational Behaviour and Human Decision Processes*, 50, 179–211.

Bandura, A. (1977). *Social Learning Theory*. Englewood Cliffs, NJ: Prentice Hall, p. 247.

Baumeister, R. F. & Bargh, J. A. (2014). Conscious and unconscious: Toward an integrative understanding of human mental life and action. *In:* Sherman, J. W., Gawronski, B., Trope, Y., Sherman, J. W., Gawronski, B. & Trope, Y. eds. *Dual-Process Theories of the Social Mind*. New York, NY: Guilford Press, 35–49.

Becker, M. H. ed. (1974). The health belief model and personal health behaviour. *Health Education Monographs*, 2, 324–508.

Cameron, D. S., Bertenshaw, E. J. & Sheeran, P. (2017). Positive affect and physical activity: Testing effects on goal setting, activation, prioritisation, and attainment. *Psychology and Health*. 33(2), 258–274.

Charante, E.P.M., Edo, R., Eurelings, L.S., van Dalen, J-W., Ligthart, S.A., van Bussel, E.F., *et al.* (2016). Effectiveness of a 6-year multidomain vascular care intervention to prevent dementia (preDIVA): A cluster-randomised controlled trial. *The Lancet*, 388(10046) (August), 20–26, 797–805.

Conner, M., Gaston, G., Sheeran, P. & Germain, M. (2013). Some feelings are more important: Cognitive attitudes, affective attitudes, anticipated affect, and blood donation. *Health Psychology*, 32, 264–272. doi:10.1037/a0028500.

Connor, M. & Norman, P. (2017). Health behaviour: Current issues and challenges. *Psychology and Health*, 32(8), 895–906. http://dx.doi.org/10.1080/08870446.2017.1336240.

Deckers, K., Van Boxtel, M. P.J., Schiepers, O. J. G., *et al.* (2015). Target risk factors for dementia prevention: A systematic review and Delphi consensus study on the evidence from observational studies. *International Journal of Geriatrics Psychiatry*, 30, 234–246.

Fishbein, M. (Ed.). (1967). *Readings in attitude theory and measurement*. New York: Wiley.

Gochman, D. S. ed. (1997). *Handbook of Health Behavior Research (vols 1–4)*. New York, NY: Plenum.

Gollwitzer, P. M. (1993). Goal Achievement: The Role of Intentions. *European Review of Social Psychology*, 4(1), 141–185. https://doi.org/10.1080/14792779343000059

Heider, F. (1944). Social perception and phenomenal causality. *Psychological Review*, 51, 358–374.

Hobbs, N., Godfrey, A., Lara, J., Errington, L., Meyer, T., Rochester, L. & Sniehotta, F. (2013). Are behavioral interventions effective in increasing physical activity at 12 to 36 months in adults aged 55 to 70 years? A systematic review and meta-analysis. *BMC Medicine*, 11(1), 75.

In-MINDD Team, O'Donnell, C. A., Browne, S., Pierce, M., McConnachie, A., Deckers, K., . . . Irving, K. (2015). Reducing dementia risk by targeting modifiable risk factors in mid-life: study protocol for the Innovative Midlife Intervention for Dementia Deterrence

(In-MINDD) randomised controlled feasibility trial. *Pilot and Feasibility Studies*, 1(1). https://doi.org/10.1186/s40814-015-0035-x

Janz, N. K., & Becker, M. H. (1984). The Health Belief Model: a decade later. *Health Education Quarterly*, 11(1), 1–47. https://doi.org/10.1177/109019818401100101

Johnston, M. (1994). Current trends in health psychology. *The Psychologist*, 7, 114–118.

Kelley. (1967, 1971). Leventhal, H., Rabin, C., Leventhal, E. A. & Burns, E. (2001). Health risk behaviours and ageing. *In:* Birren, J. E. & Schaie, K. W. eds. *Handbook of the Psychology of Ageing*, 5th edn. San Diego, CA: Academic Press, 186–214.

Lynch, A. D., Coley, R. C., Sims, J., Lombardi, C. M. & Mahalik, J. R. (2015). Direct and interactive effects of parent, friend and schoolmate drinking on alcohol use trajectories. *Psychology & Health*, 30, 1183–1205. doi:10.1080/08870446.2015.1040017 [Taylor & Francis Online].

Ngandu, T., Lehtisalo, J., Solomon, A., Levälahti, E., Ahtiluoto, S., Antikainen, R., Bäckman, L., Hänninen, T., Jula, A., Laatikainen, T., Lindström, J., Mangialasche, F., Paajanen, T., Pajala, S., Peltonen, M., Rauramaa, R., Stigsdotter-Neely, A., Strandberg, T., Tuomilehto, J., Soininen, H. & Kivipelto, M. (2015). A 2 year multidomain intervention of diet, exercise, cognitive training, and vascular risk monitoring versus control to prevent cognitive decline in at-risk elderly people (FINGER): A randomised controlled trial. *The Lancet*, 385(9984) (6–12 June), 2255–2263. doi.org/10.1016/S0140-6736(15)60461-5.

Prevention of Alzheimer's disease: An analysis of population-based data. *The Lancet Neurology*, 13, 788–794.

Ogden, J. (2012). *Health Psychology: A Textbook*, 5th edn. Maidenhead Berkshire England: Open University Press Hill House Shoppenhangers Road.

Orbell, S. & Sheeran, P. (1998). 'Inclined abstainers': A problem for predicting health-related behaviour. *British Journal of Social Psychology*, 37, 151–165. doi:10.1111/j.2044-8309.1998.tb01162.x.

Prochska, J. O. & DiClemente, C. C. (1982). Transtheoretical therapy: Toward a more integrative model of change. *Psychotherapy: Theory Research and Practice*, 19, 276–288.

Rhodes, R. E. & Dickau, L. (2012). Experimental evidence for the intention – behavior relationship in the physical activity domain: A meta-analysis. *Health Psychology*, 31(6), 724–727. doi:10.1037/a0027290.

Rhodes, R., Janssen, I., Bredin, S., Warburton, D. & Bauman, A. (2017). Physical activity: Health impact, prevalence, correlates and interventions. *Psychology & Health*, 32, 942–975. doi:10.1080/08870446.2017.1325486 [Taylor & Francis Online].

Richard, E., den Heuvel, Esther Van, Moll van Charante, Eric P., Achthoven, Lenny, Vermeulen, Marinus, Bindels, Patrick J, Van Gool, Willem A. (2009). Prevention of Dementia by Intensive Vascular Care (PreDIVA): A cluster-randomized trial in progress *Alzheimer disease & associated disorders*: July–September, 23(3), 198–204. doi:10.1097/WAD.0b013e31819783a4

Richard, E., Jongstra, S., Soininen, H., Brayne, C., Moll van Charante, E. P., Meiller, Y., van der Groep, B., Beishuizen, Cathrien R. L., Mangialasche, F., Barbera, M., Ngandu, T., Coley, N., Guillemont, J., Savy, S., Dijkgraaf, M. G. W., Peters, R. J. G., van Gool, W. A., Kivipelto, M. & Andrieu1, S. (2016). Healthy ageing through internet counselling in the elderly: The HATICE randomised controlled trial for the prevention of cardiovascular disease and cognitive impairment. *BMJ*, 6(6).

Rosenstock, I. M. (1966). Why people use health services. *Millbank Memorial Fund Quarterly*, 44, 94–124.

Schiepers, O. J., Köhler, Deckers, Irving, O'Donnell, van den Akker, Verhey, Vos, de Vugt & van Boxtel, M. P. (2017). Lifestyle for Brain Health (LIBRA): A new model for dementia prevention. *International Journal of Geriatrics Psychiatry*, (February 28). doi:10.1002/gps.4700. [Epub ahead of print]

Sheeran, P., Godin, G., Conner, M. & Germain, G. (2017). Paradoxical effects of experience: Past behavior both strengthens and weakens the intention – behavior relationship. *Journal of the Association for Consumer Behavior*. 2(3) doi:https://doi.org/10.1086/691216

Sheeran, P. & Webb, T. L. (2016). The Intention-Behaviour gap. *Social and Personality Psychology Compass*. 10(9), 503–518.

Schwarzer, R. (2008). Modelling health behaviour change: How to predict and modify the adoption and maintenance of health behaviours. *Applied Psychology*, 57(1), 1–20.

Sniehotta, F. F., Presseau, J., & Araújo-Soares, V. (2014). Time to retire the theory of planned behaviour. *Health Psychology Review*, 8(1), 1–7. https://doi.org/10.1080/17437199.2013.869710

Vellas, B., Carrie, I., Gillette-Guyonnet, S., Touchon, J., Dantoine, T., Dartigues, J. F., Cuffi, M. N., Bordes, S., Gasnier, Y., Robert, P., Bories, L., Rouaud, O., Desclaux, F., Sudres, K., Bonnefoy, M., Pesce, A., Dufouil, C., Lehericy, S., Chupin, M., Mangin, J. F., Payoux, P., Adel, D., Legrand, P., Catheline, D., Kanony, C., Zaim, M., Molinier, L., Costa, N., Delrieu, J., Voisin, T., Faisant, C., Lala, F., Nourhashémi, F., Rolland, Y., Abellan Van Kan, G., Dupuy, C., Cantet, C., Cestac, P., Belleville, S., Willis, S., Cesari, M., Weiner, M. W., Soto, M. E., Ousset, P. J. & Andrieu, S. (2014), Mapt study: A multidomain approach for preventing Alzheimer's disease: Design and baseline data. *The Journal of Prevention of Alzheimer's Disease*, 1(1), 13–22.

Wallston, K. A. & Wallston, B. S. (1982). Who is responsible for your health? The construct of health locus of control. *In:* Sanders, G. S. & Suls, J. eds. *Social Psychology of Health and Illness*. Hillsdale, NJ: Erlbaum, 65–95.

Weinsten, N. (1983). Reducing unrealistic optimism about illness susceptibility. *Health Psychology*, 3, 431–457.

Weinstein, N. (1987). Unrealistic optimism about illness susceptibility: Conclusions from a community wide sample. *Journal of Behavioural Medicine*, 10, 481–500.

Wood, W. & Neal, D. T. (2007). A new look at habits and the habit-goal interface. *Psychological Review*, 114(4), 843–863. doi:10.1037/0033-295X.114.4.843.

Section 2

Social, political and economic aspects

In the following section, social, political and economic aspects of dementia prevention are discussed. Chapter 9 reviews and compares international dementia prevention policies. Chapter 10 focuses on changing practice in primary care to include dementia prevention. Chapter 11 and 12 discuss the economics of dementia prevention and methodological issues in outcome assessment (Chapter 11) and modelling of cost-effectiveness (Chapter 12). Chapter 13 offers the *cognitive footprint framework*, which can be used within current economic evaluations to guide public policy. Lastly, Chapter 14 concludes this book, bringing together the different strands, from lifestyle and disease-based risk factors to behavioral and societal cost-effective change, to guide implementation of research findings into policies to prevent dementia.

Chapter 9

Existing and future health policy in dementia prevention

Maria Pierce

Introduction

It is estimated that there are about 46.8 million people with dementia worldwide, and this number is expected to reach 74.7 million in 2030 (Prince et al. 2015). Dementia is a very costly public health issue and because of the high personal, social and economic costs associated with dementia, preventing or delaying its onset would be hugely beneficial for ageing societies. The global costs of dementia have been estimated at US$604 billion in 2015, a 35% increase on 2010, much of which is concentrated in high-income countries (Prince et al. 2015). There are concerns that, in the absence of curative treatments, the global cost of dementia will rise if improved practices of prevention (as well as improved practices of care and treatment) are not developed and implemented. It is in this context that this chapter examines existing and future policy on prevention of dementia.

This chapter begins with a review of dementia prevention on the current international policy agenda, its transformation over a decade and the factors that have contributed to its transformation. An increasing number of countries around the world have now developed a national dementia strategy and this number continues to grow apace. In some countries, most notably France and Australia, national policy on dementia preceded and indeed played some part in shaping international policy on dementia. Governments around the world are now encouraged to identify dementia risk reduction as a priority area of action and introduce measures to counter risk factors for dementia. This chapter next examines the extent to which primary prevention of dementia has been identified as a priority area of action in national dementia strategies and what it looks like when incorporated. With an emphasis in international policy on the risk/protective factors for dementia that are shared with other non-communicable diseases, one cost-effective way for governments is to incorporate dementia into health promotion policies and campaigns relating to other non-communicable diseases, and the individual risk factors that these diseases share. This chapter examines the potential for greater alignment between dementia risk reduction and health promotion policy, drawing on a review of health promotion policy in two countries. Positive indications from several studies are that some higher-income countries are starting to witness a decline in the incidence of dementia, attributed in large part to better education and healthier lifestyles. However, the benefits from risk reduction are not evenly spread, and the final section of the chapter argues that the associations between risk factors for dementia and social inequalities need to become a real concern for governments.

Dementia prevention on the international policy agenda

In 2017, the World Health Organization launched the Global Action Plan on the Public Health Response to Dementia (WHO 2017). Prevention of dementia is at the heart of the WHO Plan, which envisions 'a world in which *dementia is prevented* and people with dementia and their carers live well and receive the care and support they need to fulfil their potential with dignity, respect, autonomy and equality' (p. 4). Metaphorically speaking, dementia prevention now has a leading part on the world stage, less than 10 years on from when dementia prevention was first mooted in dementia policy at a supranational level.

Policy at European Union (EU) level offers a case in point. Alzheimer's disease and the other dementias began to be identified as a domain of importance in the latter part of the 1990s and was recognized by each of the three main institutions of the European Community – the Commission, the Parliament and the Council. However, it was not until 2009 when the European Commission presented a *Communication on a European Initiative on Alzheimer's disease and the other dementias* that prevention of dementia was identified as one of the key issues where coordinated action at Community level on dementia was needed (European Commission 2009). It noted that 'people can act to help prevent dementia, especially vascular dementia and in some extent also Alzheimer's disease'. At the same time, it highlighted a lack of awareness of the importance of prevention throughout the EU.

Demographic and socio-economic factors (i.e. population ageing and the commensurate growth in the number of people with dementia together with the estimated social and economic costs associated with dementia, particularly in the area of health and social care) have likely helped concentrate the minds of policymakers and led to a greater focus in dementia policy on possible action that can be taken to reduce the number of people who develop dementia across the world. However, the contribution of a range of other major influences on the shaping of supranational policy on dementia prevention also needs to be acknowledged. The last decade has seen European and international dementia advocacy organizations seeking to influence dementia policy. In the Paris Declaration of 2006, Alzheimer Europe and its member organizations called on the EU and the WHO to recognize dementia as major public health issue and among its political priorities was a call to foster pan-European research into the causes, *prevention* and treatment of dementia (Alzheimer Europe 2009). A key influencer on the world stage has been the international non-governmental organization

(NGO), Alzheimer Disease International, which has a core belief in the possibility that the risk of developing dementia at a population level can be reduced. In its official relations with the WHO, the ADI and the WHO jointly developed the report *Dementia: A Public Health Priority*, which promotes the message that dementia may be prevented through increased adoption and more effective implementation of public health strategies, such as those focused on detecting and treating diabetes and hypertension, reducing obesity levels, smoking cessation, increasing physical activity and better education (WHO 2012). Echoing the WHO, the G8 Dementia Summit Declaration called upon all sectors to enhance their contribution to dementia care and prevention (G8 2013).

The framing of dementia as 'the greatest global challenge for health and social care in the 21st century' (see, for example, Livingston et al. 2017) and the accumulating evidence showing that people may be able to reduce their risk of dementia has had a diffuse and indirect influence on the incorporation of dementia prevention into international policy. Over the past decade, systematic reviews of observational studies and of randomized controlled trials (Kloppenborg et al. 2008; Plassman et al. 2010) have identified a range of modifiable risk factors that play a role in exacerbating, or reducing, a person's risk of developing dementia in later life. Likewise, Deckers et al. (2015), combining a review of observational studies with a Delphi consensus study, identified target risk factors for dementia prevention. Depression, midlife obesity, high cholesterol, midlife hypertension, diabetes, physical inactivity and smoking are associated with an increased risk of developing dementia in later life, with evidence relating to diet, cognitive activity, coronary heart disease and renal dysfunction being less conclusive.

The 2014 World Alzheimer Report (WAR), which critically examines the evidence for the existence of modifiable risk factors for dementia (Prince et al. 2014a), has formed the basis of the ADI's campaign for change. More recently, the publication in 2017 of an authoritative report on dementia prevention, intervention and care commissioned by the prestigious Lancet Commission has extended existing models of risk to include hearing loss (Livingston et al. 2017). Like the 2014 WAR, it too proposes a life-course model of risk. Using this model and building on previous studies calculating the population attributable risk associated with modifiable risk factors for dementia (Barnes and Yaffe 2011), Livingston et al. (2017) have calculated that it might theoretically be possible to prevent a third of cases of dementia through the elimination of the most potent modifiable risk factors. The key message of this expert project, which captured attention globally, is to 'be ambitious about prevention'.

Dementia prevention in national dementia strategies

Many countries across the world now have a national dementia strategy in place or have developed a neurodegenerative disease strategy, with some already on their second, third or fourth iteration. It is not immediately evident how many countries have included dementia risk reduction as a priority area of action in their national dementia strategies. However, the Global Dementia Observatory[1] has begun, in its profile of countries, to identify those with the inclusion of dementia risk reduction as a specific action of the dementia plan. All 13 countries with a national dementia strategy so far profiled by the Observatory were identified positively on this indicator. For example, in Australia's National Framework for Action on Dementia 2015–2019, reducing dementia risk is identified in the first of seven priority areas of action, i.e. increasing awareness and reduction risk (AHMAC 2015). With these 13 countries hailing from a range of WHO regions, dementia prevention is no longer the preserve of Western industrialized economies.

In national dementia strategies where there is a focus on risk reduction, it is common to find reference to increasing public awareness of risk factors for dementia. Several studies have found the public's knowledge of risk factors for dementia to be poor (Cahill et al. 2015), and in this context, the logic underpinning this discourse is that if the general public were to become better informed about modifiable risk factors for dementia, then they would be better equipped to take advantage of opportunities to reduce their risk of developing dementia.

The importance of having information on risk reduction that is evidence-based and on promoting research to better understand risk factors is also emphasized in many national dementia strategies. While there is now compelling evidence on modifiable risk factors for dementia, the challenge for governments is that there is still insufficient evidence to recommend specific interventions to reduce dementia risk. This may explain why in some countries, for example Scotland, now on its third national dementia strategy (Scottish Government 2017), dementia risk reduction has not been identified as a priority area of action. In other countries, though, a strong emphasis on promoting research to identify risk reduction strategies can be found in their national dementia strategies, e.g. Australia and the Netherlands (AHMAC 2015; Ministry of VWS 2013). For example, one of the goals of Memorabel, the dementia research and innovation programme of the Dutch Deltaplan (Ministry of VWS 2013), is to generate knowledge that might help reduce the future prevalence of dementia by facilitating state of the art research that would provide a better understanding of how to prevent it in addition to how it occurs (ZonMW 2013).

Even where people are aware of the risk factors for dementia, people do not always find it easy to make and sustain health behaviour change (see Chapter 8). However, prevention of dementia is not simply a matter of changing individual behaviour. As Scrambler (2012) points out, people's health behaviours are often anchored in their culture and in their social and economic circumstances and risk behaviours associated in part with material disadvantage and deprivation. Therefore, as well as encouraging people to change their behaviour, broader changes are also needed in social, economic, environmental and cultural contexts. Furthermore, despite the growing consensus that a life-course approach to dementia prevention is needed (Prince et al. 2014a; Livingston et al. 2017), a life-course approach to risk factors for dementia has found its way into few national dementia strategies. One notable exception is Finland's National Memory Programme 2012–2020, which identifies brain health as a lifelong concern (Finnish Ministry of Social Affairs and Health 2013).

Health promotion policies and the links between modifiable risk factors and dementia

So far in this chapter, it has been seen that governments around the world are being encouraged to identify primary prevention of dementia as a priority area of action and develop measures to counter risk factors for dementia. A key development at international policy level is the recognition of a clear overlap between modifiable risk/protective factors for dementia and risk/protective factors for other chronic diseases, such as cardiovascular disease and diabetes. This is illustrated by the declaration of the high-level meeting of the 66th UN General Assembly on the Prevention and Control of NCDs (UN 2011) and its follow-up document, the WHO global action plan for the prevention and control of NCDs 2013–2020 (WHO 2013), both of which highlight the four major risk factors – tobacco use, physical inactivity, the harmful use of alcohol and unhealthy diets – which are important drivers of the rise of NCDs, including dementia.

The overlap between modifiable risk factors for dementia and those for other non-communicable diseases is recognized in some national dementia strategies, including Australia and England (AHMAC 2015; Department of Health 2009). Dementia prevention programmes, such as the Your Brain Matters Program developed in Australia, the world's first publicly funded dementia prevention program, promotes the message that what's good for your health generally is good for your brain.[2]

Alongside national dementia strategies, many countries around the world, particularly those in higher-income countries, will already have existing health promotion policies to address cardiovascular disease and diabetes and to address individual risk factors for these diseases. Policy aimed at improving health in these domains is generally well developed and public awareness of the importance of lifestyle changes to prevent cardiovascular disease is high. However, as mentioned earlier, public awareness of the role that many of the same risk factors play in the promotion of brain health and the prevention of dementia is low and needs to be highlighted. It is not evident that the relevant health promotion policy that currently exists (e.g. in the domains of cardiovascular health, smoking, alcohol, physical activity, diet and nutrition) has been informed by evidence from research on modifiable risk factors for dementia or if it promotes the message that dementia can be delayed by lifestyle changes.

A review of health promotion policies in two countries, Scotland and Ireland, both with a national dementia strategy in place, can serve to illustrate this. Both countries have an overarching health promotion policy in place, Scotland since 2007 and Ireland since 2013, which mention many of the risk/protective factors associated with dementia, including alcohol, obesity, diabetes, physical inactivity, cholesterol, blood pressure, smoking, heart disease, depression and unhealthy diets and their role as risk/protective factors linked to chronic disease. However, neither includes any mention of the links between the risk/protective factors mentioned and dementia or the message that lifestyle changes can delay the onset of dementia (Pierce et al. 2014).

Similarly, for the Republic of Ireland and Scotland, when specific national level strategies, frameworks, action plans for a range of modifiable risk/protective factors including alcohol, physical activity, smoking, obesity and healthy diet are reviewed, the vast majority make no mention of the links between modifiable risk factors and dementia, nor include the message that lifestyle changes can delay the onset of dementia. This is also the case with respect to national policy or action plans on cardiovascular disease or heart health, which address the risk factors of cholesterol, hypertension and heart disease, and with respect to diabetes and strategic frameworks on renal services. The one exception is Ireland's mental health strategy, *A Vision for Change*. It highlights that Alzheimer's disease shares many of the same risk factors as cardiovascular disease. It states, 'As far as the stroke-related organic conditions of vascular origin and Alzheimer's dementia are concerned, the health promotion message is the same as that for preventing cardiovascular disease generally' (Department of Health and Children 2006, p. 117). However, there is no mention of depression as a risk factor for dementia, even though the mental health strategy includes a focus on promoting psychological well-being (Pierce et al. 2014).

Despite strong evidence on the links between modifiable risk factors and dementia, this evidence has not yet been incorporated into relevant health promotion policy documents, at least in Scotland and the Republic of Ireland. Yet, this offers governments a cost-effective way of capitalizing on existing policy to address the challenge of dementia in ageing societies and links dementia with health promotion policies and campaigns on risk reduction for other non-communicable diseases.

Health and social inequalities: an important consideration in dementia prevention

There are positive indications from several higher-income countries that incidence of dementia may be declining slowly over time (Langa et al. 2017; Manton et al. 2005; Matthews et al. 2013). For example, Matthews et al. (2013) in their study comparing prevalence of dementia in cohorts of older adults two decades apart in England found evidence that people in the more recently born cohort had a lower risk of dementia than those born earlier. The potential fall in the risk of dementia in older adults in higher-income countries may be due to better education with each generation, and the general trend in higher-income countries towards less smoking, better control of cardiovascular risk factors such as high cholesterol and hypertension, and increasing physical activity (Manton et al. 2005; Schrijvers et al. 2012; Matthews et al. 2013; Prince et al. 2015).

It cannot be assumed, however, that the trend towards falling incidence of dementia will be uniformly spread within countries as, unfortunately, evidence shows that 'the enjoyment of good health is most unequally spread' (Marmot 2015, p. 22). In the UK, variation in dementia prevalence across different areas of deprivation (Matthews et al. 2013) suggests that health inequalities over the life course may influence an older person's risk of developing dementia and that people living in more affluent areas will have benefited more than others from reduction in risk.

Numerous studies have found that low educational attainment is associated with increased risk of dementia, as is low income (Valenzuela and Sachdev 2006). Scazufca et al. (2008) found a higher prevalence of dementia among older people from poor socio-economic backgrounds in Brazil, attributed in part to low education and income. In addition, smoking, midlife hypertension and physical inactivity, all risk factors for dementia, are more common in people who are financially and educationally worse off (Cronin et al. 2011; Marmot 2010). It does not seem surprising, therefore, that people living in areas of greatest deprivation have been shown to have the highest risk of developing cognitive dysfunction (McNulty et al. 2014; McCann et al. 2018).

Despite promising trends showing a decline in incidence of dementia in some higher-income countries, there is concern that gains made as a result of an active public health approach to risk reduction will be offset by rising levels of obesity and diabetes (Prince et al. 2014a). Both of these dementia risk factors are also associated with socio-economic disparities. Many lower and middle-income countries are witnessing quite different trends to the higher-income countries. Increasing rates of stroke and cardiovascular disease, linked to obesity and increasing blood pressure levels, could potentially lead to increasing incidence of dementia in these countries (Prince et al. 2014a).

Two of the cross-cutting principles of the Global Action Plan on a Public Health Response to Dementia refer to social inequalities (WHO 2017). The first promotes equitable access to relevant services, including preventive services. The second cross-cutting principle referring to social inequalities is the principle of equity, emphasizing that all public health responses to dementia must support gender equity and 'vulnerable' people, 'specific to each national context'. These principles are significant. The distribution and prevalence of modifiable risk factors for dementia vary not only by age but also by sex and ethnicity. For example, rates of hypertension, high cholesterol and diabetes are higher in women aged over 75 years when compared with men of a similar age (Azad et al. 2007) and hypertension, diabetes, and heart disease are consistently high among people from several black, Asian and minority ethnic backgrounds (Prince et al. 2014b).

Future directions

Over a span of 10 years, dementia risk reduction has moved from a muted position and risen right up the international policy agenda where it now holds an unequivocal position. There is a discernible shift to a more even balance between dementia prevention, cure and care. Indeed, at the First WHO Ministerial Conference on Global Action Against Dementia in 2015, 'balancing prevention, risk reduction, care and cure' was identified as one of the overarching principles and approaches integral to global efforts required to promote action on dementia. It came with a stark reminder though that directing efforts towards finding effective treatments and practices and risk reduction interventions must not happen at the cost of making continuous improvements on care for people living with dementia and support for their caregivers. Nevertheless, a space has opened up for dementia prevention and, with the message loud and clear from the Lancet Commission, policymakers at international and national levels have been given the go-ahead to be ambitious about dementia prevention.

Evidence on modifiable risk factors suggests that a shift is needed so that the focus of interventions is on adults in midlife as well as older adults (Deckers et al. 2015). However, there is a growing consensus that a life-course approach to dementia prevention is needed (Livingston et al. 2017; Prince et al. 2014a). Being ambitious about dementia prevention requires that there is a focus on what happens during the earlier years of life. This is because what happens during the early years of life can have lifelong effects on many aspects of health and well-being including obesity, heart disease, mental health, educational achievement and economic status (Marmot 2010), all of which are associated with the development of dementia.

Prevention of dementia is included as a priority area of action in many national dementia strategies. Much less attention is given to potential for health promotion policy and activities to publicize the message that making and sustaining changes in lifestyle behaviours can reduce the risk of developing dementia in later life. This is a potentially cost-effective way of motivating individuals to change their health behaviours. However, being ambitious about dementia means not simply focusing on individuals and their lifestyle behaviours; it is also about creating and developing healthy places and communities in which people can live.

Achieving a goal of preventing or delaying the onset of dementia requires not only interventions to target particular risk factors for dementia, but also a broad focus on social inequalities. Dementia risk reduction policies and programs that are accessible to disadvantaged people, throughout the life course, must be implemented as a matter of urgency to cater for the needs of this population in both lower and higher-income countries. It is important that dementia risk reduction address all socially determined aspects of health through policy and that the association between risk factors for dementia and socio-economic status becomes a real concern. Through the promotion of integrated approaches to reducing health inequalities to address dementia risk reduction in disadvantaged communities at particularly high risk, there is potential for real gains to be made leading to a significant reduction in the prevalence of dementia across the world.

Conclusion

The chapter has reviewed dementia prevention on the international policy agenda and shown that it is now at the heart of international dementia policy, the culmination of 10 years of developing a collective understanding of – and enacting knowledge about – dementia prevention. Governments have begun to include dementia risk reduction as a specific action in national dementia strategies, so much so that dementia prevention is no longer the preserve of Western industrialized economies. National dementia strategies place an emphasis, to varying degrees, on public awareness of dementia risk factors for dementia, developing an evidence base and promoting research to better understand risk factors for dementia, with some countries going so far as to allocate public funds for dementia prevention programmes. Governments now have an opportunity to incorporate the strong evidence on the links between modifiable risk factors and dementia into a range of relevant health promotion policy documents. This offers a cost-effective way of capitalizing on existing policy to address the challenge of dementia in ageing societies and to link dementia with health promotion policies and campaigns on risk reduction for other non-communicable diseases. There are promising trends showing a decline in incidence of dementia in some higher-income countries, but the different trends in lower and middle-income countries are concerning, as is the evidence showing that modifiable risk factors for dementia are associated with socio-economic disparities. As health in old age is affected by inequalities across life course, more governments need to focus attention on brain health as a lifelong concern and implement dementia prevention programmes that are accessible to disadvantaged groups, throughout the life course.

Notes

1 World Health Organization. Global Dementia Observatory (GBO). Available at: http://apps.who.int/gho/data/node.dementia [accessed: 15 February 2018].
2 Dementia Collaborative Research Centres. Your Brain Matters. Available at: https://yourbrainmatters.org.au/your-brain-matters [accessed: 17 August 2018]

References

Alzheimer Europe. (2009). *Paris declaration – 2006*. [online] Available at: www.Alzheimer-europe.org/Policy-in-Practice2/Paris-Declaration-2006 [Accessed 15 February 2018].

Australian Health Ministers Advisory Council. (2015). *National Framework for Action on Dementia* 2015–2019. Australia: Department of Social Services. Available at: https://agedcare.health.gov.au/ageing-and-aged-care-older-people-their-families-and-carers-dementia/national-framework-for-action-on-dementia-2015–2019 [accessed 17 August 2018]

Azad, N. A., Al Bugami, M. & Loy-English, I. (2007). Gender differences in dementia risk factors. *Gender Medicine*, 4(2), 120–129.

Barnes, D. E. & Yaffe, K.Y. (2011). The projected effect of risk factor reduction on Alzheimer's disease prevalence. *The Lancet Neurology*, 10, 819–828.

Cahill, S., Pierce, M., Werner, P, Darley, A. & Bobersky, A. (2015). A systematic review of the public's knowledge and understanding of Alzheimer's disease and dementia. *Alzheimer Disease and Associated Disorders*, 29(3), 255–275.

Cronin, H., O'Regan, C. & Kenny, R. A. (2011). Physical and behavioural health of older Irish adults. *In:* Barrett, A., Savva, G., Timonen, V. & Kenny, R. A. eds. *Fifty Plus in Ireland 2011: First Results from The Irish Longitudinal Study on Ageing*. Dublin: TILDA, 73–154.

Deckers, K., van Boxtel, M. P. J., Schiepers, O. J. G., de Vugt, M., Muñoz Sánchez, J. L., Anstey, K. J., Brayne, C., Dartigues, J., Engedal, K., Kivipelto, M., Ritchie, K., Starr, J. M., Yaffe, K., Irving, K., Verhey, F. R. J. & Köhler, S. (2015). Target risk factors for dementia prevention: A systematic review and Delphi consensus study on the evidence from observational studies. *International Journal of Geriatric Psychiatry*, 30(3), 234–246.

Department of Health. (2009). *Living Well with Dementia: A National Dementia Strategy*. London: Department of Health.

Department of Health and Children. (2006). *A Vision for Change: Report of the Expert Group on Mental Health Policy*. Dublin: Department of Health and Children.

European Commission. (2009). Communication from the Commission COM (2009) 380/4 of 22.07.2009 to the European Parliament and the Council on a European initiative on Alzheimer's disease and other dementias.

Finnish Ministry of Social Affairs and Health. (2013). *National Memory Programme 2012–2020: Creating a "Memory Friendly" Finland*. Helsinki: Finnish Ministry of Social Affairs and Health.

G8. (2013). *G8 Dementia summit declaration*. Policy paper published on 11 December 2013 by the Department of Health. Available at: www.gov.uk/government/publications/g8-dementia-summit-agreements/g8-dementia-summit-declaration [Accessed 15 February 2018].

Kloppenborg, R. P., van den Berg, E., Kappelle, L. J. & Biessels, G. J. (2008). Diabetes and other vascular risk factors for dementia: Which factor matters most? A systematic review. *European Journal of Pharmacology*, 585, 97–108.

Langa K. M., Larson E. B., Crimmins E. M., et al. (2017). A comparison of the prevalence of dementia in the United States in 2000 and 2012. *JAMA Internal Medicine*. 177(1), 51–58. doi:10.1001/jamainternmed.2016.6807.

Livingston, G., Sommerlad, A., Orgeta, V., Costafreda, S. G., Huntley, J., Ames, D., Ballard, C., Banerjee, S., Burns, A., Cohen-Mansfield, J., Cooper, C., Fox, N., Gitlin, L. N., Howard, R., Kales, H. C., Larson, E. B., Richie, K., Rockwood, K., Sampson, E. L., Samus, Q., Schneider, L. S., Selbæk, G., Teri, L. & Mukadam, N. (2017). Dementia prevention, intervention and care. *The Lancet*, 390(11113), 2673–2734.

Matthews, F., Author, A., Barnes, L., Bond, J., Jagger, C., Robinson, L. & Brayne, C. & On behalf of the Medical Research Council Cognitive Function and Ageing Collaboration. (2013). A two-decade comparison of prevalence of dementia in individuals aged 65 years and older from three geographical areas of England: Results of the Cognitive Function and Ageing Study I and II. *The Lancet*, 382(9902), 1405–1412. http://dx.doi.org/10.1016/S0140-6736(13)61570-6.

Manton, K., Gu, X. & Ukraintseva, S. (2005). Declining prevalence of dementia in the US elderly population. *Advances in Gerontology = Uspekhi gerontologii*, 16, 30–37.

Marmot, M. (2010). *Fair Society, Healthy Lives: The Marmot Review*. London: The Marmot Review. Available at: www.instituteofhealthequity.org/Content/FileManager/pdf/fairsocietyhealthylives.pdf. [Accessed 6 January 2015].

Marmot, M. (2015). *The Health Gap: The Challenge of an Unequal World*. London: Bloomsbury.

McCann, A., McNulty, H., Rigby, J., Hughes, C. F., Hoey, L., Molloy, A. M., Cunningham, C. J., Casey, M. C., Tracey, F., O'Kane, M. J., McCarroll, K., Ward, M., Moore, K., Strain, J. J. & Moore, A. (2018). Effect of area level socioeconomic deprivation on risk of cognitive dysfunction in older adults. *Journal of the American Geriatrics Society*, [online]. http://dx.doi.org/10.1111/jgs.15258 [Accessed 12 March 2018].

McNulty, H., McCann, A., Moore, A., Hoey, L., Molloy, A. & Rogby, J. (2014). *Socioeconomic Deprivation and Risk of Age-Related Cognitive Dysfunction: Results from the TILDA Ageing Cohort Study*. Belfast: Centre for Ageing Research and Development in Ireland.

Ministry of VWS. (2013). *Deltaplan Dementie 2012–2020*. Available at: www.rijksoverheid.nl/documenten/rapporten/2013/04/04/rapport-deltaplan-dementie [Accessed 15 February 2018].

Pierce, M., Browne, S., Mattock, M., Irving, K. & O'Donnell, C. (2014). *Prevention of Dementia: Potential for Alignment with Health Promotion Policy*, 24th Alzheimer Europe Conference "Autonomy and dignity in dementia", Glasgow, Scotland, UK, 20–22 October.

Plassman, B. L., Williams, J. W., Burke, J. R., Holsinger, T. & Benjamin, S. (2010). Systematic review: Factors associated with risk for and possible prevention of cognitive decline in later life. *Annals of Internal Medicine*, 153, 182–193.

Prince, M., Albanese, E., Guerchet, M. & Prina, M. (2014a). *World Alzheimer Report 2014 Dementia and Risk Reduction: An Analysis of Protective and Modifiable Factors*. London: Alzheimer Disease International (ADI).

Prince, M., Knapp, M., Guerchet, M., McCrone, P., Prina, M., Comas-Herrera, A., Wittenberg, R., Adelaja, B., Hu, B., King, D., Rehill, A. & Salimkumar, D. (2014b). *Dementia UK: Update*. London: Alzheimer Society.

Prince, M., Wimo, A., Guerchet, M., Ali, G-C., W, Y-T. & Prina, M. (2015). *World Alzheimer Report 2015, The Global Impact of Dementia: An Analysis of Prevalence, Incidence, Cost and Trends*. London: Alzheimer Disease International (ADI).

Scazufca, M., Menezes, P. R., Vallada, H. P., Crepaldi, A. L., Pastor-Valero, M., Coutinho, L. M. S., Di Rienzo, V. D. & Almeida, O. P. (2008). High prevalence of dementia among older adults from poor socioeconomic backgrounds in Sao Paulo, Brazil. *International Psychogeriatrics*, 20(2), 394–405.

Schrijvers, E. M., Verhaaren, B. F., Koudstall, P. J., Hofman, A., Ikram, M. A. & Breteler, M. M. (2012). Is dementia incidence declining? Trends in dementia incidence since 1990 in the Rotterdam study. *Neurology*, 78, 1456–1463.

Scottish Government. (2017). *Scotland's National Dementia Strategy 2017–2020*. Edinburgh: The Scottish Government.

Scrambler, G. (2012). Health inequalities. *Sociology of Health & Illness*, 34(1), 130–146.

United Nations. (2011). *United Nations General Assembly Resolution 66/2: Political Declaration of the High-Level Meeting of the General Assembly on the prevention and Control of Non-Communicable Diseases*. Available at: www.un.org/en/ga/search/view_doc.asp?symbol=A/RES/66/2 [Accessed 9 February 2018].

Valenzuela, M. J. & Sachdev, P. (2006). Brain reserve and dementia: A systematic review. *Psychological Medicine*, 36, 441–454.

WHO. (2012). *Dementia: A Public Health Priority*. Geneva: World Health Organization.

WHO. (2013). *Global Action Plan for the Prevention and Control of Noncommunicable Diseases 2013–2020*. Geneva: World Health Organization.

WHO. (2017). *Global Action Plan on the Public Health Response to Dementia 2017–2025*. Geneva: World Health Organization.

ZonMW. (2013). *Memorabel: Programmavoorstel Onderzoeks- en Innovatieprogramma Dementie*. Den Haag: ZonMW. Available at: www.zonmw.nl/uploads/tx_vipublicaties/programmatekst_memorabel_def_met_omslagen.pdf [Accessed 15 February 2018].

Chapter 10

Changing practice in primary care

Hamish Foster and Catherine A O'Donnell

Introduction

Dementia is a growing healthcare challenge internationally. In 2015, almost 50 million people worldwide had a diagnosis of dementia; this is projected to increase to 75 million by 2030 and 132 million by 2050 (Prince et al. 2015). The scale of dementia prevalence, coupled with its rapid increase in low and middle-income countries, means dementia is now considered a major public health challenge (Williamson 2015; Frankish and Horton 2017).

While much of the focus has been on diagnosis, post-diagnostic support and palliative treatment, viewing dementia as a public health priority shifts the balance towards thinking about dementia in terms of prevention. Dementia can be described as a 'clinically silent disorder' beginning in mid-life, around 40–65 years old, with the manifestation of symptoms in later life viewed as a terminal stage of the disease (Prince 2017; Frankish and Horton 2017). This raises the possibility that more can be done to reduce risk long before clinical disease is manifest. The decrease in age-specific prevalence rates reported in the UK, compared to what had been expected, has been attributed – at least in part – to changes in health behaviour, in particular smoking, and improved management of cardiovascular disease, supporting the mantra of 'what's good for your heart is good for your head' (Banerjee 2013). This, however, raises the question of who – within a healthcare system – is best placed to address such issues? The answer, at least as far as the World Health Organization is concerned, is within primary care (World Health Organization 2016).

In this chapter, we will consider the role for primary care in the identification and management of modifiable risk factors for dementia, as well as the role that mobile health (mhealth) interventions may play in helping individuals manage their own health-related risk factors.

Modifiable risk factors and dementia

As discussed in previous chapters, there is growing evidence of an association between modifiable risk factors prevalent in mid-life and the likelihood of developing dementia in later life identified by a range of international studies (Barnes and Yaffe 2011; Norton et al. 2014; de Bruijn et al. 2015; Deckers et al. 2015; Vos et al. 2017; Livingston et al. 2017). These include hypertension, obesity, smoking and physical inactivity. In addition, pre-existing health conditions, such as cardiovascular disease, diabetes and depression, are also associated with an increased risk of developing dementia. More recent research has also highlighted the importance of educational level, hearing loss and social isolation as risk factors for dementia (Livingston et al. 2017). Taken together, Livingston et al. suggest that – over the life course – these modifiable risk factors account for 35% of the known prevalence of dementia (see Table 1.1).

This raises the possibility that interventions targeted at these risk factors may reduce the risk of developing dementia or at least delay onset. In order to tackle these risk factors effectively, it is necessary to find an arena that routinely addresses this range of modifiable risk factors, social conditions and co-existing disease – that place is, arguably, primary care.

Primary care is 'first-contact, continuous, comprehensive, and coordinated care provided to populations undifferentiated by gender, disease, or organ system' (Starfield 1994). Primary care, and in particular general practice or family medicine, is thus close to individuals and is built on a system of long-term contacts and knowledge of patients and their social environment (Stange 2009). Primary care practitioners not only deal reactively with the conditions that patients present to them during consultations; it also acts proactively, providing primary prevention for conditions that have not yet developed (World Health Organization 2008; Watt et al. 2011). This model of primary prevention is well developed for a range of chronic diseases, in particular cardiovascular disease and diabetes. In the UK, for example, primary prevention targeting such diseases was a feature of the general practice pay-for-performance incentivized care scheme known as the Quality and Outcomes Framework (Doran et al. 2006).

The recognition that primary care is already well placed to deal with issues of prevention led the World Health Organization to recommend that dementia is incorporated into existing programmes, policies and campaigns focused on non-communicable disease risk reduction and health promotion (World Health Organization 2016). This, however, requires that healthcare professionals in primary care understand the role of such modifiable risk factors in dementia and value any feasible and acceptable work in identifying and managing modifiable dementia risk factors when discussing prevention with their patients (O'Donnell et al. 2015b).

The role of primary care in managing modifiable risk factors for dementia

To date, much of the focus on the role of primary care in relation to dementia care has focused on diagnosis, post-diagnostic support and the provision of medicines that may slow the development of dementia (Koch and Iliffe 2011). In the UK, general practitioners (GPs) were incentivized to improve rates of diagnosis in primary care through a voluntary scheme whereby GPs were paid for each patient assessed for signs of early dementia and then offered a screening test (Department of Health 2012) (Mayor 2013). This opportunistic screening for a disease that, if diagnosed, could not be improved or ameliorated was thought to introduce as much harm as help for patients, with suggestions that such screening could increase anxiety (Brunet et al. 2012; Fox et al. 2013). Of course, such anxiety can be ameliorated through access to post-diagnostic support, both for patients and their carers/families.

However, less attention has been paid to the role that primary care might play in the primary prevention of dementia. Given the role of modifiable factors such as obesity, smoking and physical inactivity, as well as the contribution of pre-existing diseases, such as cardiovascular disease and diabetes, it would seem logical to add dementia to the group of non-communicable diseases that primary care considers when planning programmes of primary prevention. This led the WHO, in its Global Action Plan for Dementia, to call for the reduction and control of modifiable dementia risk factors to be integrated into national healthcare planning processes and development agendas (World Health Organization 2016). This approach is supported in the UK by the National Institute for Health and Health Care Excellence (NICE) in its 2015 guideline 'Dementia, Disability and Frailty in Later Life – Mid-life Approaches to Prevention' (Box 10.1).

Box 10.1 Recommendations from the National Institute for Health and Healthcare Excellence (National Institute for Health and Care Excellence 2015)

Health and social care providers, and relevant national third-sector organizations, should:

- Include dementia in strategy documents aimed at preventing other non-communicable chronic conditions, such as cardiovascular disease, type 2 diabetes, stroke and chronic obstructive pulmonary disease.
- Make clear that some common unhealthy behaviours can increase the risk of dementia and that addressing behaviours will reduce the likelihood of developing dementia and other non-communicable chronic conditions.

- Ensure interventions and programmes to prevent non-communicable chronic conditions state that the risk of dementia can be reduced by encouraging health behaviours (reducing smoking and alcohol consumption, increasing physical activity, adopting a healthy diet and maintaining a healthy weight), including reducing loneliness, by leading a physical and mentally active life.

This approach provides an opportunity to develop a more joined-up strategy to dementia prevention. For example, dementia prevention was set out as a key priority in NHS England and in Public Health England awareness campaigns. The awareness campaigns targeting primary care professionals, patients and the public have been developed by a number of third-sector organizations and Alzheimer's Disease charities.

Integrating dementia prevention with existing programmes is not always reflected in national policy documents. An analysis of healthcare policies in Ireland and Scotland found that national policies on non-communicable diseases rarely considered dementia alongside other diseases such as cardiovascular disease, diabetes and cancer (Pierce, personal communication). This is a missed opportunity, especially when it is known that the prevalence of key risk factors such as obesity, smoking and physical inactivity is high in the European population; over half of Europeans aged over 50 have two or more modifiable risk factors (Linardakis et al. 2013). Without a clear national strategy that places dementia firmly alongside other non-communicable chronic diseases, the lack of awareness of dementia prevention among healthcare professionals, patients and the public will persist.

Primary prevention and dementia: How well known is the link?

Research has found that both healthcare professionals and the wider public are largely unaware of the link between modifiable risk factors and dementia risk in later life. With respect to practitioners, studies have focused on GPs' views and educational needs with respect to diagnosis and management of dementia. Studies in the UK exploring GPs' attitudes towards dementia reported that they had difficulties discussing dementia with patients, as well as dealing with behavioural problems and co-ordinating support services (Turner et al. 2004). While older GPs were more confident in dealing with diagnosis and advising patients, GPs of all ages felt they would benefit from more training in dementia advice, diagnosis and post-diagnostic support (Turner et al. 2004; Ahmad et al. 2010). Similar findings were found in a study of Irish GPs (Foley et al. 2017).

There has been less work exploring professionals' views of dementia prevention. In a survey of public health practitioners in England, half of the participants thought their colleagues were unaware that dementia was preventable. While awareness of some behavioural risk factors, including smoking, alcohol consumption, physical inactivity and poor diet was good, awareness of other factors, including hypertension, obesity and diabetes, was much lower (UK Health Forum 2014). As a result, most of the survey respondents did not include dementia in prevention activities. Furthermore, there is a lack of evidence in relation to the views of others working in primary care. In particular, the views of general practice nurses, who often lead on chronic disease management programmes within practices, remain largely unknown.

Awareness of dementia prevention might improve through the development of risk scores using healthcare data routinely collected in primary care. Dementia risk algorithms using primary care data, including sociodemographic variables, lifestyle risk factors and pre-existing health conditions have now been developed (Walters et al. 2016; Schiepers et al. 2017; Vos et al. 2017). Such risk scores perform well in terms of risk prediction for those in mid-life and later life, but less well for the oldest age groups. However, these risk scores need to be further tested and their acceptability to both practitioners and patients explored. A related issue might be the well-recognized reluctance of doctors and nurses working in primary care to discuss issues that are viewed as difficult, including weight management and alcohol consumption (Dewhurst et al. 2017). Such reluctance might be compounded when the clinical condition being discussed is dementia.

If practitioners are to be able to address primary prevention with patients, patients themselves (and the wider public) also need to know and understand the association of modifiable risk factors with dementia development in later life. To date, the evidence suggests this link is not widely recognized.

Several countries have now run national campaigns highlighting the need to look after one's 'brain health', including in Ireland, the UK, Australia and the US (see examples in Smith et al. 2014). Despite these, it appears that neither patients nor the public are fully aware of the links between mid-life health-related behaviour and dementia. Alzheimer's Australia found that while 41% of Australians believe risk reduction was possible, there was greater awareness of the beneficial impact of increasing mental activity (57%) compared to physical activity (31%) and much lower awareness of the role of a healthy diet or other cardiovascular risk factors (Smith et al. 2014). Lack of awareness for the roles of physical activity and healthy eating was also found in a survey of the public in Northern Ireland (McParland et al. 2012), in surveys conducted in the US (Anderson et al. 2009) and in a qualitative study of perceptions of risk reduction carried out with adults aged 52–90 years living in Australia (Kim et al. 2015). A more recent survey of 1,641 US adults aged 50 and over did find a greater percentage who were aware of the benefits of keeping mentally active (61.4% rating this very effective), eating a healthy diet (44.3% rating this very effective) and keeping physically active (40.6%) (Roberts et al. 2014). However, 20.5% of those surveyed thought that taking vitamins and supplements was an effective strategy to reduce dementia risk, for which there is no evidence. Awareness of risk factors was greater in females, lower in younger respondents and in those with a lower level of education. A systematic review of studies exploring public knowledge has confirmed these findings; in the 21 studies which reported on awareness of risk factors and/or prevention strategies, most found moderate or low levels of knowledge (Cahill et al. 2015).

One key source of information for people is the media. This information source is, at best ambiguous, when it comes to dementia prevention. A comparative analysis of Australian media reporting in 2000/2001 and 2006/2007 found that the quality of reporting of dementia itself improved over time and was less sensationalist; however, there did not appear to be any coverage of prevention (Doyle et al. 2012). In the UK, newspapers appeared to focus on either a catastrophic view of dementia's impact on individuals and their families, or on individual behaviour change need to 'ward off' dementia (Peel 2014). This information on behaviour change was, however, often sensationalist and lacked a clear evidence base. Thus, it is likely that individuals will be left confused about the key messages in dementia prevention and unable to have meaningful discussions with their primary care practitioners. Even if they are able to seek reliable and relevant information, there is one major challenge still to address – that of achieving and maintaining behaviour change and, for healthcare professionals, effectively supporting patients on that journey.

Health behaviour change in relation to dementia risk reduction

Making and sustaining health behaviour changes can be difficult (Elwood et al. 2013; Fineberg 2013). Although wider social and structural determinants of health are recognized as important, much attention has focussed on individual behaviour change, generally in relation to single risk factors (Sniehotta et al. 2017). However, there are particular challenges when patients are faced with making changes over multiple risk factors, with patients having to make decisions about which risk factors to address, in what order and when (Goldstein et al. 2004; Koshy et al. 2012). Successful interventions need to be patient centred, tailored, proactive, culturally acceptable, multilevel and on-going (Glasgow et al. 2004). However, in increasingly busy and resource stretched healthcare systems, it is not always possible to deliver such interventions in face-to-face settings. This has led to increasing interest in the development of interventions employing mobile health (mhealth) approaches. Such interventions may be delivered by internet-based programmes, social media or apps and are increasingly viewed as an approach to support individuals trying to make and maintain lifestyle changes (OECD 2013; E-Health Initiative 2012; European Union 2014; European Commission 2014).

Web-based and e-health interventions can be effective in supporting behaviour change, at least in the short-term, and are viewed as convenient, easily accessible and can preserve anonymity and privacy (Murray 2012). A systematic review of web-based interventions targeting cardiovascular risk factors in adults aged 50 and over found small, but significant decreases in blood pressure, HbA1c levels, LDL cholesterol, weight and a small increase in physical activity (Beishuizen et al. 2016). However, these changes were most pronounced in the first 12 months and then tended to disappear. Mhealth interventions also show some promise in targeting lifestyle factors, diabetes, raised cholesterol and hypertension; however, results were often modest and there was a lack of long-term outcomes (Webb et al. 2010; Aalbers et al. 2011; Rehman et al. 2017b; Rehman et al. 2017a).

In terms of interventions targeting aspects of dementia prevention, Farrow reported on the impact of a website designed by Alzheimer's Australia to improve knowledge about modifiable risk factors for dementia (Farrow 2013). In a survey of 123 adults who used the site, both knowledge about the links between risk factors and dementia and intentions to make lifestyle changes increased after visiting the website. The European Commission funded Innovative Midlife Intervention for Dementia Deterrence project (In-MINDD 2012) combined an on-line risk profiler which provided participants with a tailored global 'brain health' score and profile (LIBRA: Lifestyle for Brain Health score) as well as a web-based on-line support environment and goal setting (O'Donnell et al. 2015a). A feasibility RCT showed that this intervention was acceptable to participants and supported them to initiate lifestyle changes such as improving diet and increasing physical activity.

Future directions

The link between modifiable health-related behaviours in mid-life and the development of dementia in later life is becoming clearer, with cardiovascular risk factors making a particular contribution. Primary care, both at the level of policy and practitioners, has a crucial role to play in making this link more visible. At a policy level, programmes and strategies targeting non-communicable chronic disease should routinely address dementia alongside other diseases such as cardiovascular disease and type 2 diabetes. The emerging evidence of a link between dementia and social factors such as social isolation deserves further exploration and, if found to be salient, should be considered more explicitly in policies integrating health and social care. At the practice level, dementia should be discussed within consultations which target primary prevention and risk factor reduction, for example, as part of national health check programmes. However, dementia may present particular challenges to healthcare professionals when discussing long-term risks with patients. Therefore, research to explore what practitioners and patients think about conversations dealing with dementia prevention is urgently needed, as is the need to identify, and address, training needs for professionals.

Finally, the on-going development and scaling up of mhealth interventions to support behaviour change offer potentially tailorable solutions for individuals trying to make and sustain long-term lifestyle changes. In addition, internet and social media channels may offer powerful platforms on which to engage the public and offer evidence-based information on risk factors, lifestyle and dementia.

References

Aalbers, T., Baars, M. A. & Rikkert, M. G. (2011). Characteristics of effective Internet-mediated interventions to change lifestyle in people aged 50 and older: A systematic review. *Ageing Research Reviews*, 10, 487–497.

Ahmad, S., Orrell, M., Iliffe, S. & Gracie, A. (2010). GPs' attitudes, awareness, and practice regarding early diagnosis of dementia. *British Journal of General Practice*, 60, e360–e365.

Anderson, L. A., Day, K. L., Beard, R. L., Reed, P. S. & Wu, B. 2009. The public's perceptions about cognitive health and Alzheimer's disease among the U.S. population: A national review. *The Gerontologist*, 49, S3–S11.

Banerjee, S. (2013). Good news on dementia prevalence – we can make a difference. *The Lancet*, 382, 1384–1386.

Barnes, D. E. & Yaffe, K. (2011). The projected effect of risk factor reduction on Alzheimer's disease prevalence. *The Lancet Neurology*, 10, 819–828.

Beishuizen, C. R. L., Stephan, B. C. M., Van Gool, W. A., Brayne, C., Peters, R. J. G., Andrieu, S., Kivipelto, M., Soininen, H., Busschers, W. B., Moll Van Charrante, E. P. & Richard, E. (2016). Web-based interventions targeting cardiovascular risk factors in middle-aged and older people: A systematic review and meta-analysis. *Journal of Medical Internet Research*, 18, e55.

Brunet, M. D., McCartney, M., Heath, I., Tomlinson, J., Gordon, P., Cosgrove, J., Deveson, P., Gordon, S., Marciano, S-A., Colvin, D., Sayer, M., Silverman, S. & Bhattia, N. (2012). There is no evidence base for proposed dementia screening. *BMJ*, 345, e8588.

Cahill, S., Pierce, M., Werner, P., Darley, A. & Bobersky, A. (2015). A systematic review of the public's knowledge and understanding of Alzheimer's disease and dementia. *Alzheimer Disease and Associated Disorders*, 29, 255–275.

De Bruijn, R. F. A. G., Bos, M. J., Portegies, M. L. P., Hofman, A., Franco, O. H., Koudstaal, P. J. & Ikram, M. A. (2015). The potential for prevention of dementia across two decades: The prospective, population-based Rotterdam Study. *BMC Medicine*, 13, 132.

Deckers, K., Van Boxtel, M. P. J., Schiepers, O. J. G., De Vugt, M., Munoz Sánchez, J. L., Anstey, K. J., Brayne, C., Dartigues, J-F., Engendal, K., Kivipelto, M., Ritchie, K., Starr, J. M., Yaffe, K., Irving, K., Verhey, F. R. J. & Kohler, S. (2015). Target risk factors for dementia prevention: A systematic review and Delphi consensus study on the evidence from observational studies. *International Journal of Geriatric Psychiatry*, 30, 234–246.

Department of Health. (2012). *Prime Minister's Challenge on Dementia: Delivering Major Improvements in Dementia Care and Research by 2015*. London: Department of Health.

Dewhurst, A., Peters, S., Devereux-Fitzgerald, A. & Hart, J. (2017). Physicians' views and experiences of discussing weight management within routine clinical consultations: A thematic synthesis. *Patient Education and Counseling*, 100, 897–908.

Doran, T., Fullwood, C., Gravelle, H., Reeves, D., Kontopantelis, E., Hiroeh, U. & Roland, M. (2006). Pay-for-performance programs in family practices in the United Kingdom. *The New England Journal of Medicine*, 355, 375–384.

Doyle, C. J., Dunt, D. R., Pirkis, J., Dare, A., Day, S. & Wijesundara, B. S. (2012). Media reports on dementia: Quality and type of messages in Australian media. *Australasian Journal on Ageing*, 31, 96–101.

E-Health Initiative. (2012). *A Study and Report on the Use of e-Health Tools for Chronic Disease Care Among Socially Disadvantaged Populations*. Final report. CA. Available at: https://ehi-rails-app.s3.amazonaws.com/uploads/article/file/8/2013-04-03_-_CHCF_-_A_Study_on_the_Use_of_eHealth_Tools_for_Chronic_Disease_Care_Among_Socially_Disadvantaged_Populations_-_Final_-_Report.pdf.

Elwood, P., Galante, J., Pickering, J., Palmer, S., Bayer, A., Ben-Schlomo, Y., Longley, M. & Gallacher, J. (2013). Healthy lifestyles reduce the incidence of chronic diseases and dementia: Evidence from the Caerphilly cohort study *PLoS One*, 8.

European Commission. (2014). *Green Paper on Mobile Health ("mHealth")*. Brussels: European Commission. Available at: https://ec.europa.eu/digital-single-market/en/news/green-paper-mobile-health-mhealth.

European Union. (2014). *EU Task Force on eHealth: Redesigning Health in Europe for 2020*. Luxembourg: Publications Office of the European Union, 2012. Available at: https://e-health-com.de/fileadmin/user_upload/dateien/Downloads/redesigning_health-eu-for2020-ehtf-report2012_01.pdf.

Farrow, M. (2013). User perceptions of a dementia risk reduction website and its promotion of behavior change. *JMIR Research Protocols*, 2, e15.

Fineberg, H.V. (2013). The paradox of disease prevention: Celebrated in principle, resisted in practice. *JAMA*, 310, 85–90.

Foley, T., Boyle, S., Jennings, A. & Smithson, W. H. (2017). "We're certainly not in our comfort zone": A qualitative study of GPs' dementia-care educational needs. *BMC Family Practice*, 18, 66.

Fox, C., Lafortune, L., Boustani, M. & Brayne, C. (2013). The pros and cons of early diagnosis in dementia. *BJGP*, 63, e510.

Frankish, H. & Horton, R. (2017). Prevention and management of dementia: A priority for public health. *The Lancet*. 390(10113), 2614–2615. DOI: 10.1016/S0140-6736(17)31756-7.

Glasgow, R. E., Goldestein, M. G., Ockene, J. K. & Pronk, N. P. (2004). Translating what we have learned into practice: Principles and hypotheses for interventions addressing multiple behaviors in primary care. *American Journal of Preventive Medicine*, 27, 88–101.

Goldstein, M. G., Whitlock, E. P. & Depue, J. (2004). Multiple behavioral risk factor interventions in primary care: Summary of research evidence. *American Journal of Preventive Medicine*, 27, 61–79.

In-MINDD. (2012). *Innovative Midlife Interventions for Dementia Deterrence*. Available at: www.inmindd.eu [Accessed 3 May 2018].

Kim, S., Sargent-Cox, K. A. & Anstey, K. J. (2015). A qualitative study of older and middle-aged adults' perception and attitudes towards dementia and dementia risk reduction. *Journal of Advanced Nursing*, 71, 1694–1703.

Koch, T. & Iliffe, S. (2011). Dementia diagnosis and management: A narrative review of changing practice. *British Journal of General Practice*, 61, e513–e525.

Koshy, P., Mackenzie, M., Leslie, W., Lean, M. & Hankey, C. (2012). Eating the elephant whole or in slices: Views of participants in a smoking cessation intervention trial on multiple behaviour changes as sequential or concurrent tasks. *BMC Public Health*, 12, 500.

Linardakis, M., Smpokos, E., Papadaki, A., Komninos, I. D., Tzanakis, N. & Philalithis, A. (2013). Prevalence of multiple behavioral risk factors for chronic diseases in adults aged 50+, from eleven European countries: The SHARE study (2004). *Preventive Medicine*, 57, 168–172.

Livingston, G., Sommerland, A., Orgeta, V., Costafreda, S. G., Huntley, J., Ames, D., Ballard, C., Banerjee, S., Burns, A., Cohen-Mansfield, J., Cooper, C., FOX, N., Gitlin, L. N., Howard, R., Kales, H. C., Larson, E. B., Ritchie, K., Rockwood, K., Sampson, E. L., Samus, Q., Schneider, L. S., Serlbaek, G., Teri, L. & Mukadam, N. (2017). Dementia prevention, intervention, and care. *The Lancet*. 390(10113), 2673–2734. DOI: https://doi.org/10.1016/S0140-6736(17)31363-6

Mayor, S. (2013). Government's plan to raise dementia diagnoses gets mixed response. *BMJ*, 346.

McParland, P., Devine, P., Innes, A. & Gayle, V. (2012). Dementia knowledge and attitudes of the general public in Northern Ireland: An analysis of national survey data. *International Psychogeriatrics*, 24, 1600–1613.

Murray, E. (2012). Web-based interventions for behavior change and self-management: Potential, pitfalls, and progress. *Journal of Medical Internet Research*, 1.

National Institute for Health and Care Excellence. (2015). *Dementia, Disability and Frailty in Later Life – Mid-Life Approaches to Prevention*. London: NICE.

Norton, S., Matthews, F. E., Barnes, D. E., Yaffe, K. & Brayne, C. (2014). Potential for primary prevention of Alzheimer's disease: An analysis of population-based data. *The Lancet Neurology*, 13, 788–794.

O'Donnell, C. A., Browne, S., Pierce, M., McConnachie, A., Deckers, K., Van Boxtel, M. P. J., Manera, V., Koehler, S., Redmond, M., Verhey, F. R. J., Van Den Akker, M., Power, K., Irving, K. & and The IN-MINDD Team. (2015a). Reducing dementia risk by targeting modifiable risk factors in mid-life: Study protocol for the *In*novative *M*idlife *In*tervention for *D*ementia *D*eterrence (In-MINDD) randomised controlled trial. *Pilot and Feasibility Studies*, 1, 40.

O'Donnell, C. A., Manera, V., Kohler, S. & Irving, K. (2015b). Promoting modifiable risk factors for dementia: Is there a role for general practice? *British Journal of General Practice*, 65, 567–568.

OECD. (2013). *ICTs and the Health Sector: Towards Smarter Health and Wellness Models*. Paris, France: OECD Publishing. Available at: https://read.oecd-ilibrary.org/science-and-technology/icts-and-the-health-sector_9789264202863-en#page4

Peel, E. (2014). 'The living death of Alzheimer's' versus 'Take a walk to keep dementia at bay': Representations of dementia in print media and carer discourse. *Sociology of Health & Illness*, 36, 885–901.

Prince, M. (2017). Progress on dementia – leaving no one behind. *The Lancet*, 39, 10113.

Prince, M., Wimo, A., Guerchet, M., Ali, G-C., Wu, Y-T. & Prina, M. (2015). The global impact of dementia: An analysis of prevalence, incidence, cost & trends. *In: World Alzheimer Report 2015*. London: Alzheimer's Disease International (ADI).

Rehman, H., Kamal, A. K., Morriss, P. B., Sayani, S., Merchant, A. T. & Virani, S. S. (2017a). Mobile health (mHealth) technology for the management of hypertension and hyperlipidemia: Slow start but loads of potential. *Current Atherosclerosis Reports*, 19, 12.

Rehman, H., Kamal, A. K., Sayani, S., Morris, P. B., Merchant, A. T. & Virani, S. S. (2017b). Using mobile health (mHealth) technology in the management of diabetes mellitus, physical inactivity, and smoking. *Current Atherosclerosis Reports*, 19, 16.

Roberts, J. S., McLaughlin, J. & Connell, C. M. (2014). Public beliefs and knowledge about risk and protective factors for Alzheimer's disease. *Alzheimer's & Dementia*, 10, S381–S389.

Schiepers, O. J. G., Kohler, S., Deckers, K., Irving, K., O'Donnell, C. A., Van Den Akker, M., Verhey, F. R. J., Vos, S. J. B., De Vugt, M. E. & Van Boxtel, M. P. J. (2017). Lifestyle for Brain

Health (LIBRA): A new model for dementia prevention. *International Journal of Geriatric Psychiatry*. 33(1): 167–175. DOI: 10.1002/gps.4700

Smith, B., Ali, S. & Quach, H. (2014). Public knowledge and beliefs about dementia risk reduction: A national survey of Australians. *BMC Public Health*, 14, 661.

Sniehotta, F. F., Araújo-Soares, V., Brown, J., Kelly, M. P., Michie, S. & West, R. (2017). Complex systems and individual-level approaches to population health: A false dichotomy? *The Lancet Public Health*, 2, e396–e397.

Stange, K. C. (2009). The generalist approach. *Annals of Family Medicine*, 7, 198–203.

Starfield, B. (1994). Is primary care essential? *The Lancet*, 344, 1129–1133.

Turner, S., Iliffe, S., Downs, M., Wilcock, J., Bryans, M., Levin, E., Keady, J. & O'Carroll, R. (2004). General practitioners' knowledge, confidence and attitudes in the diagnosis and management of dementia. *Age and Ageing*, 33, 461–467.

UK Health Forum. (2014). *Knowledge and Awareness Among the Public Health Workforce in the UK About the Prevention of Dementia*. Available at: http://www.ukhealthforum.org.uk/EasysiteWeb/EasysiteWeb/getresource.axd?AssetID=58933&servicetype=Attachment

Vos, S. J. B., Van Boxtel, M. P. J., Schiepers, O. J. G., Deckers, K., De Vugt, M., Carriere, I., Dartigues, J. F., Peres, K., Artero, S., Ritchie, K., Galluzzo, L., Scafato, E., Frisoni, G. B., Huisman, M., Comijs, H. C., Sacuiu, S. F., Skoog, I., Irving, K., O'Donnell, C. A., Verhey, F. R. J., Visser, P. J. & Kohler, S. (2017). Modifiable risk factors for prevention of dementia in midlife, late life and the oldest-old: Validation of the LIBRA index. *Journal of Alzheimers Disease*, 58, 537–547.

Walters, K., Hardoon, S., Petersen, I., Iliffe, S., Omar, R. Z., Nazareth, I. & Rait, G. (2016). Predicting dementia risk in primary care: Development and validation of the Dementia Risk Score using routinely collected data. *BMC Medicine*, 14, 6.

Watt, G., O'Donnell, C. & Sridharan, S. (2011). Building on Julian Tudor Hart's example of anticipatory care. *Primary Health Care Research & Development*, 12, 3–10.

Webb, T. L., Joseph, J., Yardley, L. & Michie, S. (2010). Using the internet to promote health behavior change: A systematic review and meta-analysis of the impact of theoretical basis, use of behavior change techniques, and mode of delivery on efficacy. *Journal of Medical Internet Research*, 12, e4.

Williamson, T. (2015). Dementia, public health and public policy – making the connections. *Journal of Public Mental Health*, 14, 35–37.

World Health Organization. (2008). *Primary Health Care: Now More Than Ever*. Geneva: The World Health Organization. Available at: http://www.who.int/whr/2008/en/

World Health Organization. (2016). *Draft Global Action Plan on the Public Health Response to Dementia*. Geneva: The World Health Organization. Available at: http://www.who.int/mental_health/neurology/dementia/action_plan_2017_2025/en/.

Chapter 11

The economics of preventing dementia

Dominic Trépel

Introduction

As of this year (2018), projections suggest that the costs of dementia will reach $1 trillion USD worldwide (Wimo et al. 2017) and, as a result, debates on strategies for dementia seem to have become inextricably linked to the associated economic consequences of the disease. Stakeholders and policymakers are justifiably concerned, and there has been a steady increase in level of substantive global actions for dementia.[1]

Economics is a discipline that aims to inform how to make best use of limited resources and economic analysis commonly applies mathematical techniques to inform these issues of *scarcity*. In the case of dementia prevention, such a question may be,

> *What strategies are likely to represent the best value for money in reducing the risk, incidence and outcomes of dementia, compared to other potential investment decisions?*

This question acknowledges that the risk of dementia varies between individuals, that the profile of risk factors drive incidence rate (and therefore may represent targets of potential interventions) and ultimately the outcomes of dementia in society may also be altered by intervening throughout individuals' life course. However, active intervention will have some form of direct cost that must be justified and, drawing finances from a limited budget, will entail competing for investment where such decisions might be based on a rational comparison to other ways resources could alternatively be utilized.

This section of *Dementia Prevention* provides three chapters to review the current state of the art of the application of economic concepts to preventing dementia. This chapter introduces the economic concerns that dementia creates, what economic evidence currently informs decision-makers, whether the demand for finding dementia prevention strategies can be sustained and, if so, what might *preventing dementia* actually look like? Thereafter, in the next chapter, Handels and Wimo review worked examples of health-economic models of dementia prevention and discusses available evidence, the challenges faced by researchers and policymakers and provide recommendations for future studies.

In the last chapter of this section, Knapp, Kung, Rossor and Stoner present an alternative framework to guide public policy – entitled the *Cognitive Footprint* – in which the authors argue that policy needs to consider the cognitive effects of experiences, events and interventions across individuals' life course.

What economic concerns does dementia create?

Dementia encompasses a number of unique disease states (American Psychiatric Association. and American Psychiatric Association. DSM-5 Task Force 2013). Alzheimer's disease and vascular dementia make up the majority of cases, followed by Lewy body and frontotemporal dementias. While the symptoms of each type of dementia vary, they generally include loss of memory, impaired judgment, loss of daily functioning and inappropriate behavior. The progressive symptomology increases dependence on others due to loss of physical and mental abilities. The progressive loss of function that individuals experience creates a demand for formal support by services (e.g. health and social care) and places increasing demand on *informal carers* (e.g. families, and the wider community) to facilitate living in the community (Trépel 2011).

Dementia is a major – and a relatively unique – economic challenge and as there is currently no known cure, high economic cost and limited evidence on the economic benefit of the available treatment in seeking to provide symptom control (Trépel 2017). Whilst there will be a considerable change in the world's demographic profile over the next century (see Figure 11.1), consensus

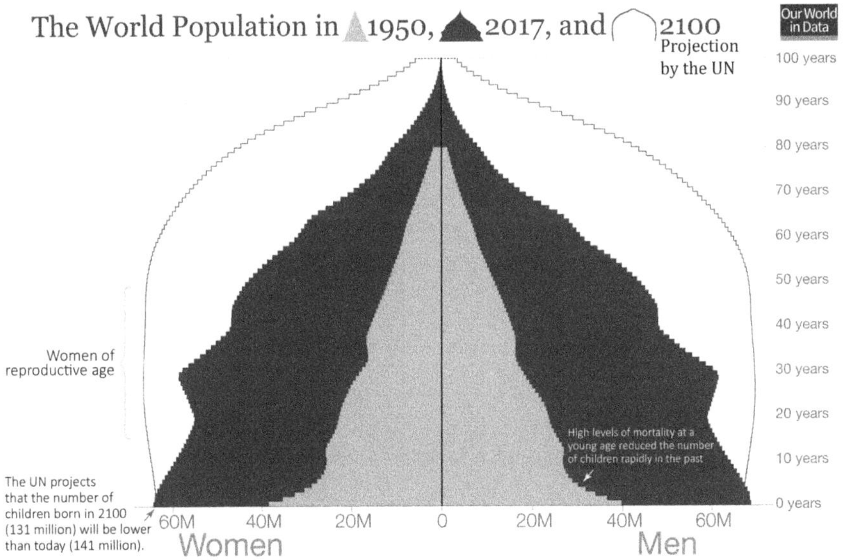

Figure 11.1 World population growth

Source: www.ourworldindata.org

amongst leading experts agreed it is unlikely that there will be a cure within the next half of the century.[2]

To contextualize the world's demographic shift, the largest changes in the world's older population should be anticipated in low- and middle- income countries. As a result, globally, the variation in the prevalence of dementia will be largely driven by country-level changes in its demographics profile (Prince et al. 2015). As the strongest predictor of dementia is that the likelihood doubles with every five-year increase over 65 years of age (Gao et al. 1998), the *International Global AgeWatch Index* is a good indication of where the largest future demand will lie (see Figure 11.2).

Over the next three decades, the older population will increasingly affect lesser-developed economies where scarcity of resources creates even greater demand for the prevention of chronic non-communicable diseases (Guerchet et al. 2017). By 2050, it is estimated that 68% of all dementia cases will be found in low- and middle-income countries (Prince et al. 2015). This will

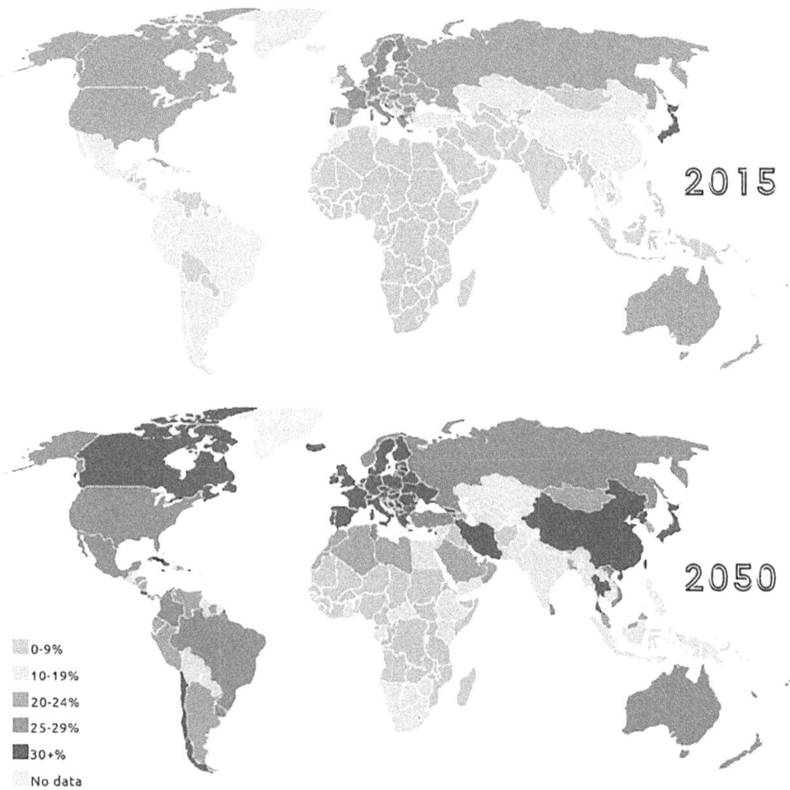

Figure 11.2 Proportions of the population aged over 60, by country.

Source: International Global AgeWatch Index 2015, Age International, London.

raise important questions on the economic feasibility of treatment following a diagnosis, the reimbursement thresholds for dementia strategies in resource-limited countries (Woods et al. 2016) and preferences to allocate resources toward prevention over an immediate treatment need, particularly in the face of uncertain outcomes.

Current economic evidence to inform investment decisions in dementia

The purpose of economic evaluation is to inform decisions intended to improve healthcare and health (Drummond et al. 2015). Health systems face analytical and policy challenges in seeking to allocate resources efficiently and fairly. Given that only a small number of studies exist to inform primary prevention, it is currently difficult to make evidence-based recommendations on allocation toward prevention strategies versus treatment (Handels and Wimo 2017). Furthermore, Cost-Effectiveness Analysis is less common in dementia relative to other disease states (e.g. cancer), which may in part explain the growing gap between budget allocation and the economic burden placed on society (Saxena et al. 2007).

Systematic searches are applied to identify, quantify and appraise evidence (Higgins 2008), and despite numerous reviews over the last decade (Knapp et al. 2013; Laver et al. 2016; Oremus 2008; Schaller et al. 2015; Tilford et al. 2012), there remains a paucity of economic evaluations in dementia. The most recent published review of dementia studies containing both cost and outcomes found that a total of only 56 papers met their inclusion criteria (Knapp et al. 2013). Since that time (January 2012), further emerging research has been identified (Trépel 2017), and whilst no formal quality assessment was conducted, it seems evident that the paucity of research efforts continues and issues of methodological quality are not being addressed.

Whether resource allocation decisions to *active* prevention of dementia may be currently supported by available economic evidence is presented in detail in the next chapter, but to consider all alternative options in dementia, let us first examine the economic evidence supporting treatment for dementia disorders.

In the absence of any curative intervention for dementia, common pharmacological interventions that alter the course of dementia progress fall into two categories: *acetylcholinesterase inhibitors (AChEI)*, which address deficits in cerebral acetylcholine by inhibiting its breakdown and raising its concentration in brain synapses. *N-methyl-D-aspartate (NMDA) receptor antagonists* that selectively inhibit the production of glutamate. Memantine is currently the only NMDA receptor antagonist licensed treatment with indications in moderate-to-severe Alzheimer's disease.

Evidence of the cost-effectiveness of these pharmaceutical treatments have been a source of sustained argument for the executive non-departmental public body of the Department of Health in the United Kingdom, the National

Institute for Health and Care Excellence (NICE). NICE has a strong international reputation in developing clinical guidelines and, unlike the American equivalent, *Patient-Centered Outcomes Research Institute* (Neumann and Weinstein 2010), NICE encourages the use of economic evidence to inform national health policy decisions. Based on the available evidence, NICE will make recommendations, such as interventions: a) must (or must not) be used (i.e. where there is a legal duty to apply the recommendation), b) should (or should not) be used (i.e. where use may be 'advised') and c) could be used (i.e. where use will do more good than harm and should be 'considered') (NICE 2012). In part, economic evidence on cost-effectiveness and the quality of the evidence will also inform recommendations on non-pharmacological approaches.

In 2004, NICE conducted an appraisal regarding the market for AChEI and NMDA receptor inhibitors. Following a judicial review, NICE restricted the use of memantine on the basis of uncertainty surrounding it's clinical- and cost-effectiveness (NICE 2009). Memantine was licensed for use *only in research*, such as clinical trials (Walker et al. 2012). However, as a result of political pressure, NICE later developed the '*Assessment of Health Economics in Alzheimer's Disease*' or AHEAD model and, in 2010, NICE guidelines broadened indications for AChEI and allowed NMDA receptor antagonists in routine practice. However, attempts to replicate the models' conclusions raised debate in the literature (Getsios et al. 2007). To summarize how and why these arguments for dementia changed over time, Table 11.1 shows evidence on cost-effectiveness in 2004 and 2010 for these pharmaceutical products.

Table 11.1 Comparison of the effectiveness and cost-effectiveness of Alzheimer's disease drugs in 2004 and 2010.

Year	*Measures*	*Summary evidence of cost-effectiveness, by pharmacological treatment*			
		Donepezil	*Galantamine*	*Rivastigmine*	*Memantine*
2004	Cost	£2,895	£2,648	£2,121	*
	QALY	0.036	0.039	0.037	*
	Cost/QALY	£80,941	£68,042	£57,985	£37,000–53,000
2010	Cost	−£588	−£620	−£534	£405
	QALY	0.036	0.033	0.029	0.013
	Cost/QALY	dominates**	dominates**	dominates**	£32,100

* Not reported
** The situation where a treatment is more effective and less costly than the alternative and therefore the new treatment 'dominates' over the alternative
Source: Hyde et al. 2013

NICE works with an explicit reimbursement threshold of £20,000 to £30,000 per quality-adjusted life year (QALY) – referred to as 'incremental cost effect ratio' or ICER – to indicate what should be funded by the health service (Claxton et al. 2013). Comparison using the aforementioned evidence shows that, whilst the level of effectiveness remained relatively similar, the 2010 estimates identified a total reduction in costs to healthcare, largely as a result of *drug acquisition* and *the costs of full time institutionalized care*, thus resulting in the new guidance after 2010. Since that time, further research has identified additional clinical effectiveness evidence, but conclusions concerning cost-effectiveness remain highly uncertain and definitive evidence from RCT (including time to institutionalization) was recommended.

NICE guidelines on these pharmaceutical treatments were updated on 20 June 2018 (NICE, 2018). NICE also developed separate guidelines, pathways and quality standards and advice for dementia (NICE, 2017) and, most recently, issued guidance on Dementia – assessment, management and support for people living with dementia and their carers (NICE, 2018).

Reviews have shown that there is a limited number of economic evaluations of non-pharmacological interventions for people with dementia available in the current literature (Knapp et al. 2013). Knapp and colleagues' searches identified that economic studies of cognitive stimulation therapy, tailored activity programs and occupational therapy were more cost-effective compared to usual care. Since that time, further studies have also examined the effect of gingko biloba, reminiscence therapies and interventions for agitation (Trépel 2017).

As we shall see in the next chapter, there has been limited work by health economists to explore the cost-effectiveness of dementia prevention strategies to date. In October 2015, NICE issued guidelines on 'dementia, disability and frailty in later life – mid-life approaches to delay or prevent onset'.[3] However, given the paucity of research, their current economic model is restricted to examining 'costs and benefits of increasing physical activity to prevent the onset of dementia: a modeling analysis' (Van Baal & Hoogendoorn 2014). As a result, the only formal recommendation by NICE is to '*promote a healthy lifestyle*' (e.g. stop smoking, be more active, reduce their alcohol consumption, improve their diet and maintain a healthy weight). However, this recommendation is passive (i.e. places the emphasis on the individual to change their behavior) and is therefore cost neutral to the healthcare budget. In part, there may be limited evidence to support the investment by healthcare, however, it may be argued that to improve health across individuals' life course may merit investment beyond heath care; Knapp and colleagues' chapter on *Cognitive Footprint* argues that policymakers may need to consider the effects of investment outside of healthcare on cognition.

Nevertheless, the absence of evidence on the cost-effectiveness of active dementia prevention strategies does not necessarily imply that any *active* dementia prevention strategy will not be cost-effective. The next chapter will present the current evidence base of emerging research on the economics of dementia prevention. As accepting that good quality and reliable evidence that supports investing in dementia prevention may still be required, the next section discusses whether the demand to identify options which may prevent dementia is likely to be sustained.

Will the demand to find ways to prevent dementia be sustained?

Comptroller and Auditor General, National Audit Office, 2007 has been cited to have said that 'parallels can be drawn between dementia now and cancer in the 1950s, when there were few treatments and patients were commonly not told the diagnosis for fear of distress'(Committee of Public Accounts 2008, p. 1). This statement points to the current state of affairs for people living with dementia and, more importantly, lags in appropriate investment to identify solutions. There has been an inequity of effort to solve dementia compared to other conditions. Researchers from the University of Oxford illustrated this disparity of efforts by highlighting that, for every £10 of health and social care costs attributable to the disease, cancer received £1.08 in research funding, chronic heart disease received £0.65, stroke received £0.19 (or £0.11 depending on care costs of stroke used) and, finally, dementia received £0.08 (Luengo-Fernandez et al. 2012). In other words, relative to the economic impact of the disease, these UK figures would suggest cancer has received 13.5 times more support than dementia.

Whilst more research funding in the United Kingdom is currently directed toward cancer and other diseases, priorities seem to be shifting. The National Institute for Health (NIH) 'state-of-the-science conference' called for increased research into the prevention of Alzheimer's disease and cognitive decline. The panel have concluded the need for more large-scale population-based studies and RCTs to investigate strategies to

> *maintain cognitive function in individuals at risk for decline, to identify factors that may delay the onset of Alzheimer's disease among persons at risk, and to identify factors that may slow the progression of Alzheimer's disease among persons in whom the condition is already diagnosed.*
>
> (Daviglus et al. 2010, p. 2)

So, the question is then, can we expect the attention on prevention of dementia to be sustained for a sufficient time to find any meaningful solutions? Reviewing the evidence, dementia prevention is starting from a relatively low base of funding. However, Figure 11.3 aims to illustrate a shifting in the demand for this, which it is felt will be attributed to a variety of factors currently occurring.

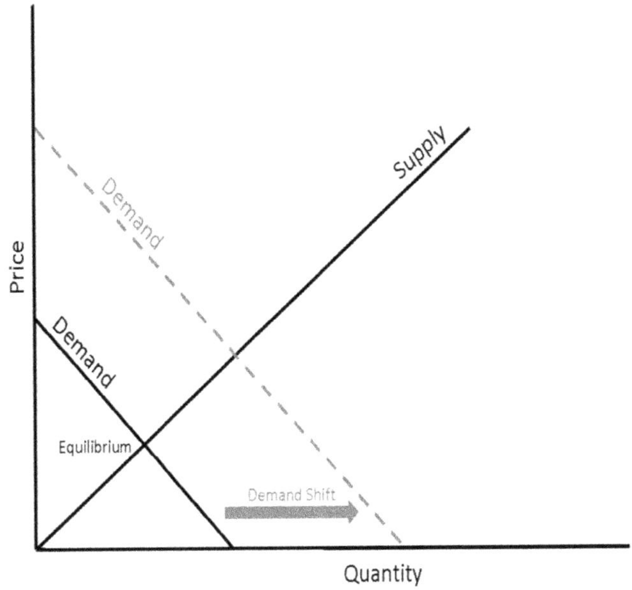

Figure 11.3 Supply and demand curve

Firstly, the world's population continues to expand and also the proportion of the older population is growing, thus resulting in more cases of dementia. Secondly, with projected increases in the prevalence of dementia, a larger proportion of the world total resources (as indicated by GDP) will be consumed by dementia and thus in an attempt to mitigate loss of resources to managing dementia, the case for prevention is becoming increasingly accepted and sought. And, finally, expert consensus has anticipated that it is unlikely that there will be a *cure* for dementia soon. With an increase in the demand for dementia prevention, the supply of resources deployed for prevention can be anticipated to continue to increase and, in the face of increasing value placed on prevention, one might anticipate a growth in the number of suppliers (e.g. research, policies and services with the common aim of reducing the incidence of dementia).

Health economics defines the demand for healthcare as a *derived* demand for health, in the sense that a consumer is motivated by the awareness of what constitutes 'good health' and, from that, the demand for healthcare goods and services is derived (Grossman 1972). This concept – termed by the Grossman model – prolifically defined *health* as a commodity that is both consumed and produced. In this context, the demand for dementia prevention may also be considered a *derived* demand for improved *brain health*.

Whilst the term *brain health* may lack a consensus on its scope and definition, it should be considered useful in defining a specific subset of one's overall health. Adopting the *cognitive ageing* paradigm, one might consider *brain health* as a relative concept whereby one might compare one's *cognitive age* to the individuals' *chronological age*, whereby the production of *brain health* keeps cognition closer (or ideally under) one's current age (i.e. a positive stock of *brain health*). However, in line with Grossman's original thinking, one must invest in developing such a stock of *brain health*, and therefore the investment decision may mean forgoing some other source of utility (Marshall 1960).

In fact, objectively measuring *brain health* is not straightforward so it may be best considered as a latent construct, in which one's *cognitive age* is simply an indicator of one's brain health status, but will only be one of a variety of potential biomarkers and degree of *cognitive reserve*, many of which are currently still being discovered by neuroscientists (Bigio et al. 2002; Robertson 2013; Stern 2009).

Nevertheless, uncertainties surrounding what is truly in demand (i.e. increased brain health that reduces the chance of cognitive decline and dementia), does not remove the forces driving this. Policymakers must be responsive to this emerging societal demand and, with research suggesting that public health interventions may prevent 28.2% (95% confidence interval 14.2% to 41.5%) of projected cases worldwide in the next two decades (Norton et al. 2014), one must then ask, if we were managing to prevent dementia, how would we know?

How might 'preventing dementia' be detected and measured?

Firstly, if *prevention* is the outcome of interest in the case of dementia, let us first consider the underlying motivation. In preparation for the G8 Dementia Summit legacy event, analysis from the UK's Office of Health Economics suggested that delaying the onset of dementia by five years would both reduce the number of cases by a third and alleviate economic costs by 36% by 2050 (Lewis et al. 2014). Given the projections that suggest dementia may consume 1% GDP globally (Wimo et al. 2013), this creates a strong call to action and, in the United Kingdom, has resulted in a significant investments in dementia research (NIHR 2018) and prevention (Ritchie and Ritchie 2012). But if economics is a key consideration in dementia, we need tangible *outcomes* to help guide policy on appropriate prevention strategies. Given the complexity to conduct comparative research related to prevention, in order to make the required resource allocation decisions, policy may often necessitate risk factors and outcomes to be considered independently. This makes the accuracy of future projections of dementia prevalence (and associated costs) vital to policymakers, as their objective may be to *alter* the expected trajectory.

There continues to be extensive debate amongst epidemiologists on the basis, empirical methods and accuracy of future projections. The basis of many projections comes from the trends in incidence and prevalence to date. However, population-based studies must apply the same diagnostic and research methods consistently over time. As an illustration, one systematic review searched for reports of Alzheimer's disease or dementia in China between 1990 and 2010 and concluded that dementia was increasing faster than is generally assumed by the international health community (Chan et al. 2013) – on this basis, policy would be fuelled by an anticipated high future demand. However, the reliability of these trends was subsequently criticized for not controlling for methodological factors including changes in diagnostic criteria (Wu et al. 2017), which drew credibility from applying meta-regression techniques to control for heterogeneity across studies and refined estimates (Wu et al. 2013). This shows that our understanding of population-level projections and trends is complex and therefore cannot be taken with complete certainty with regards to making future projections, particularly if such trends were to form a baseline to determine the success of efforts to prevent dementia.

In comparing two-decade dementia incidence, evidence from the Medical Research Council funded *Cognitive Function and Ageing Study* (CFAS) has recently reported a 20% drop in incidence (95% CI: 0%–40%) and the research team concluded that the reduction was largely attributed to men across all ages above 65 years of age (Matthews et al. 2016). As a result, the study suggested that the number of new cases in the United Kingdom were 209,600 (suggesting a net reduction of around 40,000 based on previous figures). This raises the question: is this evidence of prevention, or is it that we are refining our projections? Such findings may suggest that, if a policy initiative is performed now, is it influencing future trends in dementia? *Knowing* (or at least *estimating*) with some degree of certainty of the projected outcome (e.g. incidence or prevalence of dementia) must therefore precede any inference on causality.

Unlike experimental paradigms, such as *RCT* (results of which are commonly used by clinicians to make assertions on causality of an intervention), economists face the methodological issue that our experiments cannot randomize entire societies into comparative arms of a study to examine outcomes (like changes in dementia). As the risk of dementia is associated with a mix of genetic factors, events occurring over the individuals' life course (commonly described as modifiable risk) and their interaction with the environment, the degree of heterogeneity of risk over their life course is extremely difficult to capture or control for in any one experiment.

Adopting alternative empirical approaches, economists examine the *marginal effects* of covariates (e.g. modifiable risk factors) on the outcome of interest (e.g. diagnosis of dementia). Such studies must be highly resource incentive in order to collect sufficiently sized samples to be representative of the population and allow for individual differences in risk, and thereafter repeat data collection over time for a sufficient duration to allow for causal inference of any given *risk* (i.e. where the outcome of interest is some years in the future). Furthermore, within this framework, intervention on any specific *risk factor* requires knowledge of the *counterfactual* (Holland et al. 1985). Such research would be costly and requires many years of follow-up. However, with the growing number of successful longitudinal studies following individuals aged 50 and over,[4] secondary data analysis may present greater opportunities than conducting primary studies of prevention.

In the absence of robust empirical evidence, early evidence of the potential benefit of investing in dementia prevention may need to rely on simulation studies drawing on the best available evidence. In the next chapter, Handels and Wimo review recently identified examples of health-economic models of dementia prevention.

Notes

1 Advances on dementia policy include G8 dementia summit: global action against dementia (www.gov.uk/government/publications/g8-dementia-summit-global-action-against-dementia/g8-dementia-summit-global-action-against-dementia-11-december-2013); UK prime minister launches and backs 'Dementia challenge' www.gov.uk/government/news/dementia-challenge-launched; Global action plan on the public health response to dementia 2017–2025 (www.who.int/mental_health/neurology/dementia/action_plan_2017_2025/en/);WHO heads the development of the Global Dementia Observatory (www.who.int/mental_health/neurology/dementia/GDO/en/); Atlantic Philanthropies Gives $177M to Establish Global Brain Health Institute to Fight Dementia: (www.gbhi.org); Life Changes Trust £50m. endowment from the Big Lottery Fund (www.lifechangestrust.org.uk/); Bill Gates invest $100 m in dementia research (http://fortune.com/2017/11/13/bill-gates-alzheimers-50-million-investment-dementia-research/).

2 In 2010, when Comas-Herrera et al. asked a panel of international experts to reach a consensus on the potential impact of scientific advances, the panel were only moderately optimistic about the chances of Alzheimer's disease disappearing in the next 50 years; as a result, this work raised concerns of the projected costs of dementia and anticipated that services may fall short of the required increase (Comas-Herrera et al. 2011).

3 National Institute for Health and Care Excellence (NICE). Dementia, disability and frailty in later life – mid-life approaches to delay or prevent onset (www.nice.org.uk/guidance/ng16/evidence)

4 Gateway to Global Aging Data (https://g2aging.org/?section=surveyOverview).

References

American Psychiatric Association. & American Psychiatric Association. DSM-5 Task Force. (2013). *Diagnostic and Statistical Manual of Mental Disorders: DSM-5*. Washington, DC: American Psychiatric Association.

Bigio, E. H., Hynan, L. S., Sontag, E., Satumtira, S., & White, C. L. (2002). Synapse loss is greater in presenile than senile onset Alzheimer disease: implications for the cognitive reserve hypothesis. *Neuropathology and Applied Neurobiology*, 28(3), 218–227. https://doi.org/10.1046/j.1365-2990.2002.00385.x

Chan, K.Y., Wang,W., Wu,J.J., Liu, L., Theodoratou, E., Car,J., Middleton, L., Russ,T. C., Deary,I.J., Campbell, H., Wang,W. & Rudan,I. 2013. Global Health Epidemiology Reference Group (GHERG). Epidemiology of Alzheimer's disease and other forms of dementia in China, 1990–2010: A systematic review and analysis. *The Lancet*, 381(9882), 2016–2023. https://doi.org/10.1016/S0140-6736(13)60221-4.

Claxton, K., Martin S., Soares, M., Rice, N., Spackman, E., Hinde, S., Devlin, N., Smith, P. C. & Sculpher, M. (2013). *Methods for the Estimation of the NICE Cost Effectiveness Threshold Revised Report Following Referees Comments*. Available at: www.york.ac.uk/media/che/documents/reports/resubmitted_report.pdf.

Comas-Herrera, A., Northey, S., Wittenberg, R., Knapp, M., Bhattacharyya, S. & Burns, A. (2011). Future costs of dementia-related long-term care: Exploring future scenarios. *International Psychogeriatrics*, 23(1), 20–30. https://doi.org/10.1017/S1041610210000025.

Committee of Public Accounts. (2008). *Improving Services and Support for People with Dementia: Sixth Report of Session 2007–2008: Report, Together with Formal Minutes, Oral and Written Evidence*. London: Stationery Office Books.

Daviglus, M. L., Bell, C. C., Berrettini, W., Bowen, P. E., Connolly, E. S. Jr, Cox, N. J., Dunbar-Jacob, J. M., Granieri, E. C., Hunt, G., McGarry, K., Patel, D., Potosky, A. L., Sanders-Bush, E., Silberberg, D. & Trevisan, M. (2010). NIH state-of-the-science conference statement: Preventing Alzheimer's disease and cognitive decline. *NIH Consensus and State-of-the-Science Statements*, 27(4), 1–30.

Drummond, M., Sculpher, M., Claxton, K. & Stoddart, G. (2015). *Methods for the Economic Evaluation of Health Care Programmes*. Available at: https://books.google.com/books?hl=en&lr=&id=yzZSCwAAQBAJ&oi=fnd&pg=PP1&dq=Methods+for+the+Economic+Evaluation+of+Healthcare+Programmes+Fourth+Edition&ots=_aNipJ9oII&sig=eQ9tzYaMBb1dNhUKw7FM8ftVc6g.

Gao, S., Hendrie, H. C., Hall, K. S. & Hui, S. (1998). The relationships between age, sex, and the incidence of dementia and Alzheimer disease: A meta-analysis. *Archives of General Psychiatry*, 55(9), 809–815.

Getsios, D., Migliaccio-Walle, K. & Caro, J. J. (2007). NICE cost-effectiveness appraisal of cholinesterase inhibitors: Was the right question posed? Were the best tools used? *Pharmaco Economics*, 25(12), 997–1006.

Grossman, M. (1972). On the concept of health capital and the demand for health. *Journal of Political Economy*, 80(2), 223–255. https://doi.org/10.1086/259880.

Guerchet, M. M., Mayston, R., Lloyd-Sherlock, P., Prince, M. J., Aboderin, I., Akinyemi, R., . . . Ezeah, P. (2017). *Dementia in sub-Saharan Africa: challenges and opportunities*. London: Alzheimer's Disease International.

Handels, R. & Wimo, A. (2017). Challenges and recommendations for the health-economic evaluation of primary prevention programmes for dementia. *Aging & Mental Health*, 1–7. https://doi.org/10.1080/13607863.2017.1390730.

Higgins, J. G. S. (2008). *Chapter 15: Incorporating Economics Evidence: Cochrane Handbook for Systematic Reviews of Interventions Version 5.0.1* [updated September 2008]. Chichester, England: The Cochrane Collaboration.

Holland, P. W., Glymour, C. & Granger, C. (1985). Statistics and Causal inference*. *ETS Research Report Series*, (2), 1–72. https://doi.org/10.1002/j.2330-8516.1985.tb00125.x.

Hyde, C., Peters, J., Bond, M., Rogers, G., Hoyle, M., Anderson, R., Jeffreys, M., Davis, S., Thokala, P. & Moxham, T. (2013). Evolution of the evidence on the effectiveness and cost-effectiveness of acetylcholinesterase inhibitors and memantine for Alzheimer's disease: Systematic review and economic model. *Age and Ageing*, 42(1), 14–20. https://doi.org/10.1093/ageing/afs165.

Knapp, M., Iemmi, V. & Romeo, R. (2013). Dementia care costs and outcomes: A systematic review. *International Journal of Geriatric Psychiatry*, 28(6), 551–561. https://doi.org/10.1002/gps.3864.

Laver, K., Dyer, S., Whitehead, C., Clemson, L. & Crotty, M. (2016). Interventions to delay functional decline in people with dementia: A systematic review of systematic reviews. *BMJ Open*, 6(4), e010767. https://doi.org/10.1136/bmjopen-2015-010767.

Lewis, F., Schaffer, S. K., Sussex, J., Neill, P. O., Cockcroft, L. & Org, J. (2014). *The trajectory of Dementia in the UK – Making a Difference*. Available at: www.Alzheimersresearchuk.org/wp-content/uploads/2015/01/OHE-report-Full.pdf.

Luengo-Fernandez, R., Leal, J. & Gray, A. M. (2012). UK research expenditure on dementia, heart disease, stroke and cancer: Are levels of spending related to disease burden? *European Journal of Neurology*, 19(1), 149–154. https://doi.org/10.1111/j.1468-1331.2011.03500.x.

Marshall, A. (1960). *Principles of economics*. Palgrave Macmillan. Retrieved from http://www.springer.com/gp/book/9780333056462

Martin Prince, A., Wimo, A., Guerchet, M., Gemma-Claire Ali, M., Wu, Y.-T., Prina, M., Yee Chan, K. & Xia, Z. (2015). *World Alzheimer report 2015: The Global Impact of Dementia an Analysis of Prevalence, Incidence, Cost and Trends*.

Matthews, F. E., Stephan, B. C. M., Robinson, L., Jagger, C., Barnes, L. E. & Arthur, A. (2016). A two decade dementia incidence comparison from the Cognitive Function and Ageing Studies I and II. *Nature Communication*, 7, 1–8. https://www.nature.com/articles/ncomms11398.pdf.

Neumann, P. J., & Weinstein, M. C. (2010). Legislating against use of cost-effectiveness information. *The New England Journal of Medicine*, 363(16), 1495–1497. https://doi.org/10.1056/NEJMp1007168

NICE. (2018). Donepezil, galantamine, rivastigmine and memantine for the treatment of Alzheimer's disease: Technology appraisal guidance [TA217]. Publication date: 23 March 2011. Last updated: 20 June 2018. https://www.nice.org.uk/guidance/ta217.

Norton, S., Matthews, F. E., Barnes, D. E., Yaffe, K. & Brayne, C. (2014). Potential for primary prevention of Alzheimer's disease: An analysis of population-based data. *The Lancet Neurology*, 13(8), 788–794. https://doi.org/10.1016/S1474-4422(14)70136-X.

Oremus, M. (2008). Systematic review of economic evaluations of Alzheimer's disease medications. *Expert Review of Pharmacoeconomics & Outcomes Research*, 8(3), 273–289. https://doi.org/10.1586/14737167.8.3.273.

Robertson, I. H. (2013). A noradrenergic theory of cognitive reserve: implications for Alzheimer's disease. *Neurobiology of Aging*, 34(1), 298–308. https://doi.org/10.1016/j.neurobiolaging.2012.05.019

Saxena, S., Thornicroft, G., Knapp, M. & Whiteford, H. (2007). Resources for mental health: Scarcity, inequity, and inefficiency. *The Lancet* (London, England), 370(9590), 878–889. https://doi.org/10.1016/S0140-6736(07)61239-2.

Schaller, S., Mauskopf, J., Kriza, C., Wahlster, P. & Kolominsky-Rabas, P. L. (2015). The main cost drivers in dementia: A systematic review. *International Journal of Geriatric Psychiatry*, 30(2), 111–129. https://doi.org/10.1002/gps.4198.

Stern, Y. (2009). Cognitive reserve. *Neuropsychologia*, 47(10), 2015–2028. https://doi.org/10.1016/j.neuropsychologia.2009.03.004

Tilford, J. M., Payakachat, N., Kovacs, E., Pyne, J. M., Brouwer, W., Nick, T. G., Bellando, J. & Kuhlthau, K. A. (2012). Preference-based health-related quality-of-life outcomes in children with autism spectrum disorders: A comparison of generic instruments. *PharmacoEconomics*, 30(8), 661–679. https://doi.org/10.2165/11597200-000000000-00000.

Trépel, D. (2011). Informal cost of dementia care – a proxy-good valuation in Ireland. *Economic and Social Review*, 42(4).

Trépel, D. (2017). Cost-effectiveness of interventions for the treatment of dementia disorders. *In:* Denise, R. ed. *Mental Health Economics: The Costs and Benefits of Psychiatric Care*. Cham, Switzerland: Springer, 339–351. https://doi.org/10.1007/978-3-319-55266-8_22

Van Baal, P., & Hoogendoorn, M. (2014). *Costs and benefits of increasing physical activity to prevent the onset of dementia: a modelling analysis*. Retrieved from https://www.nice.org.uk/guidance/ng16/evidence/economic-modelling-report-pdf-552745261

Walker, S., Sculpher, M., Claxton, K. & Palmer, S. (2012). Coverage with evidence development, only in research, risk sharing, or patient access scheme? A framework for coverage decisions. *Value in Health: The Journal of the International Society for Pharmacoeconomics and Outcomes Research*, 15(3), 570–579. https://doi.org/10.1016/j.jval.2011.12.013.

Wimo, A., Guerchet, M., Ali, G. C., Wu, Y.T., Prina, A. M., Winblad, B., Jönsson, L., Liu, Z. & Prince, M. (2017). The worldwide costs of dementia 2015 and comparisons with 2010. *Alzheimer's & Dementia: The Journal of the Alzheimer's Association*, 13(1), 1–7. https://doi.org/10.1016/j.jalz.2016.07.150.

Wimo, A., Jönsson, L., Bond, J., Prince, M., Winblad, B. & Alzheimer Disease International. (2013). The worldwide economic impact of dementia 2010. *Alzheimer's & Dementia : The Journal of the Alzheimer's Association*, 9(1), 1–11.e3. https://doi.org/10.1016/j.jalz.2012.11.006.

Woods, B., Revill, P., Sculpher, M., & Claxton, K. (2016). Country-Level Cost-Effectiveness Thresholds: Initial Estimates and the Need for Further Research. *Value in Health*, 19(8), 929–935. https://doi.org/10.1016/j.jval.2016.02.017

Wu, Y-T., Beiser, A. S., Breteler, M. M. B., Fratiglioni, L., Helmer, C., Hendrie, H. C., Brayne, C. (2017). The changing prevalence and incidence of dementia over time – current evidence. *Nature Reviews Neurology*, 13(6), 327–339. https://doi.org/10.1038/nrneurol.2017.63.

Wu, Y-T., Lee, H., Norton, S., Chen, C., Chen, H., He, C. & Brayne, C. (2013). Prevalence studies of Dementia in Mainland China, Hong Kong and Taiwan: A Systematic Review and Meta-Analysis. *PLoS One*, 8(6), e66252. https://doi.org/10.1371/journal.pone.0066252.

Chapter 12

Health-economics of dementia prevention using modelling

Ron Handels and Anders Wimo

Introduction

With a global prevalence of 47 million and a corresponding economic impact of US $818 billion, dementia has a substantial burden on societies worldwide (Prince et al. 2015; Wimo et al. 2017). There has been a growing interest in the primary prevention of dementia by means of interventions aimed at reducing risk factors for dementia. Various studies are currently evaluating the effectiveness of such programs by following cohorts of participants who were exposed to programs targeting at improving lifestyle and cardiovascular disease management. Among them is the Finnish Geriatric Intervention Study to Prevent Cognitive Impairment and Disability (FINGER) (Ngandu et al. 2015). This study has found that people aged 60–77 who were at risk for dementia and who received a multi-domain intervention (including elements of diet, exercise, cognitive training and vascular risk monitoring) showed an 0.20 improvement in the z-score of a neuropsychological test battery after two years, which was higher than the control group. The Prevention of Dementia by Intensive Vascular care (preDIVA) study did not report a significant difference in dementia incidence between a nurse-led, multi-domain cardiovascular intervention and usual care among people aged 70–78 years, who had been recruited from general practices, and were assessed after a six-year follow-up (van Charante et al. 2016).

The cost-effectiveness of the FINGER intervention has not been established. This leaves policy makers in uncertainty as to whether spending public healthcare resources to bring this innovation to patients will result in sufficient health gains to justify the investment.

We aimed to discuss methods to assess the incremental cost-effectiveness of interventions targeted at the primary prevention of dementia. We mainly relied on the results from a literature review on health-economic evaluations of (hypothetical) intervention programs for the primary prevention of dementia (Handels and Wimo 2017). The methods of this literature review entailed a specific search of studies reporting economic outcomes of existing or hypothetical dementia prevention programmes. The following databases were searched for publications published between 2000 and April 2017: PubMed, Modelling

Outcome and Cost Impacts of Interventions for Dementia toolkit evidence database, Tufts Medical Centre's Cost-effectiveness Analysis Registry and The Centre for Reviews and Dissemination database. In addition, references and citations were reviewed including the 2014 Alzheimer Disease International report on dementia and risk reduction (Prince et al. 2014).

Available evidence

The review identified three publications reflecting the potential of primary prevention of dementia. These publications sketched a hypothetical scenario in which an effect on dementia risk reduction was assumed by a plausible intervention program. The studies had different purposes as explained next.

The first study (Zhang et al. 2011) focussed on estimating the cost-effectiveness of a combination of a health promotion program and pharmacological treatment of cardiovascular risk factors in Sweden. Their goal was to evaluate whether large health trends in dementia would impact health-economic outcomes by assuming a hypothetical intervention effect. They assumed that a natural 20-year risk of developing dementia of 4.2% in people aged 50 would be reduced to 1%.

The second study (Van Baal et al. 2016) hypothesized that primary prevention programs increase the life expectancy of people in the UK and this exposes them to other diseases and the costs related to those diseases. This indicates the importance of including effects of primary prevention beyond dementia. Therefore, in their evaluation of the burden of dementia associated with physical inactivity they also explicitly took the additional costs due to increased life expectancy into account.

The third study (Lin et al. 2014) highlighted that cardiovascular diseases and dementia share common risk factors. Therefore, programs targeting cardiovascular risk factors potentially have benefits for reducing the burden related to dementia, which they have referred to as "unintended benefits". Although insufficient evidence withholds recommending such interventions specifically for dementia, they argued that anticipating on such effects could help policy makers to assess future care needs and public planning related to dementia. They simulated a 10% reduction in the prevalence of diabetes, hypertension and cardiovascular diseases, and a reduction of body mass index, as this hypothetical effect size corresponded to the effect size of an existing diabetes prevention programme.

A detailed overview of the methods and results of the studies is given in the following paragraphs.

Overview of methods

Cost-effectiveness of primary prevention

Zhang et al. aimed to "estimate the cost-effectiveness of a potential preventive intervention program meant to lower the score related to increased dementia risk". The natural probability of developing dementia was estimated using the CAIDE (Cardiovascular Risk Factors, Aging, and Incidence of Dementia) risk score (Kivipelto et al. 2006) and the single 20-year risk score was transformed into 20 1-year risk scores. In concordance with estimates from the literature, they assumed this risk of developing dementia doubled with each 5-year age increments. This allowed them to simulate the incidence of dementia in a virtual cohort in annual steps from the age of 50 onwards. They applied age-specific mortality estimates to simulate the proportion survival, and assumed a similar mortality rate in dementia as well as non-dementia. They applied previously established estimates of care costs specifically for age and dementia status. Lastly, they applied age-specific estimates of health-related quality of life in the general population and assumed a similar age-trend for estimates of health-related quality of life estimates in dementia.

The model was used to simulate the annual costs and quality-adjusted life years (QALYs) from age 50 to 70 in annual steps for a situation reflecting usual care and a situation reflecting a hypothetical intervention to lower the risk of dementia. The results indicated that in usual care 4.8% had developed dementia and 12% had died after 20 simulation years, while in the scenario of the hypothetical primary prevention program 1.2% developed dementia and the same proportion died. This was estimated to go alongside with a cost reduction and a gain of QALYs. The authors concluded that the hypothetical multi-domain preventive intervention was expected to result in less costs and better QALYs. This was considered promising for future research on programs targeting the primary prevention of dementia.

Care consumption in saved life years

Van Baal et al. aimed to "estimate the burden of dementia in England associated with physical inactivity and assess the potential health benefits and changes in health care and social care expenditures associated with increasing physical inactivity levels". They developed a three-state model reflecting the state of no dementia, dementia and death. The level of physical inactivity determined the probability of converting from no dementia to dementia and the probability of converting from no dementia to death. Evidence to support this association was obtained from published studies. The state of dementia was associated with an increased mortality risk and increase use of care. Health care costs for comorbidities were estimated using age- and gender-specific average costs of comorbidities. The model started with reflecting a population aged 40 in England in 2012 with a distribution of levels of physical activity similar to observed levels in this population.

The model allowed the calculation of life years gained due to increased life expectancy, years with dementia, costs related to dementia and costs related to other diseases over the life span of the starting cohort. These outcomes were obtained by multiplying the number of people in each state in each year by the care related costs in the respective states. They estimated the outcomes in a situation reflecting usual practice and compared the results to situations in which part of the population was assumed to become physically more active. The results indicated that an inactive person was estimated to live one additional year with dementia, with its corresponding increase of dementia-related costs, but was also estimated to have a reduced life expectancy of two years, with its corresponding absence of care costs due to comorbidities. Persons who were physically more active were estimated to have increased life expectancy, with corresponding increase in costs due to comorbidities, but decreased dementia-related costs due to the reduced dementia incidence.

The authors discussed that when inactive people become low active, dementia-related savings outweighed the additional care spending in life years gained. However, when low active become somewhat active and when somewhat active become more active and meet the recommended amount of physical activity, dementia-related savings did not outweigh the additional care spending in the life years gained. The authors further discuss that preventing dementia likely diverts people into another expensive later-life trajectory.

Unintended benefits of cardiovascular risk management

Lin et al. aimed to anticipate the possible consequences of addressing modifiable risk factors for Alzheimer's disease and related dementias. They used a cohort-based simulation model to simulate a reduction of possible dementia risk factors and its corresponding effect on the onset and duration of dementia, and care costs. The modifiable dementia-related risk factors included overweight or obesity, diabetes, hypertension and cardiovascular diseases.

They constructed three prediction models using data from longitudinal cohorts. First, a so-called Dynamic Aging Process simulation was developed to track the development of dementia risk factors over time. This was based on a framework similar to that of the RAND Future Elderly Model. Second, they developed a regression model to predict dementia in a particular year based on the aforementioned dementia risk factors, as well as demographic characteristics, comorbidities and acute medical events. Third, a regression model was developed to estimate the annual care costs for those with dementia and those without dementia, correcting for the same factors as in the second model. Combining the three models allowed the estimation of the natural development of dementia and other diseases, as well as the effects of a hypothetical reduction in risk factors related to dementia. To extract those costs related to dementia, they performed a counterfactual simulation to estimate care costs using the identical model, although without the development of dementia and subtracted this from the first simulation.

The results indicated that the hypothesized prevention program would reduce the probability of developing and/or the duration of dementia as well as the care costs for a reduction in each of the four risk factors. The authors concluded that their findings highlight potential health gains and saving opportunities as a result of managing risk factors associated with dementia.

Comparison

Van Baal et al. and Zhang et al. included care costs due to other diseases during the time gained in which persons did not have dementia (i.e. dementia-free years), and Van Baal et al. and Lin et al. also included the costs during the life years gained. Although the model by Lin et al. estimated costs due to other diseases, they explicitly omitted these costs by isolating the dementia-related costs, as this was the aim of their study. Zhang et al. assumed identical life expectancy in people with and without dementia, based on studies reporting no association between treatment and mortality in (pharmacological) intervention studies of dementia. They did, however, explore dementia-related mortality in a sensitivity analysis and reported that the hypothetical program would still likely be cost-effective. Plausible costs of the intervention programme were only examined by Zhang et al., while the other studies did not reflect such costs.

Informal care was only examined by Zhang et al. The value attached to that comprised 40% of the total costs (Wimo et al. 2013, 2014) and might have influenced the health-economic results in terms of savings gained by reducing the dementia risk. Only the study by Zhang et al. included QALYs and estimated the relation between incremental costs and incremental QALYs as a result of reducing the hypothetical risk. Only the results of this study can be used to evaluate whether the potential QALY gain from prevention programmes is worth the costs of such programmes. For example, the various situations examined by Van Baal et al. resulted in higher costs, which does not necessarily reflect a negative outcome, as the potential QALYs gained by increased life expectancy might be considered worthwhile these additional costs.

Methodological challenges

The evidence on the potential health-economic effects of primary dementia prevention is scarce and characterized by a variety in methods and results. This is challenging the assessment of the cost-effectiveness of current multi-domain primary prevention programmes, such as those addressed by the FINGER, Pre-DIVA, Multi-domain Alzheimer Preventive Trial (MAPT) (Vellas et al. 2014) and Healthy Ageing Through Internet Counselling in the Elderly (Richard et al. 2016) projects. The results from the literature review led to the identification of various challenges (Handels and Wimo 2017).

Long-term effects

What perhaps can be considered the largest challenge is caused by the fact that primary prevention trials follow-up people who initially do not have dementia (at around the age of 60) for a relatively short time (two to six years), while health-economic effects mainly occur in stages of dementia (at around the age of 80). This requires extrapolation of short-term effects in intermediate outcomes to long-term effects on dementia incidence and mortality, to ensure the largest part of the health-economic effects is incorporated.

The three studies described earlier have assumed an effect of a lifestyle program on the reduction of risk factors for dementia (the hypothetical part) and subsequently predicted the reduction of dementia incidence corresponding to this reduction in risk factors (the extrapolation part). Various dementia risk equations have been reviewed (Imtiaz et al. 2014), which can be used to estimate the probability of developing dementia given a specific status of a set of risk factors. Although this method seems plausible and has face validity, it is limited as it assumes a fully causal relation between a risk factor and the development of dementia. Evidence on risk factors is based on longitudinal cohort research. Outcomes may be biased due to unobserved confounding factors. If confounding is present, the reduction in dementia incidence is overestimated, leading to an overestimation of health-economic benefits.

Representative risk factors

The method of combining a model that reflects the change in risk factors with a model that predicts dementia incidence corresponding to a specific set of risk factor statuses requires that both parts speak the same language. In other words, the specific set of risk factors should ideally be identical in the two parts. However, not all available modifiable risk factors may have been included as outcome measures in the current prevention trials and not all outcome measures may have been included as a risk factor in dementia risk equations. For example, the current dementia prevention studies all include a measure of cognition, among which a composite z-score of a neuropsychological test battery, specific neuropsychological tests or global cognition measured by the Mini-Mental State Examination, while only few dementia risk models include baseline cognition as a risk factor. Even if a risk equation includes cognition, such as the CAIDE risk score, it only includes global cognition and not the specific neuropsychological tests. Mapping methods are required to estimate the change in global cognition corresponding to a change in specific neuropsychological test battery outcomes.

Indirect effects

Various effects are considered indirect. First, mortality has been associated with dementia, especially with severe states of dementia (Garcia-Ptacek et al. 2014). Thus, reducing dementia incidence can be expected to extend life expectancy. Second, if prevention interventions are able to reduce the incidence of dementia, it could be considered plausible they can reduce the speed of progression once dementia is present. Slower progression is expected to result in lower age-specific prevalence of severe dementia, which is then expected to decrease mortality and increase life expectancy. Third, during the gained life years other diseases could occur. The gained years drive an increase in QALYs but the incidence of other diseases increases care costs. However, risk factors associated to dementia incidence share common ground with risk factors for cardiovascular diseases, and potentially could reduce the incidence of cardiovascular disease. The three health-economic models have taught us this can be incorporated by explicitly modelling comorbidities or using age-specific overall care costs. These indirect effects have received attention in the last years (Sköldunger et al. 2013; Gustavsson et al. 2017) and urge the use of age-specific estimates in health-economic simulation related to dementia.

Other methodological challenges

Various other more generic challenges for modelling intervention effects are present. Among them is the persistence of intervention effectiveness. It is uncertain whether any benefits will persist if people drop out from a prevention program. Another challenge is the representation of usual care. Participating in a control group might trigger the Hawthorne effect of making one aware of their risk and anticipating it by changing their behaviour which one would not do if not participating in the trial. Also, finding the optimal target population is challenging. Responsiveness to a prevention program might be dependent on certain demographic risk factors or behavioural characteristics. These could distinguish subgroups with high and low cost-effectiveness.

Challenges for policy makers

Based on the results and challenges from the review (Handels and Wimo 2017) we have identified various challenges for policy making, even if a dementia prevention program has been estimated as being cost-effective. A relatively large number of people would likely need to be exposed to an intervention program in order to prevent a single case of dementia. Figure 12.1 reflects the ratio of people without and with dementia in the general population relying on the annual dementia incidence based on multi-cohort, age-specific incidence estimates (Launer et al. 1999) and age-specific death gathered from Swedish Statistics. This already indicates the challenge of finding financial resources as well as developing infrastructures to ensure access to a prevention program. It also indicates the potential importance of distinguishing those people who are at increased risk of developing dementia (i.e. and exclude those who will likely never develop dementia in their lifetime from the intervention program).

Resources to finance a new cost-effective intervention can come from different sources. The obvious choice is to use the care savings from those who have been prevented to develop dementia. This is relatively uncomplicated for

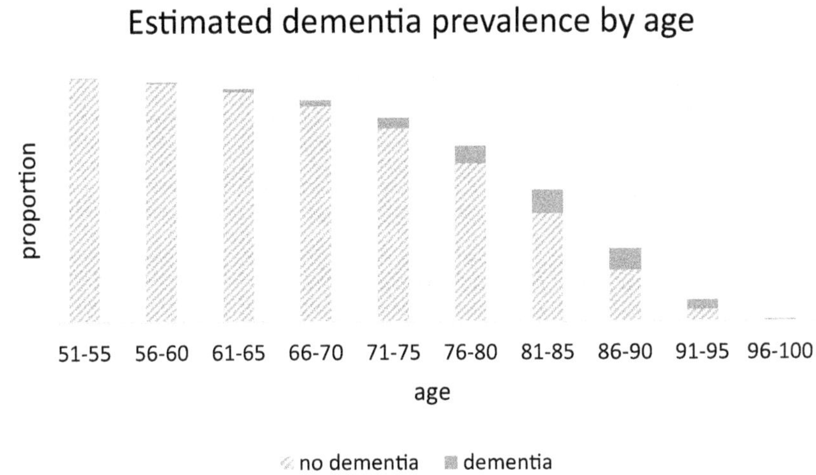

Figure 12.1 The proportion persons without dementia (blue diagonal stripes) and with dementia (solid orange) by 5-year age groups over lifetime

care savings in the medical sector as a prevention program is likely operationalized within the same sector and budgets could likely be shifted relatively easy within a sector. Prevented care from the social care sector, such as home and institutionalized care, require a cross-sector shift of financial resources. Even more challenging is to employ the economic resources reflected by the value of informal caregiving hours that became "available" due to preventing dementia, as this is not a financial budget that can be shifted. An intervention is considered cost-effective if the additional resources (i.e. investment) required to gain 1 QALY is lower than a willingness to pay cut-off. Nevertheless, the resources for this investment must be made available. The idea is that in order to operationalize a new more efficient intervention, a current less efficient intervention will be omitted in order to use the released resources to finance the new intervention. However, only few examples exist of omitting care due to inefficiency and thus also form a challenge for policy making (Elshaug et al. 2007). At last, any significant benefits of a primary prevention program will likely occur years to decades later than the investment in operationalizing such a program. This is a further challenge to translating savings into resources available to employ a prevention program.

Figure 12.2 shows the simulated lifetime effects on costs and QALY value of a hypothetical scenario in which a primary dementia prevention program was implemented compared to the care as usual. The program was assumed to reduce the annual dementia incidence by 5% and was provided to a group of persons aged 50 for a duration of 10 years at 300 Euro/year. These results were estimated using an illness-death Markov model. This graph reflects the costs of the intervention program in those aged 51–60. It shows the savings in dementia

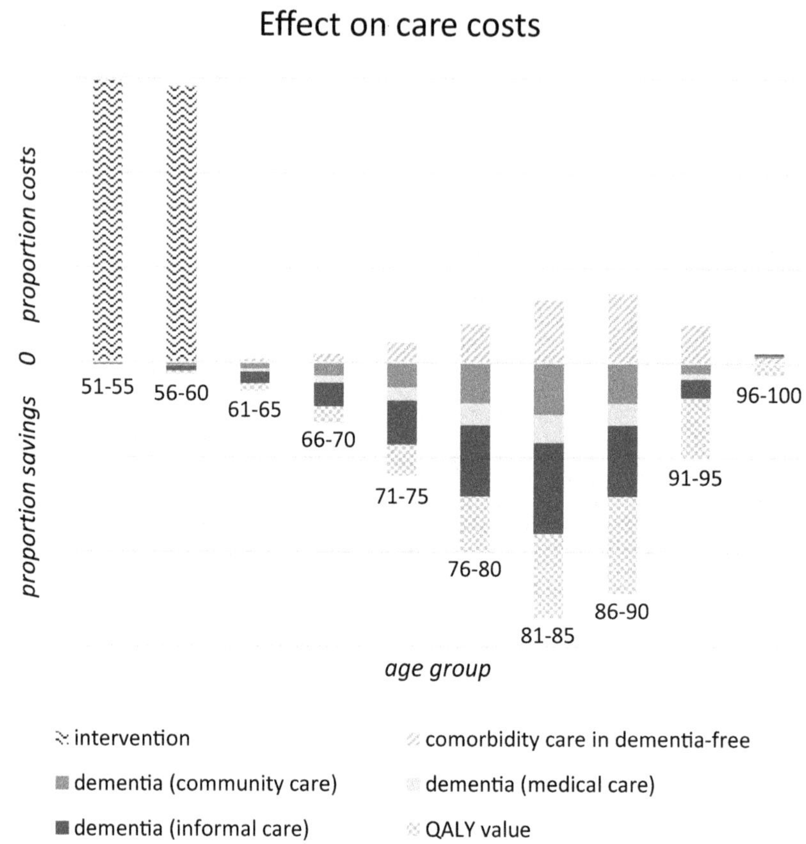

Figure 12.2 The simulated lifetime effects on care costs of a hypothetical scenario in which a primary dementia prevention program was provided to a group of persons age 50 for a duration of 10 years.

care across the three care sectors due to a proportion of the years living with dementia being prevented. It also shows the care costs in the dementia-free as well as life years gained in the at-risk population. At last, it reflects the willingness to pay of 40,000 Euro/QALY for the gained QALYs due to the proportion dementia being prevented and the life years gained due to the reduced proportion of dementia-related decreased life expectancy.

Recommendations

Several studies have evaluated or are currently evaluating the effectiveness of programs targeting the primary prevention of dementia. Various challenges exist in estimating their cost-effectiveness, among which are causality between risk factor and dementia incidence; representativeness of a risk factor in a trial and a risk factor in a risk equation (and mapping techniques); indirect effects on mortality, dementia disease progression and cardiovascular diseases and associated effects on costs and quality of life during gained life years; and other challenges, such as persistence of effectiveness, representation of usual care and optimal target population.

Three studies have reported on simulations that indicated the potential cost-effectiveness if a hypothetical prevention effect would be realized. Although they apply different methods, they all provided a valuable contribution to the methodological discussion on how to deal with these challenges. Future studies could rely on these methods and provide sensitivity analyses to reflect the impact of uncertainties in the methods and assumptions required to estimate long-term effects of primary dementia prevention interventions. Meanwhile, new data and evidence is being generated, which can help develop and validate methods for extrapolating risk factors to dementia incidence.

Evidence on the potential health-economic impact of primary dementia prevention could aid in the discussion on how to finance primary dementia prevention programs if they have been proved effective. This discussion seems important as such interventions likely generate several challenges for policy making.

References

Elshaug, A. G., *et al.* (2007). Challenges in Australian policy processes for disinvestment from existing, ineffective health care practices. *Australia and New Zealand Health Policy*, 4(1), 23. doi:10.1186/1743-8462-4-23.

Garcia-Ptacek, S., *et al.* (2014). Mortality risk after dementia diagnosis by dementia type and underlying factors: A cohort of 15, 209 patients based on the Swedish Dementia Registry. *Journal of Alzheimer's Disease : JAD*, 41(2), 467–477. doi:10.3233/JAD-131856.

Gustavsson, A., *et al.* (2017). Current issues and future research priorities for health economic modelling across the full continuum of Alzheimer's disease. *Alzheimer's & Dementia*, 13(3), 312–321. doi:10.1016/j.jalz.2016.12.005.

Handels, R. & Wimo, A. (2017). Challenges and recommendations for the health-economic evaluation of primary prevention programmes for dementia. *Aging & Mental Health*, 1–7. doi:10.1080/13607863.2017.1390730.

Imtiaz, B., *et al.* (2014). Future directions in Alzheimer's disease from risk factors to prevention. *Biochemical Pharmacology*, 88(4), 661–670. doi:10.1016/j.bcp.2014.01.003.

Kivipelto, M., *et al.* (2006). Risk score for the prediction of dementia risk in 20 years among middle aged people: A longitudinal, population-based study. *The Lancet Neurology*, 5(9), 735–741. doi:10.1016/S1474-4422(06)70537-3.

Launer, L. J., *et al.* (1999). Rates and risk factors for dementia and Alzheimer's disease: Results from EURODEM pooled analyses. EURODEM Incidence Research Group and Work Groups. European Studies of Dementia. *Neurology*, 52(1), 78–84. Available at: www.ncbi.nlm.nih.gov/pubmed/9921852 [Accessed 15 March 2018].

Lin, P-J., *et al.* (2014). Unintended benefits: The potential economic impact of addressing risk factors to prevent Alzheimer's disease. *Health Affairs (Project Hope)*, 33(4), 547–554. doi:10.1377/hlthaff.2013.1276.

Ngandu, T., *et al.* (2015). A 2 year multidomain intervention of diet, exercise, cognitive training, and vascular risk monitoring versus control to prevent cognitive decline in at-risk elderly people (FINGER): A randomised controlled trial. *The Lancet* (London, England), 385(9984), 2255–2263. doi:10.1016/S0140-6736(15)60461-5.

Prince, M., Guerchet, M. & Prina, M. (2015). *The Epidemiology and Impact of Dementia: Current State and Future Trends*. Geneva: World Health Organization. Available at: www.who.int/mental_health/neurology/dementia/dementia_thematicbrief_epidemiology.pdf.

Prince, M., *et al.* (2014). *World Alzheimer Report 2014*. London. Available at: www.alz.co.uk/research/WorldAlzheimerReport2014.pdf.

Richard, E., *et al.* (2016). Healthy ageing through Internet counselling in the elderly: The HATICE randomised controlled trial for the prevention of cardiovascular disease and cognitive impairment. *BMJ Open*, 6(6), e010806. doi:10.1136/bmjopen-2015-010806.

Sköldunger, A., *et al.* (2013). Mortality and treatment costs have a great impact on the cost-effectiveness of disease modifying drugs in Alzheimer's disease. *Current Alzheimer Research*, 10(2), 207–216.

Van Baal, P. H. M., Hoogendoorn, M. & Fischer, A. (2016). Preventing dementia by promoting physical activity and the long-term impact on health and social care expenditures. *Preventive Medicine*, 85, 78–83. doi:10.1016/j.ypmed.2016.01.013.

van Charante, E. P. M., *et al.* (2016). Effectiveness of a 6-year multidomain vascular care intervention to prevent dementia (preDIVA): A cluster-randomised controlled trial. *The Lancet* (London, England). doi:10.1016/S0140-6736(16)30950-3.

Vellas, B., *et al.* (2014). Mapt study: A multidomain approach for preventing Alzheimer's disease: Design and baseline data. *The Journal of Prevention of Alzheimer's Disease*, 1(1), 13–22.

Wimo, A., *et al.* (2013). The worldwide economic impact of dementia 2010. *Alzheimers Dementia the Journal of the Alzheimers Association*, 9, 1–11. e3. doi:10.1016/j.jalz.2012.11.006.

Wimo, A., *et al.* (2014). Health economic evaluation of treatments for Alzheimer's disease: Impact of new diagnostic criteria. *Journal of Internal Medicine*, 275(3), 304–316. doi:10.1111/joim.12167.

Wimo, A., *et al.* (2017). The worldwide costs of dementia 2015 and comparisons with 2010. *Alzheimer's & Dementia : The Journal of the Alzheimer's Association*, 13(1), 1–7. doi:10.1016/j.jalz.2016.07.150.

Zhang, Y., *et al.* (2011). Cost-effectiveness of a health intervention program with risk reductions for getting demented: Results of a Markov model in a Swedish/Finnish setting. *Journal of Alzheimer's Disease: JAD*, 26(4), 735–744. doi:10.3233/JAD-2011-110065.

Chapter 13

Cognitive footprint

A framework to guide public policy

Martin Knapp, Claryn S. J. Kung, Martin Rossor and Charlotte R. Stoner

Introduction

Cognition is obviously a key domain when considering the effects of dementia, but it has much wider relevance. It is fundamental to how each of us functions from day to day, and it has enormous influence on what we are able to achieve in our lives – in the spheres of education, employment, interpersonal relationships, social roles and economic status, for instance – with consequences for our overall quality of life.

Cognition is not just memory, but a broader spectrum that includes language, perception, creativity and social function. We have previously proposed the concept of a *'cognitive footprint'* to bring together the myriad positive and negative influences on cognition, not just in older age, but over the entire life course (Rossor and Knapp 2015). One potential use of such a cognitive footprint would be to feed into public policy discussions across a range of areas. The strong and complex interconnections between cognitive ability, family context, childhood experiences, educational attainment, employment status, earnings, health and independence in daily activities, for example, clearly also have major implications for what a country achieves in terms of the level and distribution of economic and psychological wellbeing (Hanushek and Woessmann 2008).

In this chapter, we discuss how an overarching *cognitive footprint* framework might be used to consider the cognitive effects of experiences, events and interventions across the life course. Education, for instance, would clearly have a large and lasting impact on cognition. However, a plethora of other influences, which early evidence has illustrated to have some impact, remains less well-researched. We have chosen five particular influences on cognition to illustrate the diverse range of experiences that would need to be taken into consideration: adverse side effects of medications, loneliness, pollution, perinatal mental illness and traumatic brain injury. One of our arguments is that, whilst the (generally) late-life cognitive damage associated with dementia must certainly remain a key concern of public policy, as is now the case in most high-income countries, it is also important not to neglect cognitive impacts earlier in life and in non-health domains. An effective policy framework would investigate cognition and what affects it *across the life span*, rather than just as a characteristic of dementia, and we argue that an empirically based cognitive footprint can support policy discussion and development by allowing comparison and aggregation of the various such effects and what might be done to mitigate them.

We first go through the five illustrative areas in turn and then discuss what a cognitive footprint might look like, particularly from an economic standpoint.

Side effects of medications

Medications are widely used in high- and middle-income countries: in England, for example, an average of 18.6 items per head was prescribed in 2015 (Baker 2016). Numerous drugs affect cognition, intentionally or as a side effect, and can be evaluated within a footprint framework, by weighing the effects on cognition against beneficial outcomes. Medication effects on cognition begin during pregnancy, the most well-known example being sodium valproate and its adverse neonatal outcomes (Cummings et al. 2011; Meador et al. 2009). Chemotherapy has also been noted as potentially inducing cognitive impairment (Hutchinson et al. 2012; Orchard et al. 2017), although longitudinal evidence is lacking (Wefel and Schagen 2012).

Later in life, statins are widely taken, with their use increasingly encouraged for reducing the risk of dementia (Lincoln et al. 2014). However, a clear relationship is yet to be documented (McGuinness et al. 2016) and small adverse effects on cognition have been noted (Swiger et al. 2013). Anticholinergic drugs, commonly prescribed for older adults, also have a substantial impact on cognition (Risacher et al. 2016; Chuang et al. 2017). With at least one in four older adults with dementia (Sura et al. 2013) or mild cognitive impairment (Green et al. 2016) in some countries taking a medication with potential anticholinergic action, cognitive side effects should be weighed against any improvement in the primary indication.

Although many drugs negatively impact cognition, stimulants and unintended benefits should additionally be included in the cognitive footprint. For example, therapeutic nicotine has a positive footprint in healthy adults (Heishman et al. 2010), nootropics are increasingly used to enhance cognition (Saiz Garcia et al. 2017) and off-label trials have noted the effects of Modafinil in enhancing some aspects of working memory among healthy adults (Battleday and Brem 2015).

Whilst many cognitive side effects are minor, when medicines are prescribed over long periods of time, they may have a sizeable impact on cognition. Employing the cognitive footprint framework would enable the identification of unexpected benefits and negative effects, as seen, for example, with the association of Metformin (prescribed for diabetes) with a lower cancer risk (Franciosi et al. 2013). Thus, the cognitive footprint could be a valuable tool in health technology assessments, particularly where there is equal efficacy for the primary indication.

Loneliness

Loneliness is linked to, but is not the same as, social isolation: it is the distressing feeling accompanying the perception that one's social needs are not met by one's social engagements (Hawkley and Cacioppo 2010). Recent studies have demonstrated harmful associations between loneliness and cognitive function, such as poorer memory, lower processing speed and general ability, and increased risk of dementia (Boss et al. 2015). Loneliness has also been linked to other health problems, including depression and cardiovascular disease (Courtin and Knapp 2017), and mortality (Holt-Lunstad et al. 2015).

It is important to emphasise that the literature has yet to ascertain the true effect of loneliness on cognition (Global Council on Brain Health 2017). First, the reverse association is plausible, where poorer cognition leads to greater loneliness (Schnittger et al. 2012; Hawkley and Cacioppo 2010). Second, loneliness is a subjective construct that is only weakly correlated with objectively measured social isolation (Coyle and Dugan 2012), although there is a question here about reporting error: for example, loneliness might be under-reported to project a more socially desirable profile, which can then lead to overestimates of its effects. Third, interventions targeting loneliness are often accompanied by other cognition-enhancing activities, such as physical activity and skills training (Masi et al. 2010), so it may not be straightforward to attribute improvements in cognition to reduced loneliness *per se*.

It is nonetheless crucial that loneliness is considered in the context of preserving cognition. Up to 40% of non-institutionalised European adults aged over 65 report feeling lonely at least some of the time, with around 12% feeling lonely most or all of the time (Sundström et al. 2009). Moreover, and contrary to seemingly popular assumption, loneliness is not limited to older people: prevalence of loneliness among adults aged below 25 is similar to that of those above 55 (Dykstra 2009; Victor and Yang 2012), and – worryingly – chronic loneliness can lead to poorer cognition than temporary loneliness (Zhong et al. 2016). The cognitive footprint of loneliness would therefore offer useful information for policy makers, urban designers and community organisations to justify, with the help of quantitative evidence, the costs of creating and/or increasing meaningful social engagement opportunities.

Pollution

Another topical example upon which we can build a measure of cognitive footprint makes the link across to the carbon footprint. There is evidence suggesting that pollution – from ambient pollutants including fine particulate matter, to heavy metals, such as lead – is detrimental to cognitive function among children (Huang et al. 2012; Grönqvist et al. 2017; Bharadwaj et al. 2017), adults (Ebenstein et al. 2016; Liu and Lewis 2014; Chen and Schwartz 2009) and older people (Ailshire and Clarke 2015; Wilker et al. 2015; Cacciottolo et al. 2017). In the long term, there are non-trivial spillover effects on educational attainment, employment and lifetime earnings potential, which create additional losses to individuals, families and societies (Peet 2017; Currie et al. 2014). Ultimately, there are also suggestions of an increased risk of dementia (Chen et al. 2017; Fuller-Thomson and Jopling 2017).

Estimating the effects of early life exposure to pollution on later-life cognition is clearly important, given that clean air is a public good that can (potentially) be managed by policy. Clean air legislation in the UK and US, and the phasing out of leaded gasoline in Sweden, are examples of public policy responses. However, recent reviews have shown that even at levels below regulatory limits, including traffic-related exposure studies (Alvarez-Pedrerol et al. 2017; Ranft et al. 2009), associations between pollution and cognitive ability are still detectable, although a meta-analysis is yet to be conducted due to heterogeneity between studies (Power et al. 2016; Suades-González et al. 2015).

More research is also required on the cumulative impacts on cognition over the life course (Currie et al. 2014). How might, for instance, the cognitive effects of early life exposure (e.g. foetal origins hypothesis; Bharadwaj et al. 2017) compare with chronic exposure (e.g. long-term residents in polluted cities or near busy roads; Calderón-Garcidueñas et al. 2008) or contemporaneous exposure (e.g. transitory pollution exposure on the day of cognitive assessment; Ebenstein et al. 2016)?

Understanding the cognitive footprint of pollution would not only aid in cost-benefit analyses of regulating or reducing pollution (i.e. to preserve cognition, and prevent or delay cognitive decline) but also further incentivise individuals and nations to reduce their carbon footprint.

Perinatal mental illness

Mental disorders, especially non-psychotic disorders, are among the most common morbidities of the perinatal period (i.e. during pregnancy and up to one year after childbirth). Perinatal depression, for instance, affects at least 1 in 10 women worldwide, with greater prevalence in low- and middle-income countries. Various anxiety disorders, and to a smaller extent, eating, personality and psychotic disorders, are also prevalent during the perinatal period (O'Hara and Wisner 2014; Howard et al. 2014; Jones et al. 2014; Bauer et al. 2014). Evidence on how maternal mental disorders affect the long-term cognitive development of offspring is mixed: several studies on maternal depression reveal significantly worse offspring cognition from infancy up to adolescence, particularly among boys (Murray et al. 2010; Hay et al. 2008; Perra et al. 2015; Grace et al. 2003), while others find very small or non-significant associations (Letourneau et al. 2013; Evans et al. 2012). Fewer studies have looked at perinatal (maternal) *anxiety* on offspring cognition (note that comorbidity is high, where up to two-thirds of perinatal depression cases involve anxiety disorders; Wisner et al. 2013), but they point towards significant associations (Buss et al. 2011; Galler et al.

2004). Virtually no studies exist on maternal psychotic disorders and offspring cognition (Stein et al. 2014).

The costs of cognitive impacts on offspring can be larger than the costs of emotional or behavioural maladjustment associated with perinatal mental illness (Bauer et al. 2015). More research should nonetheless be conducted, as conclusions regarding causality have been limited to adjusted associations and short-term follow-ups of interventions targeting perinatal mental health (Stein et al. 2014; Bauer et al. 2016). A causal link between perinatal mental disorders and offspring cognitive impairment is indeed plausible, given how chronic exposure to stress hormones, even from the prenatal period, can have lifelong negative impacts on cognition (Lupien et al. 2009; Weinstock 2008). Moreover, the growing epigenetics literature suggests that the ancestral environment can affect the physical health of future generations (Kaati et al. 2002), which would theoretically include cognition as a secondary, if not primary, dimension. Further gaps in the literature relate to potential mediators, including parenting quality (Stanley et al. 2004), and moderators, such as socioeconomic status (Stein et al. 2008); a good grasp of these factors would facilitate better investigation of causal mechanisms to inform the design of, and investment in, more cost-effective interventions.

Quantifying the cognitive footprint of perinatal mental disorders on children, including its economic impacts, might help encourage societies to address perinatal (and indeed ancestral; Johnston et al. 2013) mental health and stressors, and in that way preserve the cognition of future generations.

Traumatic brain injury

Governing and professional bodies in many sports are paying increasing attention to traumatic brain injuries, including concussions (i.e. mild traumatic brain injury (TBI) and repetitive 'subconcussive' head impacts), and to a better understanding of their consequences (Lancet Neurology 2014). There is growing academic and public recognition of the short- and long-term neurodegenerative consequences (Ling et al. 2017; Sahler and Greenwald 2012; Mez et al. 2017; Broglio and Puetz 2008) of contact sports, including boxing, football, American football and rugby. These adverse consequences are not limited to professional athletes: among US youth below the age of 20, the annual incidence of nonfatal, sports- and recreation-related traumatic brain injuries has been (conservatively) estimated to reach a quarter of a million (Gilchrist et al. 2011). A wide-ranging review of evidence reported that, in general, a higher incidence of TBI is seen among females than males, among school athletes than university athletes, during competition than during training (except, apparently, for the sport of cheerleading) and among those with a history of prior concussion (Institute of Medicine and National Research Council 2014).

Understanding the cognitive footprint of sport would benefit society at large, especially to bring about awareness of cognitive damage from sport and recreational activities, and to alter attitudes towards precautionary measures. There is a disconcerting 'culture of resistance' to reporting concussions and complying with treatment plans, such as to avoid letting team mates down (Institute of Medicine and National Research Council 2014). Moreover, the literature provides evidence for what has been called 'risk-compensation behaviour' pertaining to protective headgear, where users eliminate one brain injury risk factor but, due to perceptions of safety, create or increase from a previously lower level another risk factor. This is seen among athletes (Verhagen et al. 2010; Hagel and Meeuwisse 2004) and (non-sport) cyclists alike (Gamble and Walker 2016; Phillips et al. 2011). This is worrying, considering that protective headgear can reduce, but not completely eliminate, the risk of TBI (Olivier and Creighton 2017); indeed, some of the protective sports headgear in widespread use may not even offer sufficient protection from concussions (Rowson et al. 2014). An additional complication is that enforcing protective headgear can deter enthusiasts, including cycle commuters (Fyhri et al. 2012) – due to discomfort, for instance (Bogerd et al. 2014) – which decreases the risk of injury, but also decreases the benefits of participation.

This topical example also demonstrates the need to take a broad approach to cognitive footprint research: inherent to participation in most sports are the benefits of increased physical activity and a sense of community belonging (Eime et al. 2013; Bailey 2005). Additionally, in the case of cycle commuting, lower levels of pollution can be achieved (Johansson et al. 2017). These mechanisms can be linked to cognitive benefits (Lees and Hopkins 2013; see also references for cognitive footprint of loneliness and pollution). Accounting for these factors when estimating the *net* cognitive footprint of sport would more accurately inform public and private decisions on sports participation towards preserving and enhancing cognition.

Discussion

There is no simple or single measure of cognition, nor would this be desirable given its complex, multidimensional nature, but there is nevertheless a case for seeking an overarching indication of what cognition means for individuals, societies and economies. In particular, we argue that there is considerable merit in bringing together evidence on the multifarious influences on cognition, both positive and negative, and the similar multiplicity of consequences, again both positive and negative – and in both cases across the whole of the life course – in order to inform public policy discussion.

There is some equivalence in these arguments to the carbon footprint concept – indeed, the choice of terminology for a cognitive footprint was not accidental – and the way that it has generated a very public debate about the environmental impacts of modern human lifestyles. Those impacts are multi-dimensional (as are the causes), yet it has been found to be convenient to use CO_2 levels as a simple 'headline' indicator of global environmental damage.

We are not proposing that there should be just one measure of cognition – say memory or creativity – as some equivalent, but we draw other parallels to point to the advantage of being able to bring together many different effects in one simplifying argument.

Are there common, overarching consequences of cognitive enhancement or damage? One possible numéraire for assessing the cognitive consequences of different experiences and events across the life course would be money. The empirical questions would then be of this kind: what is the monetary impact of enhancing cognition through better early years schooling, or expansion of university education or a commitment to lifelong learning? One immediate economic impact is the likely higher productivity of the workforce, with benefits both for the individuals concerned (higher wages) and for the country (greater economic growth). Similarly, what is the monetary impact, measured in terms of the costs of providing health and social care services, of damaged cognition resulting from unintended injuries in childhood or road traffic accidents in adulthood? Such incidents will probably also affect the ability to contribute productively, with further ('monetisable') consequences.

Of course, not all cognitive impacts across the life course can be measured in monetary terms. But where this *is* possible, there is then the opportunity for comparison with other life experiences and events which may themselves not have discernible cognitive effects, but might perhaps increase service-related costs or improve worker productivity. In turn, this allows public policy makers to value and trade-off (some of) the effects of different options: whether to improve safety in the home or on the roads or to encourage technological development so as to improve industrial processes, for instance. Indeed, given the growing pervasiveness of cost-benefit, cost-effectiveness and other analyses to evaluate policy scenarios and spending decisions, it makes a lot of sense to evaluate cognition-related actions in a similar way.

A well-known challenge for economic evaluation is how to measure outcomes in units that allow comparison across different fields or systems. In the healthcare domain, economists have proposed the quality-adjusted life year (QALY) as a generic measure of health-related quality of life, making it possible to compare the costs and effects of preventive or treatment interventions targeted on different health domains (see Chapter 11). With the QALY it then becomes possible to compare the *cost-effectiveness* (sometimes called the *cost-utility*) of, say, therapies for people with dementia with medications for people with breast cancer or interventions for heart disease.

When making comparisons outside the healthcare domain, economists often use *cost-benefit analysis* which aims to measure the effects of a policy or action in monetary terms. The costs of the intervention are then compared with the monetised benefits to see whether it makes sense from a resource efficiency standpoint to invest in the intervention or policy. Two or more interventions can be compared by computing the net benefit (monetised benefits minus costs) for each of them and then recommending the intervention with the greater net benefit. Not surprisingly, cost-benefit analysis becomes difficult when the effects of an intervention cannot be measured in units of money or when the attempted monetisation of those effects stretches credibility.

An alternative approach now being discussed more widely, and attempted in a growing number of empirical studies, is to measure the effects of public policy decisions in terms of their effects on *psychological wellbeing* of the population (or those members of the population affected by the decision). Among other things, this approach has encouraged exploration of empirical measures of an overall wellbeing construct (particularly hedonic measures) as well as research into the causes and consequences of better wellbeing.

It may not be the case that *all* cognitive impacts of an event or intervention would have identifiable wellbeing effects, although we are not aware of extensive research on this issue, but we see this as a potentially fruitful avenue to explore further. Evidence on the wellbeing impacts of cognitive enhancement or damage, alongside evidence on the costs of the alternatives being compared, could usefully inform policy discussions about how to invest society's scarce resources for the greater public good.

We are ourselves beginning to explore economic and other aspects of a cognitive footprint, which we see as a helpful way to view, compare, sum and trade-off the many positive and negative, transitory and enduring, profound and trivial influences on cognition. Cognitive capital can be accumulated by judicious investment in education, healthcare, cleaner environments, better housing, urban design, safer roads and many other areas. In a post-industrial context, cognitive ability is one of the most valuable resources available to a society.

References

Ailshire, J. A. & Clarke, P. (2015). Fine particulate matter air pollution and cognitive function among U.S. older adults. *The Journals of Gerontology: Series B*, 70(2), 322–328.

Alvarez-Pedrerol, M., Rivas, I., López-Vicente, M., Suades-González, E., Donaire-Gonzalez, D., Cirach, M., de Castro, M., Esnaola, M., Basagaña, X., Dadvand, P., Nieuwenhuijsen, M. & Sunyer, J. (2017). Impact of commuting exposure to traffic-related air pollution on cognitive development in children walking to school. *Environmental Pollution*, 231(Part 1), 837–844.

Bailey, R. (2005). Evaluating the relationship between physical education, sport and social inclusion. *Educational Review*, 57(1), 71–90.

Baker, C. (2016). Medicine statistics: GP prescribing by constituency, 2015. *House of Commons Library Research Paper*. Available at: goo.gl/CU1dU9 [Accessed 1 February 2018].

Battleday, R. M. & Brem, A. K. (2015). Modafinil for cognitive neuroenhancement in healthy non-sleep-deprived subjects: A systematic review. *European Neuropsychopharmacology*, 25(11), 1865–1881.

Bauer, A., Knapp, M. & Parsonage, M. (2016). Lifetime costs of perinatal anxiety and depression. *Journal of Affective Disorders*, 192(Suppl C), 83–90.

Bauer, A., Parsonage, M., Knapp, M., Iemmi, V. & Adelaja, B. (2014). *Costs of Perinatal Mental Health Problems*. London: Centre for Mental Health and London School of Economics and Political Science.

Bauer, A., Pawlby, S. J., Plant, D. T., King, D., Pariante, C. M. & Knapp, M. (2015). Perinatal depression and child development: Exploring the economic consequences from a South London cohort. *Psychological Medicine*, 45(1), 51–61.

Bharadwaj, P., Gibson, M., Graff Zivin, J. & Neilson, C. (2017). Gray matters: Fetal pollution exposure and human capital formation. *Journal of the Association of Environmental and Resource Economists*, 4(2), 505–542.

Bogerd, C. P., Walker, I., Brühwiler, P. A. & Rossi, R. M. (2014). The effect of a helmet on cognitive performance is, at worst, marginal: A controlled laboratory study. *Applied Ergonomics*, 45(3), 671–676.

Boss, L., Kang, D-H. & Branson, S. (2015). Loneliness and cognitive function in the older adult: A systematic review. *International Psychogeriatrics*, 27(4), 541–553.

Broglio, S. P. & Puetz, T. W. (2008). The effect of sport concussion on neurocognitive function, self-report symptoms and postural control. *Sports Medicine*, 38(1), 53–67.

Buss, C., Davis, E. P., Hobel, C. J. & Sandman, C. A. (2011). Maternal pregnancy-specific anxiety is associated with child executive function at 6–9 years age. *Stress*, 14(6), 665–676.

Cacciottolo, M., Wang, X., Driscoll, I., Woodward, N., Saffari, A., Reyes, J., Serre, M. L., Vizuete, W., Sioutas, C., Morgan, T. E., Gatz, M., Chui, H. C., Shumaker, S. A., Resnick, S. M., Espeland, M. A., Finch, C. E. & Chen, J. C. (2017). Particulate air pollutants, APOE alleles and their contributions to cognitive impairment in older women and to amyloidogenesis in experimental models. *Translational Psychiatry*, 7, e1022.

Calderón-Garcidueñas, L., Solt, A. C., Henríquez-Roldán, C., Torres-Jardón, R., Nuse, B., Herritt, L., Villarreal-Calderón, R., Osnaya, N., Stone, I., García, R., Brooks, D. M., González-Maciel, A., Reynoso-Robles, R., Delgado-Chávez, R. & Reed, W. (2008). Long-term air pollution exposure is associated with neuroinflammation, an altered innate immune response, disruption of the blood-brain barrier, ultrafine particulate deposition, and accumulation of amyloid β-42 and α-synuclein in children and young adults. *Toxicologic Pathology*, 36(2), 289–310.

Chen, H., Jessiman, B., Copes, R., Villeneuve, P. J. & Burnett, R. T. (2017). Exposure to lead in petrol and increased incidence of dementia – Authors' reply. *The Lancet*, 389(10087), 2372–2373.

Chen, J-C. & Schwartz, J. (2009). Neurobehavioral effects of ambient air pollution on cognitive performance in US adults. *NeuroToxicology*, 30(2), 231–239.

Chuang, Y-F., Elango, P., Gonzalez, C. E. & Thambisetty, M. (2017). Midlife anticholinergic drug use, risk of Alzheimer's disease, and brain atrophy in community-dwelling older adults. *Alzheimer's & Dementia: Translational Research & Clinical Interventions*, 3(3), 471–479.

Courtin, E. & Knapp, M. (2017). Social isolation, loneliness and health in old age: A scoping review. *Health and Social Care in the Community*, 25(3), 799–812.

Coyle, C. E. & Dugan, E. (2012). Social isolation, loneliness and health among older adults. *Journal of Aging and Health*, 24(8), 1346–1363.

Cummings, C., Stewart, M., Stevenson, M., Morrow, J. & Nelson, J. (2011). Neurodevelopment of children exposed in utero to lamotrigine, sodium valproate and carbamazepine. *Archives of Disease in Childhood*, 99, 643–647.

Currie, J., Graff Zivin, J., Mullins, J. & Neidell, M. (2014). What do we know about short- and long-term effects of early-life exposure to pollution? *Annual Review of Resource Economics*, 6(1), 217–247.

Dykstra, P. A. (2009). Older adult loneliness: Myths and realities. *European Journal of Ageing*, 6(2), 91.

Ebenstein, A., Lavy, V. & Roth, S. (2016). The long-run economic consequences of high-stakes examinations: Evidence from transitory variation in pollution. *American Economic Journal: Applied Economics*, 8(4), 36–65.

Eime, R. M., Young, J. A., Harvey, J. T., Charity, M. J. & Payne, W. R. (2013). A systematic review of the psychological and social benefits of participation in sport for children and adolescents: Informing development of a conceptual model of health through sport. *International Journal of Behavioral Nutrition and Physical Activity*, 10(1), 98.

Evans, J., Melotti, R., Heron, J., Ramchandani, P., Wiles, N., Murray, L. & Stein, A. (2012). The timing of maternal depressive symptoms and child cognitive development: A longitudinal study. *Journal of Child Psychology and Psychiatry*, 53(6), 632–640.

Franciosi, M., Lucisano, G., Lapice, E., Strippoli, G. F. M., Pellegrini, F. & Nicolucci, A. (2013). Metformin therapy and risk of cancer in patients with Type 2 diabetes: Systematic review. *PLoS One*, 8(8), e71583.

Fuller-Thomson, E. & Jopling, S. A. (2017). Exposure to lead in petrol and increased incidence of dementia. *The Lancet*, 389(10087), 2371.

Fyhri, A., Bjørnskau, T. & Backer-Grøndahl, A. (2012). Bicycle helmets – A case of risk compensation? *Transportation Research Part F: Traffic Psychology and Behaviour*, 15(5), 612–624.

Galler, J. R., Ramsey, F. C., Harrison, R. H., Taylor, J., Cumberbatch, G. & Forde, V. (2004). Postpartum maternal moods and infant size predict performance on a national high school entrance examination. *Journal of Child Psychology and Psychiatry*, 45(6), 1064–1075.

Gamble, T. & Walker, I. (2016). Wearing a bicycle helmet can increase risk taking and sensation seeking in adults. *Psychological Science*, 27(2), 289–294.

Gilchrist, J., Thomas, K. E., Xu, L., McGuire, L. C. & Coronado, V. (2011). Nonfatal traumatic brain injuries related to sports and recreation activities among persons aged ≤19 years – United States, 2001–2009. *Morbidity and Mortality Weekly Report*, 60(39), 1337–1342.

Global Council on Brain Health. (2017). *The brain and social connectedness: GCBH recommendations on social engagement and brain health*. Available at: goo.gl/UMfvjE [Accessed 1 September 2017].

Grace, S. L., Evindar, A. & Stewart, D. E. (2003). The effect of postpartum depression on child cognitive development and behavior: A review and critical analysis of the literature. *Archives of Women's Mental Health*, 6(4), 263–274.

Green, A. R., Oh, E., Hilson, L., Tian, J. & Boyd, C. M. (2016). Anticholinergic burden in older adults with mild cognitive impairment. *Journal of the American Geriatrics Society*, 64(12), e313–e314.

Grönqvist, H., Nilsson, J. P. & Robling, P-O. (2017). Early lead exposure and outcomes in adulthood. *Institute for Evaluation of Labour Market and Education Policy Working Paper*. Available at: goo.gl/yUUykP [Accessed 15 May 2017].

Hagel, B. E. & Meeuwisse, W. (2004). Risk compensation: A "side effect" of sport injury prevention? *Clinical Journal of Sport Medicine*, 14(4), 193–196.

Hanushek, E. A. & Woessmann, L. (2008). The role of cognitive skills in economic development. *Journal of Economic Literature*, 46(3), 607–668.

Hawkley, L. C. & Cacioppo, J. T. (2010). Loneliness matters: A theoretical and empirical review of consequences and mechanisms. *Annals of Behavioral Medicine*, 40(2), 218–227.

Hay, D. F., Pawlby, S., Waters, C. S. & Sharp, D. (2008). Antepartum and postpartum exposure to maternal depression: Different effects on different adolescent outcomes. *Journal of Child Psychology and Psychiatry*, 49(10), 1079–1088.

Heishman, S. J., Kleykamp, B. A. & Singleton, E. G. (2010). Meta-analysis of the acute effects of nicotine and smoking on human performance. *Psychopharmocology*, 210(4), 453–469.

Holt-Lunstad, J., Smith, T. B., Baker, M., Harris, T. & Stephenson, D. (2015). Loneliness and social isolation as risk factors for mortality. *Perspectives on Psychological Science*, 10(2), 227–237.

Howard, L. M., Molyneaux, E., Dennis, C-L., Rochat, T., Stein, A. & Milgrom, J. (2014). Non-psychotic mental disorders in the perinatal period. *The Lancet*, 384(9956), 1775–1788.

Huang, P-C., Su, P-H., Chen, H-Y., Huang, H-B., Tsai, J-L., Huang, H-I. & Wang, S-L. (2012). Childhood blood lead levels and intellectual development after ban of leaded gasoline in Taiwan: A 9-year prospective study. *Environment International*, 40(Suppl C), 88–96.

Hutchinson, A. D., Hosking, J. R., Kichenadasse, G., Mattiske, J. K. & Wilson, C. (2012). Objective and subjective cognitive impairment following chemotherapy for cancer: A systematic review. *Cancer Treatment Reviews*, 38(7), 926–934.

Institute of Medicine and National Research Council. (2014). *Sports-Related Concussions in Youth: Improving the Science, Changing the Culture*. Washington, DC: The National Academies Press.

Johansson, C., Lövenheim, B., Schantz, P., Wahlgren, L., Almström, P., Markstedt, A., Strömgren, M., Forsberg, B. & Sommar, J. N. (2017). Impacts on air pollution and health by changing commuting from car to bicycle. *Science of The Total Environment*, 584–585(Suppl C), 55–63.

Johnston, D. W., Schurer, S. & Shields, M. A. (2013). Exploring the intergenerational persistence of mental health: Evidence from three generations. *Journal of Health Economics*, 32(6), 1077–1089.

Jones, I., Chandra, P. S., Dazzan, P. & Howard, L. M. (2014). Bipolar disorder, affective psychosis, and schizophrenia in pregnancy and the post-partum period. *The Lancet*, 384(9956), 1789–1799.

Kaati, G., Bygren, L. O. & Edvinsson, S. (2002). Cardiovascular and diabetes mortality determined by nutrition during parents' and grandparents' slow growth period. *European Journal of Human Genetics*, 10, 682–688.

Lancet Neurology. (2014). Tackling the sports-related concussion crisis. *The Lancet Neurology*, 13(8), 747.

Lees, C. & Hopkins, J. (2013). Effect of aerobic exercise on cognition, academic achievement, and psychosocial function in children: A systematic review of randomized control trials. *Preventing Chronic Disease*, 10, 130010.

Letourneau, N. L., Tramonte, L. & Willms, J. D. (2013). Maternal depression, family functioning and children's longitudinal development. *Journal of Pediatric Nursing*, 28(3), 223–234.

Lincoln, P., Fenton, K., Alessi, C., Prince, M., Brayne, C., Wortmann, M., Patel, K. & Deanfield, J. (2014). The blackfriars consensus on brain health and dementia. *The Lancet*, 383, 1805–1806.

Ling, H., Morris, H. R., Neal, J. W., Lees, A. J., Hardy, J., Holton, J. L., Revesz, T. & Williams, D. D. R. (2017). Mixed pathologies including chronic traumatic encephalopathy account for dementia in retired association football (soccer) players. *Acta Neuropathologica*, 133(3), 337–352.

Liu, J. & Lewis, G. (2014). Environmental toxicity and poor cognitive outcomes in children and adults. *Journal of Environmental Health*, 76(6), 130–138.

Lupien, S. J., McEwen, B. S., Gunnar, M. R. & Heim, C. (2009). Effects of stress throughout the lifespan on the brain, behaviour and cognition. *Nature Reviews Neuroscience*, 10, 434–445.

Masi, C. M., Chen, H-Y., Hawkley, L. C. & Cacioppo, J. T. (2010). A meta-analysis of interventions to reduce loneliness. *Personality and Social Psychology Review*, 15(3), 219–266.

McGuinness, B., Craig, D., Bullock, R. & Passmore, P. (2016). Statins for the prevention of dementia. *The Cochrane Database of Systematic Reviews*, 1(CD003160), 1–46.

Meador, K. J., Baker, G. A., Browning, N., Clayton-Smith, J., Combs-Cantrell, D. T., Cohen, M., Kalayjian, L. A., Kanner, A., Liporace, J. D., Pennell, P. B., Privitera, M. & Loring, D. W. (2009). Cognitive function at 3 years of age after fetal exposure to antiepileptic drugs. *New England Journal of Medicine*, 360(16), 1597–1605.

Mez, J., Daneshvar, D. H., Kiernan, P.T., *et al.* (2017). Clinicopathological evaluation of chronic traumatic encephalopathy in players of American football. *JAMA*, 318(4), 360–370.

Murray, L., Arteche, A., Fearon, P., Halligan, S., Croudace, T. & Cooper, P. (2010). The effects of maternal postnatal depression and child sex on academic performance at age 16 years: A developmental approach. *Journal of Child Psychology and Psychiatry*, 51(10), 1150–1159.

O'Hara, M. W. & Wisner, K. L. (2014). Perinatal mental illness: Definition, description and aetiology. *Best Practice & Research Clinical Obstetrics & Gynaecology*, 28(1), 3–12.

Olivier, J. & Creighton, P. (2017). Bicycle injuries and helmet use: A systematic review and meta-analysis. *International Journal of Epidemiology*, 46(1), 278–292.

Orchard, T. S., Gaudier-Diaz, M. M., Weinhold, K. R. & Courtney DeVries, A. (2017). Clearing the fog: A review of the effects of dietary omega-3 fatty acids and added sugars on chemotherapy-induced cognitive deficits. *Breast Cancer Research and Treatment*, 161(3), 391–398.

Peet, E. D. (2017). *Environment and Human Capital: The Effects of Early-Life Exposure to Pollutants in the Philippines*. Available at: goo.gl/JeGHRk [Accessed 1 September 2017].

Perra, O., Phillips, R., Fyfield, R., Waters, C. & Hay, D. F. (2015). Does mothers' postnatal depression influence the development of imitation? *Journal of Child Psychology and Psychiatry*, 56(11), 1231–1238.

Phillips, R. O., Fyhri, A. & Sagberg, F. (2011). Risk compensation and bicycle helmets. *Risk Analysis*, 31(8), 1187–1195.

Power, M. C., Adar, S. D., Yanosky, J. D. & Weuve, J. (2016). Exposure to air pollution as a potential contributor to cognitive function, cognitive decline, brain imaging, and dementia: A systematic review of epidemiologic research. *NeuroToxicology*, 56(Suppl C), 235–253.

Ranft, U., Schikowski, T., Sugiri, D., Krutmann, J. & Krämer, U. (2009). Long-term exposure to traffic-related particulate matter impairs cognitive function in the elderly. *Environmental Research*, 109(8), 1004–1011.

Risacher, S. L., McDonald, B. C., Tallman, E. F., West, J. D., Farlow, M. R., Unverzagt, F. W., Gao, S., Boustani, M., Crane, P. K., Peterson, R. C., Jack, C. R. J., Jaqust, W. J., Aisen, P. S., Weiner, M. W., Saykin, A. J. & Initiative, A. S. D. N. (2016). Association between anticholinergic medication use and cognition, brain metabolism, and brain atrophy in cognitively normal older adults. *JAMA Neurology*, 73(6), 721–732.

Rossor, M. & Knapp, M. (2015). Can we model a cognitive footprint of interventions and policies to help to meet the global challenge of dementia? *The Lancet*, 386(9997), 1008–1010.

Rowson, S., Duma, S. M., Greenwald, R. M., Beckwith, J. G., Chu, J. J., Guskiewicz, K. M., Mihalik, J. P., Crisco, J. J., Wilcox, B. J., McAllister, T. W., Maerlender, A. C., Broglio, S. P., Schnebel, B., Anderson, S. & Brolinson, P. G. (2014). Can helmet design reduce the risk of concussion in football? *Journal of Neurosurgery*, 120(4), 919–922.

Sahler, C. S. & Greenwald, B. D. (2012). Traumatic brain injury in sports: A review. *Rehabilitation Research and Practice*, 659652, 1–10.

Saiz Garcia, H., Montes Reula, L., Portilla Fernandez, A., Pereira Sanchez, V., Olmo Lopez, N., Mancha Heredero, E., Rosero Enriquez, A. S. & Martinez Parreño, M. E. (2017). Nootropics: Emergents drugs associated with new clinical challenges. *European Psychiatry*, 41(Suppl), S877–S878.

Schnittger, R. I. B., Wherton, J., Prendergast, D. & Lawlor, B. A. (2012). Risk factors and mediating pathways of loneliness and social support in community-dwelling older adults. *Aging & Mental Health*, 16(3), 335–346.

Stanley, C., Murray, L. & Stein, A. (2004). The effect of postnatal depression on mother – infant interaction, infant response to the Still-face perturbation, and performance on an Instrumental Learning task. *Development and Psychopathology*, 16(1), 1–18.

Stein, A., Malmberg, L. E., Sylva, K., Barnes, J., Leach, P. & The FCCC team. (2008). The influence of maternal depression, caregiving, and socioeconomic status in the post-natal year on children's language development. *Child: Care, Health and Development*, 34(5), 603–612.

Stein, A., Pearson, R. M., Goodman, S. H., Rapa, E., Rahman, A., McCallum, M., Howard, L. M. & Pariante, C. M. (2014). Effects of perinatal mental disorders on the fetus and child. *The Lancet*, 384(9956), 1800–1819.

Suades-González, E., Gascon, M., Guxens, M. & Sunyer, J. (2015). Air pollution and neuropsychological development: A review of the latest evidence. *Endocrinology*, 156(10), 3473–3482.

Sundström, G., Fransson, E., Malmberg, B. & Davey, A. (2009). Loneliness among older Europeans. *European Journal of Ageing*, 6(4), 267–275.

Sura, S. D., Carnahan, R. M., Chen, H. & Aparasu, R. R. (2013). Prevalence and determinants of anticholinergic medication use in elderly dementia patients. *Drugs & Aging*, 30(10), 837–844.

Swiger, K. J., Manalac, R. J., Blumenthal, R. S., Blaha, M. J. & Martin, S. S. (2013). Statins and cognition: A systematic review and meta-analysis of short- and long-term cognitive effects. *Mayo Clinic Proceedings*, 88(11), 1213–1221.

Verhagen, E. A. L. M., van Stralen, M. M. & van Mechelen, W. (2010). Behaviour, the key factor for sports injury prevention. *Sports Medicine*, 40(11), 899–906.

Victor, C. R. & Yang, K. (2012). The prevalence of loneliness among adults: A case study of the United Kingdom. *The Journal of Psychology*, 146(1–2), 85–104.

Wefel, J. S. & Schagen, S. B. (2012). Chemotherapy-related cognitive dysfunction. *Current Neurology and Neuroscience Reports*, 12(3), 267–275.

Weinstock, M. (2008). The long-term behavioural consequences of prenatal stress. *Neuroscience & Biobehavioral Reviews*, 32(6), 1073–1086.

Wilker, E. H., Preis, S. R., Beiser, A. S., Wolf, P. A., Au, R., Kloog, I., Li, W., Schwartz, J., Koutrakis, P., DeCarli, C., Seshadri, S. & Mittleman, M. A. (2015). Long-term exposure to fine particulate matter, residential proximity to major roads and measures of brain structure. *Stroke*, 46(5), 1161–1166.

Wisner, K. L., Sit, D. Y., McShea, M. C. *et al.* (2013). Onset timing, thoughts of self-harm, and diagnoses in postpartum women with screen-positive depression findings. *JAMA Psychiatry*, 70(5), 490–498.

Zhong, B-L., Chen, S-L. & Conwell, Y. (2016). Effects of transient versus chronic loneliness on cognitive function in older adults: Findings from the Chinese Longitudinal Healthy Longevity Survey. *The American Journal of Geriatric Psychiatry*, 24(5), 389–398.

Chapter 14

Conclusion

A call to action

Kate Irving, Deborah Oliveira and Eef Hogervorst

Primary prevention of dementia has come of age. The notion of this book 10–20 years ago, not to mention the research to populate it, would have made it difficult to take seriously. At this point, ignoring the established and emerging risk factors and the impact they have on dementia incidence will further contribute to the current increasing incidence of the disease worldwide. Understanding how such factors affect human existence has implications across the lifespan. There will be a different therapeutic window for different risk factors and while a central message of this book is the importance of multimodal prevention, a better understanding of the specific impacts and mechanisms for each risk could lead to a more sophisticated strategy.

Dementia is a long process with a prognosis of between 4 and 15 years, and high human, social and economic costs (WHO 2017).[1] Existence of the physical markers in the brain span an even longer trajectory and the potential window of opportunity to develop reserves to withstand any pathology make the target years for risk reduction lifelong or also pre-natal.

It is evident in this book that because dementia prevention requires a multifactorial approach, it is not possible or even desirable to target dementia without also influencing all major chronic diseases. It is very likely that with the best practice approaches to reduction of the most potent risk factors, we will compress the clinical presentation of dementia into a much shorter period at the end of life. This would be a huge human and economic service in terms of quality of life, as it would provide people with healthier years in later life. For that reason, we advocate a combined prevention approach to all chronic diseases across the lifespan.

Dementia prevention has rarely been integrated within the chronic disease prevention discourse and its invisibility in international policy and clinical practice must be addressed. There is much we can learn from the understandings already established in health promotion for other chronic diseases. For instance, in the USA trends in tobacco use in adults has fallen consistently from just under 45% in the 1960s to just under 19% in 2014.[2] However, dementia has a different resonance with people, with specific responses of fear and dread, and thus there is also a need to understand how best to engage people in behaviour change for brain health. Reducing stigma and improving people's understanding of dementia within clinical and lay settings is paramount and should be the first step to establish good practice in dementia prevention.

A much broader understanding at the cutting edge of dementia prevention has been promoted throughout this book. For instance, there are promising emerging understandings about sleep patterns and their effect on dementia. Poor sleep has an immediate deleterious effect on wellbeing, particularly on mental wellbeing. Despite this, there is a lack of high-quality data on the exact mechanisms of such risk factors and, as highlighted in Chapter 1, filling these gaps is expensive with challenging methodological complexities. Although such studies are not more expensive than pharmacological studies, they will rarely be able to take advantage of industry/pharmaceutical investment as commercial actors are more concerned with the production of saleable products. The market forces behind research can be starkly seen in the profile of drugs in development. In cancer, where there has been good success, there are upwards of 4,000 drugs in development, whereas in dementia, that number was around 87 drugs in development in 2018.[3] This does not reflect the fact that dementia is a smaller problem in society or that it is in some sense less important, but it might be that it has not managed to come up with a product that can be sold recently. We cannot allow market forces alone to dictate the research agenda.

Not only in pharmacological research is there a discrepancy between funding for different diseases, but there is also a preponderance of the available dementia funding being directed towards basic, rather than epidemiological, research. For example, in Figure 14.1, we can see that half the European countries listed

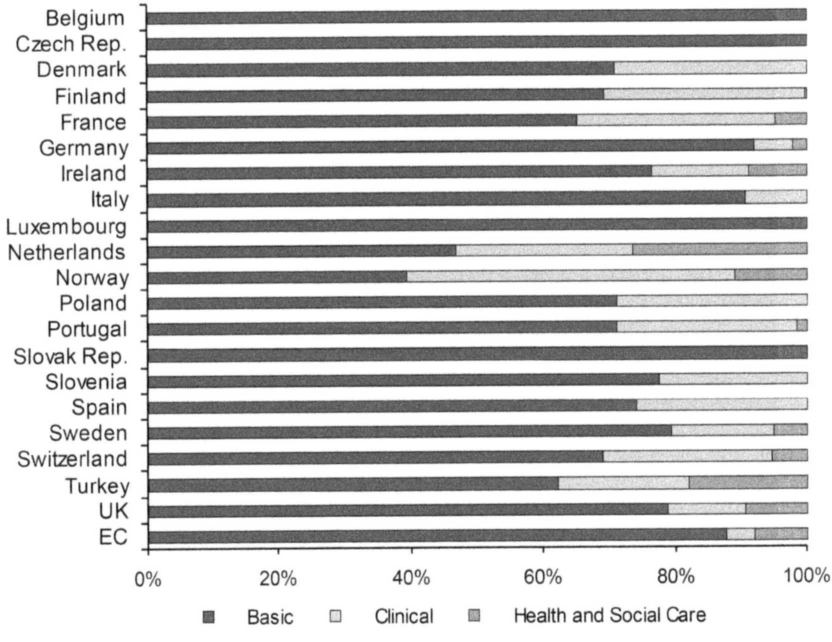

Figure 14.1 Investment by research domain by country: percentage annualised investment for JPND countries and the EC (FP7) at 1st Jan. 2011.

Source: JPND Research, *JPND Mapping Exercise*. Available at: http://www.neurodegenerationresearch.eu/fileadmin/Documents/2012/SRA-related/JPND_Mapping_Report__Final__01.pdf

have no substantive epidemiological or behaviour change research into neurodegenerative diseases. The highest percentage spending on health and social care research was in Netherlands at about 24% the lowest was 0% in a range of countries including Belgium, Poland, Denmark and Spain and the average across JPND countries was 8%.[4]

The reality for any dementia prevention approach is that we have insufficient reliable baselines across countries to evaluate any dementia prevention efforts employed over the lifespan. Better organisation would certainly help to convince policy makers of the need to redirect funding, but such organisation (such as can be seen in cancer with many countries having a national registry) would require significant funding. Dementia registries have been developed in some European countries, most notably Sweden.[5] There are huge costs involved in establishing dementia registries, and it must be acknowledged that such money needs to come from somewhere. Which budget would we choose? Patient care? Cutting-edge research into understanding risk factors, their interactions or windows of opportunity? Notwithstanding, a registry would give power to the socio-political arguments, and this is valuable, as it is perhaps necessary to convince any still to be converted decision makers. However, given the shared risk factor profile for most of the chronic diseases, it might make more sense that any such registry starts in primary care with proper coding of diseases and address multiple morbidities. Currently, however, many GPs do not feel confident in diagnosing dementia and better screening instruments are needed to aid them. Accurate diagnosis and coding for dementia would be prerequisite in the success of a dementia registry.

In low- to middle-income countries, the opportunity to form registries will likely be overshadowed by the emerging public health crisis of dementia prevalence (Prince et al 2014).[6] Alongside the improved life expectancy in these countries, dementia prevalence will increase. In keeping with the previous chapter by Knapp et al. (Chapter 13), it is likely that different countries have a different cognitive footprint than others, so it could be that there is more to be gained by ensuring longer engagement of children in education in some countries, whereas addressing obesity in other countries could have the best potential gains. This broader thinking of cognition across the lifespan points to an important aspect of primary prevention, that investment has so much more to offer society than simply delaying or preventing dementia: the investment in cognition and its impact on population wellbeing and improved productivity. However, these meta-level decisions about population or global health should not replace attempts to address multiple risk factors in primary care, responding to the risks as they affect individuals with the most appropriate approach for the individual. It does not have to be an all-or-nothing approach, or in other words, if global policy points towards primary prevention, public health and clinical guidelines still need to work towards secondary and tertiary prevention.

Given the probability that dementia will still exist within the next decades, albeit with lower incidence if we address population risk, there is a prerogative to better understand what might be achieved through secondary and tertiary prevention. However, compelling as it may be, a cure or even a significant treatment for dementia remains an unlikely event before 2025 and even such steps forward may only affect small numbers of people with specific profiles.

A major European project, European Prevention of Alzheimer's Disease Consortium (EPAD), is an initiative to create a novel environment for testing numerous interventions targeted at the prevention of Alzheimer's dementia. EPAD engages large European populations in research much earlier in life based on the hypothesis that previous trials have failed because they were initiated too late to combat brain pathology. Of course, the general public will be very appreciative of any advances in this field. However, we urge balance. We cannot wait for the fountain of youth referred to in Chapter 1. While such initiatives attract funding from drug companies and the biomarker industry, epidemiological research is less likely to attract such funding, and hence the European community and national funding schemes must focus their efforts here.

Emphasis is needed on the hardest questions of primary prevention such as, Can risks be offset? How do cumulative risks work together? What are the gender differences in risk profiles, and what weightings are there for the different risks? Importantly, some of the most common risk factors have been identified, and these are mostly related to individuals' lifestyle, and so research must look to successes in behaviour change and try to emulate these approaches where possible. Olanrewaju et al. (2015) suggest a multi-layered intervention at the levels of policy, community, household and individual, in order to address behaviours that we know to confer risk. While this may seem ambitious, we do in fact have legitimate organisations working at all these levels who currently define dementia prevention as not central to their role, if not completely outside of it. For instance, at the individual level, there are general practitioners who have shown some reticence to integrating dementia prevention within current opportunistic health promotion opportunities (O'Donnell et al. 2015). At the household and community levels, there are health visitors or public health nurses, for example. At a policy level, we have seen that there is very low visibility of dementia risk reduction messages.

Tertiary prevention has been informed by broad understandings of dementia and initiatives, such as dementia friendly towns and communities. While controversial,[7] these initiatives do point to a general willingness to engage in multi-professional, multi-layered approaches to addressing dementia when it is diagnosed. Perhaps it is a question of using these existing and emerging organisations (such as age-friendly towns and cities, active ageing and other bottom-up organisations) to address dementia risk reduction issues. Dementia prevention attempts do not need to reinvent the wheel; these can benefit from existing structures, but this may take considerable thought as to 1) where is their existing potential to promote these messages and 2) to ensure that dementia prevention for all the reasons outlined in Chapter 1 are not seen as redundant 'unmentionable' in these discourses.

Throughout this book, we have highlighted in each chapter the most promising areas for future research if we are to achieve the dementia prevention toolbox called for in Chapter 2:

> *A set of tools for different purposes and contexts: midlife or late-life risk profiles, and long-term or short-term prediction; public health, primary care, or specialized memory clinics.*
>
> (p. 40)

Implications for education

Dementia prevention needs to come in to the vernacular of health promotion alongside any other chronic disease. Students of medicine and allied services and health and social care practitioners must not only have a basic understanding of the risk factors involved in the pathogenesis of dementia, but also the skills to support people to change behaviour. Tomorrow's health practitioners need to have these skills for any chronic disease management. However, as dementia risk reduction can often seem redundant in the more established fields of cardiovascular risk reduction, education must additionally cover the particular understandings of dementia that can act as barriers to engagement in the messages and skills in engaging people in dementia risk reduction.

Implications for clinical practice

Dementia risk reduction needs to be included in all clinical guidelines for primary care practitioners. In some sense, this may naturally follow from its inclusion in national and international policies related to health promotion. However, as pointed out throughout the chapters, some thought needs to be put into considering dementia as part of the chronic disease spectrum, for better understanding and tackling risk factors in day to day care, clear pathways in primary prevention over the lifespan and secondary and tertiary prevention in later life and more focus on positive messages of brain health, rather than the term dementia prevention which needs constant clarification.

Implications for research

There are some huge knowledge gaps in how we understand the phenomenon of dementia and is pathogenesis, and we do not want to advocate a singular approach to dementia prevention. We do not know what might be achieved by investment in midlife genotyping and addressing early pathology medically early in the process. The mechanisms between risk and the dementia diseases is still not fully understood. However, we have throughout this book tried to call for balance. We have tried to demonstrate what is already known about dementia prevention from many different approaches. What remains clear after this is that the knowledge and investment in population health approaches is very low compared to the investment that has been put into drug development despite very promising avenues for population health research being documented in each chapter of this book. Epidemiological studies over time are required to understand the sociocultural effects on dementia risk and to benchmark any reduction attempts.

Understanding how to address risk factors and how to identify an individual's risk profile is an interesting research ground with great potential. Ultimately, a clear message is required and better awareness of risk and dementia. The determinants of behaviour change away from high-risk lifestyles is another fertile ground of research endeavour with clear proximal benefits for people involved. Finally, a thorough understanding of the stigma associated with dementia and the implications of this for behaviour change, clinical practice and policy must be developed.

Implications for policy

We have tried to be very clear throughout this book that a world free from dementia at any time is not only highly unlikely, but it challenges the human condition. The pursuit of a dementia-free society is quite demeaning to those who in our best predictions will still have dementia, even if all efforts are to squeeze it into a shorter period of morbidity. What does it say about the condition of ageing if the manner with which 25% of us experience old age (if we live to be 85) is something we are trying to cure? It is said that death and taxes are inevitable, but old age is a privilege. If we celebrate one type of ageing – so-called successful ageing, what does that mean for those who get dementia – are they unsuccessful? Dementia prevention discourse must run alongside a discourse with a better grasp of dementia. Not the imagined horror of a condition in ignorance of its reality or the real horror of a condition that is exacerbated by societal ignorance of the experience of actually having a complex brain disease.

At a policy level, the strong ideas put forward in the final chapter of this book call for investment in social capital, not just for disease prevention, because of the additional gains in cognition for society that result with such engagement in measures to alleviate, for instance, perinatal health, pollution or traumatic brain injury.

Notes

1 http://apps.who.int/iris/bitstream/handle/10665/259615/9789241513487-eng.pdf;jsessionid=14761811A414249BCC4AF91A7993A152?sequence=1
2 www.cdc.gov/tobacco/data_statistics/tables/trends/cig_smoking/index.htm
3 http://phrma-docs.phrma.org/files/dmfile/MID-Alz-Update_FINAL.pdf
4 www.neurodegenerationresearch.eu/fileadmin/Documents/2012/SRA-related/JPND_Mapping_Report__Final__01.pdf

5 www.alzheimer.ie/getattachment/About-Us/Research/A-National-Dementia-Registry-for-Ireland/Dementia-Registry-web-version.pdf.aspx
6 www.alz.co.uk/research/WorldAlzheimerReport2014.pdf
7 www.genio.ie/system/files/publications/Executive_Summary_Mapping_DFC_Europe.pdf

References

America's Biopharmaceutical Companies. 2017. *Medicines in development Update.* Available at: http://phrma-docs.phrma.org/files/dmfile/MID-Alz-Update_FINAL.pdf [Accessed 20 August 2018]

Centres for disease control and Prevention. 2016. *Trends in Current Cigarette Smoking Among High School Students and Adults, United states*, 1965–2014. Pages updated and reviewed March 30. [Accessed 20 August 2018]

EFID Mapping dementia-friendly communities across Europe: Summary of a Study Commissioned by the European Foundations' Initiative on Dementia (EFID). Available at: https://www.genio.ie/system/files/publications/Executive_Summary_Mapping_DFC_Europe.pdf [Accessed 20 August 2018]

Hopper, L, Hughes, S, Burke, T, Irving, K. (2016). *A National Dementia Registry for Ireland: A feasibility Study.* Alzheimer Society of Ireland. December 2016. Available at: http://www.alzheimer.ie/getattachment/About-Us/Research/A-National-Dementia-Registry-for-Ireland/Dementia-Registry-web-version.pdf.aspx [Accessed 20 August 2018].

JPND Research (EU Joint Programme on Neurodegeneration). *JPND Mapping Exercise.* Available at: http://www.neurodegenerationresearch.eu/fileadmin/Documents/2012/SRA-related/JPND_Mapping_Report__Final__01.pdf [Accessed 20 August 2018], p. 7.

O'Donnell, C. A., Browne, S., Pierce, M., McConnachie, A., Deckers, K., van Boxtel, M. P. J., Manera, V., Köhler, S., Redmond, M., Verhey, F. R. J., van den Akker, M., Power, K. & Irving, K. (2015). Reducing dementia risk by targeting modifiable risk factors in mid-life: Study protocol for the Innovative Midlife Intervention for Dementia Deterrence (In-MINDD) randomised controlled feasibility trial. *Pilot and Feasibility Studies*, 1, 40. https://doi.org/10.1186/s40814-015-0035-x.

Olanrewaju, O, Clare, L, Barnes, L. & Brayne, C. (2015). A multimodal approach to dementia prevention: A report from the Cambridge Institute of Public Health. *Alzheimer's and Dementia*, 1(3) (November), 151–156. doi:10.1016/j.trci.2015.08.003.

Prince, M Albanese, E, Guerchet, M, Prina, M. (2014) *Alzheimer Disease International (ADI) London*, September 2014. Available at: https://www.alz.co.uk/research/WorldAlzheimerReport2014.pdf [Accessed 20 August 2018]

World Health Organization. 2017. *Global Action Plan on the Public Health Response to Dementia* 2017–2025. Geneva, Licence: CC BY-NC-SA 3.0 IGO. Available at: http://apps.who.int/iris/bitstream/handle/10665/259615/9789241513487-eng.pdf;jsessionid=14761811A414249BCC4AF91A7993A152?sequence=1 [Accessed 20 August 2018]

Index

Page numbers in *italic* indicate a figure on the corresponding page. Page numbers in **bold** indicate a table or chart on the corresponding page.

For Product Safety Concerns and Information please contact our EU representative GPSR@taylorandfrancis.com
Taylor & Francis Verlag GmbH, Kaufingerstraße 24, 80331 München, Germany

www.ingramcontent.com/pod-product-compliance
Ingram Content Group UK Ltd.
Pitfield, Milton Keynes, MK11 3LW, UK
UKHW021302190926
475701UK00009B/608
9780367583200